10   Sunrise and Stormclouds

1903   1904   1905   1907

Newsweek Books New York

Editor Roger Morgan

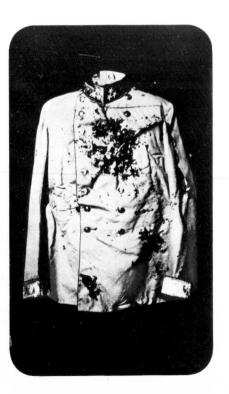

1908

1910

1914

Milestones of History

10   Sunrise and Stormclouds

1916   1917   1919

ISBN: Clothbound edition 0-88225-076-0
        Deluxe edition 0-88225-077-9
Library of Congress Catalog Card No. 74-83894

© George Weidenfeld and Nicolson Ltd, 1970 and 1975
First published 1970.   Revised and expanded edition 1975

Printed and bound in Italy by
Arnoldo Mondadori Editore – Verona

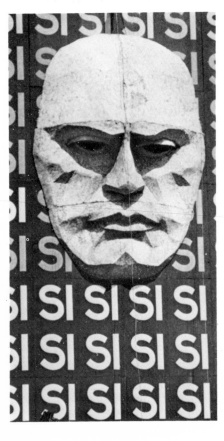

1922   1928   1929

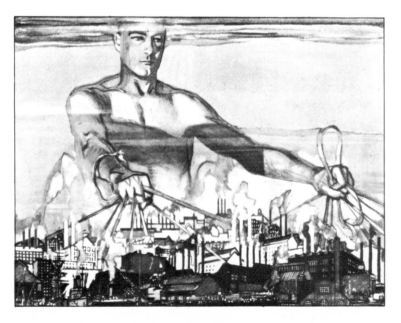

1933   1935   1936

Contents

Introduction

The twentieth century has been one of unprecedented upheavals. By the time the century had run a third of its course, most of the assumptions and beliefs current in 1900 had been severely shaken, and many of them destroyed forever. The flames of the Reichstag fire of February, 1933, consumed more than a building dating from the proud and stable years of the late nineteenth century. They symbolized, we can now see, the destruction of many of the conceptions of economic organization, constitutional politics and peaceful international relations that the nineteenth century had bequeathed to the twentieth.

In 1900, most thinking people firmly believed that the world was set on a course of progress in every aspect of life—material, scientific, social, economic, political and moral. There were still, it was clear, many shameful defects in the societies of the advanced industrial nations—poverty, inequality, the horrors of the urban slums—but it seemed equally clear that these blots would be removed by the further march of the progress that had made most people's lives in 1900 very much easier than, say, in 1850.

Scientific inventions appeared to be laying the technological foundations for further progress; economic growth could apparently be relied on to continue, and to provide greater resources for all classes in society; politically, the forces of liberalism and progress represented by the American and French republics, and by the constitutional monarchy in England, were steadily gaining ground in spreading their example to the Central and Eastern European empires of Germany, Austria-Hungary and Russia. And the pattern of relations between states, which had seen no major war since the middle years of the nineteenth century, was apparently destined to go forward to a continued era of peace and harmony. It was expected that the growth of economic wealth and the development of human reason would remove whatever causes of international strife still remained.

By the 1930s, as a glance through the chapters of this volume will show, most of these confident hopes had been revealed as illusions. Scientific and technological progress, to be sure, had continued apace: communications had been revolutionized by the development of the automobile and of air transport; radio and the cinema had transformed the lives of millions of people, and industry could call on much more technologically advanced machinery and equipment than at the start of the century. Despite all these indications of progress in the material sense, however, the first third of the twentieth century had taught bitter lessons in the fields of human society and international relations.

Even before 1914 the growth in economic wealth, which the nineteenth century had regarded as automatic, was showing some signs of faltering. It certainly seemed this way to the many thousands of workers in America and in Europe who found their wages reduced or limited by the slow development of the branch of industry they worked in, or for those thrown out of work by technological innovations. The widespread strikes of the pre-1914 era, however, were nothing compared with the industrial conflicts unleashed by the economic dislocation caused by World War I. The interruption of international trade, the destruction of productive capacity and the social and emotional disruption caused by the war, all made the early 1920s a period of great industrial turmoil. After these turbulent years there came, it is true, the brief return to "normalcy" in the later 1920s, but this was brutally interrupted in 1929 by the Great Crash and the Depression that followed. By 1933, the numbers of unemployed ran into millions in all the major industrial countries of the world. This was a catastrophe which the simple nineteenth-century belief in automatic progress toward a richer and brighter future could not survive, and from now on humanity turned toward the prophets of radically new economic policies—to John Maynard Keynes and the techniques of deficit financing, to Franklin D. Roosevelt and the New Deal, or to Joseph Stalin and the First Five-Year Plan.

In political affairs, as in economic, the twentieth century was to witness drastic transformations. Before 1914 democratic government appeared to be extending its sway throughout the world, and the prospect appeared even brighter after 1918, with the victory of those who had fought, as Woodrow Wilson expressed it, "to make the world safe for democracy." Most of the new states created after the collapse of the Central Powers in 1918—the republics of Poland and Czechoslovakia, the Kingdom of Yugoslavia, and many more —were provided with impeccably democratic constitutions, designed to bring the blessings of liberal democracy to those who had suffered under traditional autocracy. The same kind of constitution was also adopted by defeated Germany, in the regime known from its birthplace as the Weimar Republic.

Within fifteen years of the victory of 1918, these high hopes of a world safe for democracy lay in ruins. The economic and political strains of the postwar world were too powerful for the newly planted institutions to survive, and in one country after another they were swept away by more extreme creeds. In Italy, the constitutional monarchy was emasculated in 1922 by the Fascism of Benito Mussolini (and even though he claimed that Fascism was not for export, he soon found disciples throughout Europe); in Poland, parliamentary government was replaced in 1926 by the dictatorship of Marshal Pilsudski; and in Germany, the Weimar Republic succumbed in 1933 to the onslaught of the National Socialists (or Nazis) led by Adolf Hitler. One of the paradoxes of this crisis of liberal democracy was that

its earliest challenger—Marxist Communism of the type that Lenin brought to power in Russia by the October Revolution of 1917—had made very little progress outside the Soviet borders. Except for a short-lived Bolshevik regime in Hungary in 1919, the influence of Communism outside Russia was limited to noisy but not very effective Communist parties in some Western countries, of which the biggest was in Germany. They did something to weaken liberal democracy and thus to prepare the way for Fascism and Nazism, but the significant spread of Communism internationally was only to come after a second world war.

War itself was to play a part in the international life of the twentieth century that was undreamed of in 1900. The various armed conflicts that occurred from 1904 onward were on a larger scale than most of the relatively localized wars of the nineteenth century, and they were linked together in a deadly chain of cause and effect. Russia's resounding defeat by Japan in 1904–1905, as well as giving the signal for an anti-Western revolt by the colored peoples of the world that was to gather momentum as the decades passed, had the immediate effect of turning Russia's attention back from the Far East toward the Balkans. A series of clashes between Russia's small Balkan allies and the opposing powers of Turkey and Austria then led to the conflagration of 1914–18, which involved states in every part of the world from Japan to Latin America and truly deserved the name of World War.

Even this "war to end wars," however, left a string of old and new problems in its wake, which the newly founded League of Nations was unable to resolve. From the tensions of the Balkans to the simmering hostility between China and Japan in the Far East, the 1920s had only the superficial appearance of years of peace. The Great Depression added the final element of fuel to the fires of war, by increasing the resentment of the Japanese at their exclusion from access to the raw materials and markets their economy demanded. The Japanese militarists won the upper hand over the civilian authorities in Tokyo, and their attack on Manchuria in 1931 marked the start of a new era of open acts of military aggression. When Mussolini invaded Abyssinia in 1935, and when he and Hitler sent armed support for General Franco's revolt against the Spanish Republic in 1936, they were merely following the example of the Japanese acts of aggression from 1931 onward, which the League of Nations and the United States had been unable or unwilling to prevent.

The conflicts of this period were of course reflected in the early artistic and philosophical trends of the century. The mood of uncertainty, innovation and experiment, contrasting strikingly with the self-confidence normally associated with the nineteenth century, can be sensed in different ways in many of the experimental works of art, and even in the spirit of skepticism of such an intellectual achievement as Einstein's theory of relativity. The grandiose assertions of fascist art and architecture constituted a backlash against the crumbling of established social and aesthetic values. The revolutions of the right, rooted in rehashed versions of nineteenth-century concepts, sought to stifle the corrosive questioning of twentieth-century intellectual life. As the Hitlerite press wrote of the exiled Einstein: "We have no need of relativity in Germany today."

R. P. MORGAN

Wings Over Kitty Hawk 1903

With four men, a boy, a dog and his brother Wilbur as his only audience, Orville Wright revved the engine of the frail-looking biplane that the brothers had constructed, slipped the restraining wire, and set off on man's first successful powered flight in a heavier-than-air craft. Orville's flight over the sand dunes of Kitty Hawk, North Carolina, on the morning of December 17, 1903, lasted only twelve seconds and covered less than 220 feet—but in those brief seconds history was made. The brothers made three additional flights that morning, one of which lasted for almost a minute and covered 852 feet—conclusive proof that their initial feat was no accident. The Wrights' technological triumph was complete; one of man's oldest dreams had been realized. Within a few decades the brothers' invention was to revolutionize both travel and warfare and "change the face of the world."

The air age took almost exactly a century to be ushered in after Sir George Cayley laid the foundations of aerodynamics and flight control in 1799. That century progressed through widespread theory and experimentation to the masterly gliding flights of the German engineer Otto Lilienthal, and finally, in 1903, to the world's first powered, sustained and controlled flights in an airplane by the brothers Wilbur and Orville Wright.

The Wright brothers' first flight—an event that was ultimately to revolutionize transportation and warfare and to "shrink" the world—must have seemed peculiarly matter-of-fact to the two chief actors: they were merely completing the first phase of the careful experiments that had started with their wing-warping kite of 1899 and had then passed through three seasons of increasingly successful gliding.

The scene was the sandy and windy coast of the Atlantic Ocean by the Kill Devil Sand Hills, some four miles south of the small fishing village of Kitty Hawk, North Carolina. The date was Thursday, December 17, 1903, and the time was about 10:35 A.M. Wilbur and Orville had risen early and had hoisted a signal to tell the crew of the Kill Devil Life Saving Station that an attempt was to be made to fly. Four men, a boy, and a dog came over to watch; one of the men was to stand by the camera set up to record the happenings.

At about 10:15 A.M., while a brisk wind blew from the north, the final preparations were made. The aircraft—called the *Flyer*—was a biplane with a forward elevator and a double rear rudder. There was a 12-horsepower gasoline engine, lying on the lower wing, that drove two pusher airscrews (behind the wings) via bicycle chains encased in tubes. The wings could be "warped"—that is, they could be given a helical twist so that the wings on one side presented a greater angle against the airflow than those on the other. This device, used in conjunction with the rear rudder, allowed the machine to be

rolled (banked) at will and was the main achievement of the Wrights' flight-control experiments.

The frail-looking but tough little machine could not take off from the sand on wheels and was therefore fitted with skids. The brothers devised a forty-foot wooden rail, laid down into the wind, on which a wheeled yoke ran freely; the skids of the airplane were laid across this yoke. The pilot lay prone on the lower wing, and the machine was restrained by a wire until the engine had been revved up to its maximum speed. Then the wire was slipped, and the *Flyer* sped down the rail. When the craft's speed was great enough for the wings to raise it into the air, it lifted off the wheeled yoke.

For the first trial, on December 14, 1903, the brothers had flipped a coin to see who would make the attempt, and Wilbur had won. He had been too brusque with the controls, however, and the machine had stalled and ploughed into the sand just beyond the end of the rail.

Then, on December 17, it was Orville's turn; and at approximately 10:30 all was ready for the second trial. Orville had the engine going full pelt. He slipped the restraining wire, and the *Flyer* ran along the rail and was off into the air. It remained airborne for about twelve seconds. Since it was flying into a brisk wind, this meant that it actually had flown considerably more than the distance covered over the ground, which was only some 220 feet. In those brief seconds history was made. As Orville said:

This flight lasted only twelve seconds, but it was nevertheless the first in the history of the world in which a machine carrying a man had raised itself by its own power into the air in full flight, had sailed forward without reduction of speed, and had finally landed at a point as high as that from which it started.

This flight was not the end of the trials, however. In all, four flights were made that morning between 10:30 and just after noon, with the brothers taking turns as pilots. The fourth flight—which Wilbur

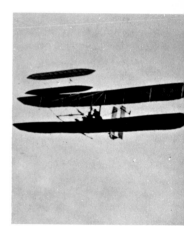

Wilbur and Orville Wright's biplane *Flyer* III in flight, September 25, 1905. This improved version constituted the first practical airplane in history.

Opposite Poster announcing an "Aviation Week" to be held at Reims, France. Aviation rapidly captured the public's imagination and demonstrations were soon held all over Europe.

Wilbur and Orville Wright, the American brothers whose powered manned flight of December 17, 1903, realized one of man's oldest dreams.

Wilbur Wright at the controls of the experimental glider at Kitty Hawk in 1901.

piloted—lasted for fifty-nine seconds and covered 852 feet of ground and over half a mile in air distance. It is both interesting and amusing to note that nobody else in the world was to remain in the air in an airplane for twelve seconds until November, 1906; no one else was to remain aloft for fifty-nine seconds until November, 1907.

In a joint statement to the Associated Press on January 5, 1904, the Wrights said:

Only those who are acquainted with practical aeronautics can appreciate the difficulties of attempting the first trials of a flying machine in a twenty-five-mile gale. As winter was already well set in, we should have postponed our trials to a more favorable season, but for the fact that we were determined, before returning home, to know whether the machine possessed sufficient power to fly, sufficient strength to withstand the shocks of landings, and sufficient capacity of control to make flight safe in boisterous winds, as well as in calm air. When these points had been definitely established, we at once packed our goods and returned home, knowing that the age of the flying machine had come at last.

From the beginning we have employed entirely new principles of control; and as all the experiments have been conducted at our own expense without assistance from any individual or institution, we do not feel ready at present to give out any pictures or detailed description of the machine.

There are four vital points about the Wright brothers that are often overlooked and that have led to a great deal of misunderstanding of these great men. The first is that these initial powered flights were the culmination of three strenuous seasons of gliding (1900–1902), by the end of which the Wrights had mastered three-axis flight control, which was the true secret of their success in aviation. In other words, before they built their first powered *Flyer* in 1903, they had learned to control pitch, yaw and roll in a glider.

Second, the naïve idea, so often expressed, that the four flights on December 17, 1903, were looked upon by the Wrights as a "final" achievement is far from the truth. The flights were only tentative and were considered simply to have proved that Orville and Wilbur's research and development had proceeded along the right lines. If the brothers had made nothing more than those four brief flights, they would have been considered significant pioneers, but not much more. Their real achievement is that they progressed through their powered *Flyer* II of 1904, to their *Flyer* III of 1905, which could easily fly for half an hour and could bank, turn, circle and do figure eights. This *Flyer* III was the first practical airplane in history; its airborne duration was not to be exceeded by any other pioneer until September, 1908.

The third consideration is a peculiar one and touches upon problems of national psychology. Americans have perhaps overworked the notion illustrated by the saying "from log cabin to White House"—the belief that there is a chance for everybody, and that everybody has a chance of becoming President. Applied to the Wright brothers, this

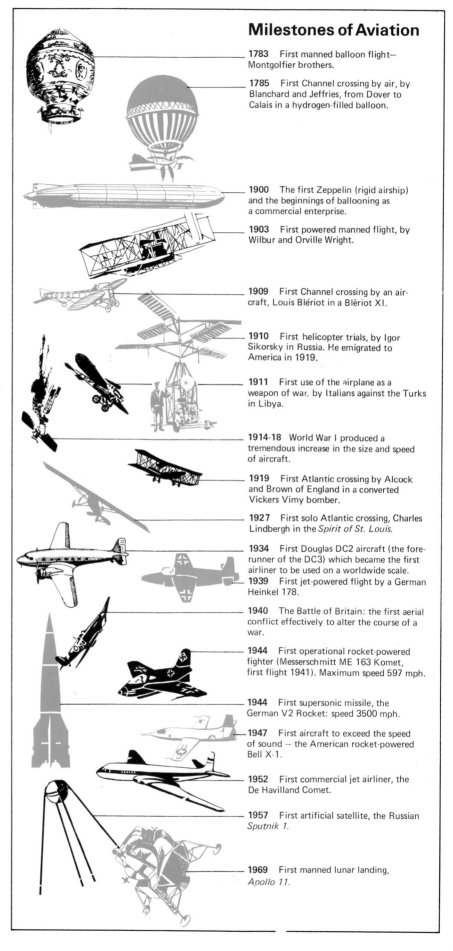

Milestones of Aviation

1783 First manned balloon flight— Montgolfier brothers.

1785 First Channel crossing by air, by Blanchard and Jeffries, from Dover to Calais in a hydrogen-filled balloon.

1900 The first Zeppelin (rigid airship) and the beginnings of ballooning as a commercial enterprise.

1903 First powered manned flight, by Wilbur and Orville Wright.

1909 First Channel crossing by an aircraft, Louis Blériot in a Blériot XI.

1910 First helicopter trials, by Igor Sikorsky in Russia. He emigrated to America in 1919.

1911 First use of the airplane as a weapon of war, by Italians against the Turks in Libya.

1914-18 World War I produced a tremendous increase in the size and speed of aircraft.

1919 First Atlantic crossing by Alcock and Brown of England in a converted Vickers Vimy bomber.

1927 First solo Atlantic crossing, Charles Lindbergh in the *Spirit of St. Louis*.

1934 First Douglas DC2 aircraft (the forerunner of the DC3) which became the first airliner to be used on a worldwide scale.

1939 First jet-powered flight by a German Heinkel 178.

1940 The Battle of Britain: the first aerial conflict effectively to alter the course of a war.

1944 First operational rocket-powered fighter (Messerschmitt ME 163 Komet, first flight 1941). Maximum speed 597 mph.

1944 First supersonic missile, the German V2 Rocket: speed 3500 mph.

1947 First aircraft to exceed the speed of sound — the American rocket-powered Bell X-1.

1952 First commercial jet airliner, the De Havilland Comet.

1957 First artificial satellite, the Russian *Sputnik 1*.

1969 First manned lunar landing, *Apollo 11*.

doctrine has emerged as the legend that they were humble lads—only one stage from being hicks. The myth pictures them as youngsters who "by guess and by golly" knocked up an odd contraption, tinkered about with it until it seemed to be promising, got in and—more by luck than good judgment—managed to take off the ground in their homemade creation. Nothing could be further from the truth.

The Wrights were bachelor sons of a widower bishop who was a member of a nonconformist sect called the United Brethren. The family also included a married son Lorin and the brothers' beloved sister Katharine, who ran the Wright household very efficiently. Their religious background produced two noticeable features in the Wright brothers. First was a strict ethic, which taught them honesty and integrity. The second was that, having been brought up with a biblical background, they both wrote excellent English—simple, straightforward, and expressive. This was to stand them in excellent stead when it came to their aeronautical studies and their correspondence with the great American aviation pioneer Octave Chanute and a growing number of men who became involved with their activities over the years.

Building on these foundations, the brothers went through the customary education of the time and then struck out on their own. They became first-class mechanics and, after setting up a successful bicycle shop, progressed to designing and manufacturing an excellent bicycle of their own—the Van Cleeve. The mechanical know-how that Wilbur and Orville acquired in the bicycle business was of great service when they took to designing and building aircraft. But of equal importance—and one of the most remarkable features of their lives—was their almost innate gift for research in aerodynamics, the results of which surprised even modern masters such as Theodore von Karman. There are thousands of notes, diagrams and letters (many of them now published) to prove that gift. Almost as remarkable —some would perhaps say *more* remarkable—was their ability as airplane pilots, an ability that rapidly

A model of a Voisin biplane built in 1908. After the Americans, the French were the most advanced aeronauts.

evolved in both brothers alike. They were not only the first men to fly, but the first true pilots; their friends have said that it was hard to choose between them when it came to piloting ability.

Perhaps most misunderstood of the four vital points concerning the brothers has been the Wrights' influence on the history of aviation. Unfortunately, certain prejudiced writers on both sides of the Atlantic have tried to show that the work of the Wrights was isolated and influenced no one. This is quite untrue. That misconception has developed because of the brothers' regrettable decision to stop flying at the end of 1905 and not to fly again until they had a guaranteed buyer for their machines. Such a buyer did not materialize until 1908. Their refusal to fly for this long period was to protect their invention.

Nevertheless, their vital influence on European experimentation had been at work ever since 1902 and 1903, when illustrations and descriptions of their gliding achievements became available in France. This material proved to be the direct inspiration for the revival of interest in aviation in Europe, especially when the grand old man of American aviation, Octave Chanute, lectured to the French pioneers in April of 1903. Chanute showed his audience excellent photographs and gave them accounts of the Wrights' masterly glider flying. The French, led by Ferdinand Ferber and Ernest Archdeacon, started to build Wright-type gliders, and with these machines the revival of European aviation was launched.

In 1908 it was decided that Orville should stay in the United States to fly the acceptance tests that had now been agreed to by the Army Signal Corps at Fort Myer, Virginia, while Wilbur was destined for Europe. Financial arrangements were completed by early 1908, and Wilbur went over to France. In August he made his first public flights, and in the words of the Count de La Vaulx—one of France's great aviation pioneers—Wilbur's wonderful new aircraft had, in a matter of weeks, "revolutionized the aviator's world." When Wilbur started to fly, no one in Europe really understood flight control— that is, the proper control of an airplane in the air, especially control in roll combined with control in yaw and pitch. The Wright airplane could be banked, turned, circled and generally maneuvered with the greatest of ease, whereas the primitive European machines had to be maneuvered with great care and could only be turned with difficulty.

European praise for the Wright machine knew no bounds, and as Wilbur piled triumph upon triumph, the continental pioneers began to realize what essential lessons had to be learned from the Wrights. Wilbur's audience was by turns astounded, dismayed and, to give them credit, repentant— repentant of their six years of disbelief and dismayed at the memory of their six years of aeronautical fumbling. With no proper control in their hands, and no image of true flight in their minds, they were now experiencing a painful moment of truth.

The veteran pioneer Léon Delagrange spoke for

A model of *Flyer* I, the original Wright biplane, with Orville lying at the controls.

all his honest countrymen when he exclaimed: "Well, we are beaten! We just don't exist." "No one can estimate," said one French spokesman, "the consequences that will result from this new method of locomotion, the dazzling beginnings of which we salute today." "For us in France," exclaimed French aviator Louis Blériot, "and everywhere, a new era in mechanical flight has commenced … It is marvelous." "It is a revelation in airplane work," said René Gasnier; "who can now doubt that the Wrights have done all they claimed? … We are as children compared with the Wrights."

The French aviation press was equally repentant and enthusiastic, noting that Wilbur's demonstration was "one of the most exciting spectacles ever presented in the history of applied science." François Peyrey wrote:

I had the good fortune to find myself at Hunaudieres on August 8th, 1908, the date of the memorable demonstration. I shall try to give an idea of the incomparable mastery of the American aviators in the marvelous art of imitating the birds. For a long time—for too long a time—the Wright brothers have been accused in Europe of bluffing; perhaps even in their own land. Today they are hallowed by France, and I feel an intense pleasure in counting myself among the first to make amends for such flagrant injustice. … It would also be just as puerile to challenge the first flight of December 17, 1903 in North Carolina as it would be to deny the experiences in La Sarthe. … From the stands [on the race course] an immense acclamation goes up from the witnesses of this prowess. …

The London *Times*, in its report of the flight demonstration in France, observed:

All accounts … published in this morning's paper from the correspondents on the spot, attest the complete triumph of the American inventor … the enthusiasm was indescribable … all accounts agree that the most admirable characteristic of yesterday's flight was the steady mastery displayed by Mr. Wright over his machine.

The Europeans thus acquired a proper understanding of flight control for the first time, and it

effected the revolution necessary to bring about the final conquest of the air. The world—not only of aviation but of politics and power—soon endorsed the now famous statement of Major B.F.S. Baden-Powell, the past president of the Royal Aeronautical Society: "That Wilbur Wright is in possession of a power which controls the fate of nations is beyond dispute."

Between August 8 and August 13, 1908, Wilbur made nine flights, the longest lasting just over eight minutes. He then received permission to use the great military ground, the Camp d'Auvours, seven miles east of Le Mans. Here, from August 21 to the last day of December, 1908, he made 104 flights and was airborne for about twenty-five and a half hours, thus making some twenty-six hours for the combined French locations that year. Wilbur's astonishing 1908 season at Auvours included: taking up passengers on some sixty occasions; fourteen flights of between one-quarter and one-half an hour's duration; six of between one-half and three-quarters of an hour; six of between one and two hours; a record flight (on December 31) of two hours, twenty minutes and twenty-three seconds; and one flight (on December 18) to gain the altitude record of 360 feet.

The influence exerted by the great inventors of the world—especially those who are the true initiators—lays the foundations upon which their followers can build and sparks them into action. This vital role of first achiever, director and energizer was admirably fulfilled in the realm of aviation by the brothers Wilbur and Orville Wright. The final word belongs to the great French aeronaut and historian Charles Dollfus:

It is therefore incontestably the Wright brothers alone who resolved, in its entirety, the problem of human mechanical flight. ... This resulted from their tests from 1903 to 1905. Men of genius—erudite, exact in their reasoning, hard workers, outstanding experimenters, and unselfish—the brothers Wilbur and Orville Wright have, more than anyone else, deserved the success which they achieved. They changed the face of the globe.

CHARLES GIBBS-SMITH

A photograph of Louis Blériot making the first powered flight across the English Channel in 1909.

Transport and communications

The potential of flight as a means of improving transport was recognized almost at once. Military possibilities, too, were not ignored: as early as 1911 the Italians made use of aircraft to help fight the Turks in Libya, and by the end of World War I aviation had made considerable progress. However, the transportation of large and heavy cargoes by air was a problem that was not quickly solved, and during the first two decades of the century commercial interest in aviation tended to concentrate more on improvements in airship design than on heavier-than-air aircraft.

Surface transportation was also improving rapidly and the cost of goods was being kept low by the use of faster and larger ships as well as by more direct routes. The construction of the Panama Canal, which was begun in 1904, but not opened until 1914, had an effect on transportation speeds almost as great as the Suez Canal had in 1869. The long delay in its building was due in large measure to Ferdinand de Lesseps' mismanagement, which had led to the Panama scandal in France in 1892 and to the work being undertaken by the United States. Smaller canals, such as the Kiel (connecting the Baltic and North Seas) and Corinth (connecting the Saronic Gulf with the Gulf of Corinth) canals, also had a substantial effect on shipping profits. Larger steam locomotives were making it possible to increase railroad speeds too, and by the outbreak of World War I the railroad was at the high point of its development. Later in the century there

Radio operator at sea, 1912. Improved radio, telephone and telegraph communication helped shrink the globe.

were to be reductions both in railroad mileage and in train speeds in most of the advanced countries in the world.

By 1900 the use of telegraphy was no longer a novelty in the world's industrialized countries, but other and newer means of communication still caused great excitement. Although the telephone was an American invention, it developed far faster in Europe than in the United States, largely because most European governments either nationalized or took a close interest in telephone companies. In 1905 London became the first city to have a large-scale underground network of telephone wires. Still newer, and more exciting as a means of communication, was the radio, whose development was largely due to Guglielmo Marconi (1874–1937), although many others had worked on ideas similar to his. In 1899 Marconi succeeded in sending a

message across the English Channel, and two years later he was able to send one across the Atlantic from England to Newfoundland. By the outbreak of World War I the value of the radio had been widely recognized, particularly at sea.

Improved transport and communication facilities were not merely the result of technological developments. There was in fact a rapidly growing need for them. The interests of the major colonial powers, Britain and France, and of their rapidly growing rivals, the United States and Germany, made first-rate transportation facilities essential. The Wright brothers, Count Ferdinand von Zeppelin and Marconi were helping to fill an important void.

Diplomatic consequences of the Boer War

Throughout the world, the colonial powers came into competition, although war was usually averted. In southern Africa, for example, where Britain and Germany were both seeking to extend their colonies, the situation was com-

with Germany and agreed to a division of any southern African territory that Portugal abandoned. This appeared to be in Germany's interest but Britain then buttressed Portugal's colonial position so that Germany gained nothing. German anger at this maneuver led to a rapid deterioration in relations between Britain and Germany. The seeds of diplomatic distrust were to bear fruit over the next few years.

This diplomatic incident had a further European dimension. At the beginning of the Boer War, France sought to take advantage of Britain's difficulty and isolation by making an alliance with Germany to heal the hostility that still existed as a result of the Franco-Prussian War of 1870. However, Germany's insistence on French recognition of the loss of Alsace-Lorraine led to a breakdown in the negotiations. The French suspected that Alsace-Lorraine would be the price of any agreement with Germany and in 1903 turned instead to Britain for support.

The actual course of the Boer War was of less importance than its

Boer refugee family at Pretoria railway station.

Charing Cross underground station, 1894. First opened in 1863, London's underground rail service was completely steam hauled until 1890. Most of the present system was constructed in the first decade of the century.

plicated by the presence of the Boers—descendants of the original Dutch settlers of the Cape. Able to rely on German sympathy and support, the Boers took a militantly anti-British line, which led to the outbreak of the Boer War in 1899. Britain and Germany disagreed over the borders of their southern African colonies, and in order to avoid the danger of German intervention in support of the Boers, Britain settled its border disputes

diplomatic consequences, but it showed how inadequate the British army had become as a serious fighting machine. Although at the outbreak of the war in the fall of 1899, Britain had only 27,000 soldiers in South Africa, while the Boers had an effective fighting force three times as large, nobody doubted that Britain would soon win. But it was not until 1902 that the British army, which by then had over 200,000 soldiers in the field,

Anglo-German distrust are sown

finally forced the Boers to accept a peace treaty. Even then the treaty was surprisingly advantageous to the Boers. The length of the war and its enormous cost to Britain had so vast an effect on public feeling that a new attitude toward colonialism and imperialism began to emerge—although it was to take decades for this attitude to be fully reflected in official thinking. A new concentration on improving the army was also apparent. A new approach became necessary: more modern equipment, up-to-date tactics, and a recognition that military virtue included the ability to win a war rather than merely march up and down a parade ground.

China

In China, too, revolution was brewing. There, as elsewhere, it was the impact of Western trade and ideas that triggered the disturbances. Like every Chinese dynasty since 200 B.C., the ruling Manchus rested on three pillars: Confucianism, agriculture and the myth of

Chinese troops on their way to fight the Boxer rebels in 1900. Despite the arrival of an international column that occupied Peking in 1901, the Boxer Rebellion had in fact postponed the dismemberment of China.

universal empire. These pillars were badly shaken in the nineteenth century when the importation of manufactured goods was coupled with a vast population explosion to create intense peasant unrest. The resulting Taiping Rebellion (1850–64) took fourteen years to crush, and by that time knowledge that powerful nations existed beyond the seas had shattered the myth of universal empire.

Defeat in the war with Japan convinced many Chinese intellectuals that their country had to be Westernized, but the Dowager Empress Tzu Hsi refused to make concessions. Peasant discontent surfaced in 1900 in the form of the Boxer Rebellion, and the "Westernizers" were shunted aside. Encouraged from abroad by their exiled leader, Sun Yat-sen (1866–1925), they continued to plot. China's government, despite its antiquity, was no longer stable. Only the support of the Western powers enabled it to survive, and violent revolution seemed likely.

Russian discontent

On July 30, 1903, the Second Congress of the All-Russian Social Democratic Party convened in a smelly, flea-infested warehouse in Brussels. After a few days, the smells, the fleas and the Belgian police caused the delegates to move to London. The Bolshevik Party, which would seize control of Russia in 1917, emerged out of the dissensions of that Congress.

At the beginning of the twentieth century Russia possessed an autocratic monarchy, a parasitic nobility and a corrupt bureaucracy —all of which exploited a vast semi-feudal peasantry. Stirrings of protest from intellectuals and students were met by police brutality, and peasant risings were put down by regiments of Cossacks; as discontent increased so did oppression.

Peasants and factory workers alike were ready recruits for revolution. Much of the best pasture, woodland and water was in the hands of aristocrats who did not bother to farm it, and few peasants had the money to live above subsistence level, let alone afford improvements. Famine was rampant. A repressed proletariat was emerging in the larger industrial areas where slum housing conditions, long working hours, child labor and low wages caused widespread discontent.

Despite the secret police and the constant threat of execution, exile or flogging, there was a flourishing revolutionary movement in existence. At first it had been an anarchist movement, primarily concerned with peasant problems. Then, in 1898, the Marxist Social Democratic Party was founded at Minsk, and a new sort of revolutionary appeared to challenge the old order. Even at the outset the new party was split. The older leaders believed the organization's main task was to make the workers aware that they were being exploited. Vladimir Ilich Ulyanov thought differently. Such a process, he said, would only lead to reformism—that is, to a series of small improvements in contemporary economic conditions rather than to a change of regime. In 1902, Ulyanov published *What Is To Be Done?* under his pen name, Lenin. In that work he claimed that the working class was incapable of creating its own revolutionary ideology, and that such a task would have to be undertaken by an elite of professional revolutionaries. The ideological conflict between Lenin and the older members of the party was raised at the Second Party Congress. Through skillful committee work and not a little underhandedness, Lenin and his followers emerged from the Congress as the *Bolshinstvo*, or majority, while those who preferred a more democratic notion of the party were left with the stigma of *Menshinstvo*, or minority. The result of this clash decided the course of revolution, for the Bolsheviks were committed to dictatorship. But the importance of this commitment lay in the future; for a time the revolution proceeded without Lenin.

In 1903, there were eighty-seven strikes in St. Petersburg, and elsewhere peasant bands burned down manor houses and murdered their landlords. The government had hoped to divert attention from domestic troubles with a successful war against Japan, but the war was not a success.

The Dragon Empress, Tzu Hsi, photographed in the Forbidden City. On the far left is Lung-yü, Kuang-hsu's empress.

The Russo-Japanese War   1904

As the nineteenth century drew to a close, Japan, emerging from isolation, began looking for areas in which to expand, notably Korea. This put her on a collision course with Russia, as the Tsar sought to take over Manchuria and perhaps Korea as well. After Russia had rejected a compromise, Japanese troops attacked the Russian army. In the ensuing fighting, the Russian army was decisively defeated, the Russian navy decimated. Although the Russians did well enough at the peace table, it was clear to all that Japan had won great power status—the first non-European nation to do so.

The enemy had finished turning. His twelve ships were in perfect order at close intervals, steaming parallel to us, but gradually forging ahead. No disorder was noticeable. It seemed to me that with my Zeiss glasses, I could even distinguish the mantlets of the hammocks on the bridges, and groups of men. But with us? I looked around. What havoc!—Burning bridges, smoldering debris on the decks, piles of dead bodies. Signaling and judging distance stations, gun-directing positions, all were destroyed. And astern of us the *Alexander* and *Borodino* were also enveloped in smoke . . . [Twenty minutes later] . . . I crossed over to the port side, between the forward twelve-inch and six-inch turrets, to have a look at the enemy's fleet. It was all there, just the same—no fires, no heeling over, no fallen bridges—as if it had been at drill instead of fighting, and as if our guns, which had been thundering incessantly for the last half-hour, had been firing—not shells, but the devil alone knows what! Feeling almost in despair, I put down my glasses and went aft.

The author of these words, Vladimir Semenov, was an officer of the Imperial Russian Navy, and the event to which he gave such vivid witness was the devastating Battle of Tsushima, fought in the China seas on May 27, 1905, between Russia and Japan. Semenov's despair was to be amply justified by the end of the battle. Torpedoes as well as fast-firing guns had proved their worth, from the Japanese point of view. And yet superior firepower was not the whole reason for Japan's success, even though it was at the time the most direct. For not only was the Russian fleet at Tsushima badly equipped and indifferently commanded; the encounter itself was the last effort of a nation already haunted by defeat.

The war between Russia and Japan had broken out a little more than a year before Tsushima, on February 10, 1904, when Japan formally declared war on Russia, though the Japanese navy had actually struck the first blow two days earlier, with a characteristically daring attack on Russia's fleet off Port Arthur. Behind the outbreak of hostilities lay a story of Japanese foreign development that

had been unfolding for some two decades, bringing her into conflict first with China, and ultimately with Russia. Japan's active interest in the Asian mainland had started in 1884, when she had attempted to intervene in Korea on behalf of a native regime rebelling against its Chinese suzerain. The threat of open conflict between Japan and China was averted on this occasion, but only by means of an agreement which, while obliging both countries to withdraw their troops from Korea, also acknowledged a joint right of intervention for the future. For Japan the intervention and its outcome marked the beginnings of a new outward-looking stance, unmatched since the "closing" of Japan in the seventeenth century, and, a concomitant of the country's new nationalism, its demand for independence and its move to modernization on Western lines.

Ten years later, in 1894, further disorders in Korea gave Japan a new opportunity to challenge China from a position of much-improved strength. In a war that lasted nine months Japan convincingly defeated China on both land and sea; yet this military success served principally to expose Japan's diplomatic weakness. The Treaty of Shimonoseki that concluded the war in April, 1895, gave Japan some useful territory in mainland China, as well as Formosa and other islands, and secured China's recognition of Korean independence, which gave Japan the right to a free hand there. Within a week of this triumph, however, a diplomatic intervention by Russia, France and Germany forced Japan to surrender all of her new mainland possessions, on the grounds that they threatened the stability of China and the security of peace in the Far East.

This "Triple Intervention" was thus a warning and a lesson to Japan; yet at the same time it could not hide the fact that Japan and Russia, two nations with equal, though differently motivated, expansionist policies, would be the main protagonists in

Russian warship captured at Tsushima and undergoing repairs at Sasebo, Japan, in 1905, after which it was commissioned as part of the Japanese fleet.

Opposite Japanese sealing the mouth of Port Arthur. Two days before Japan formally declared war on Russia on February 10, 1904, the Japanese navy attacked Russia's fleet off Port Arthur.

Defense of Port Arthur by the Russians.

The Russo-Japanese War 1904-1905 RUSSIA

By the treaty Japan was leased the Liaotung peninsula and ceded the southern part of Sakhalin; Japanese interests in Korea were recognized. Despite the parties' agreement to evacuate Manchuria, Russia's interests remained strong in the north.

the Far East. China, it was clear, was to subside into a mere field for the rivalries of others. The new balance of power in the area was marked in June, 1896, when Russia and Japan concluded an alliance of interest in the luckless Korea, similar in intent to the old Sino-Japanese convention of 1884. In May, 1896, a defensive alliance with China gave Russia an important railway concession across Manchuria. Two years later, Russia secured a lease of the Liaotung peninsula, including the valuable warm-water ports of Dalny (Dairen) and Port Arthur—precisely the prizes denied Japan in 1895.

Russia's most direct route to her new bases lay across Manchuria, and accordingly she acquired a more personal interest in the fate of that territory. Nevertheless, Japan's evident hope that this new preoccupation would divert Russia from her own interests in Korea was misplaced. In 1898 Japan proposed a trade to Russia—mutual recognition of each other's exclusive interests, Russia in Manchuria, Japan in Korea; but Russia rejected this, principally because a Japanese free hand in Korea might well menace Russia's position in the Liaotung peninsula, whose approach was dominated by the Korean coast. Instead of moving toward any mutual adjustment with Japan, Russia sought to strengthen her strategic position in relation to the peninsular ports, using the Boxer Rebellion of 1900, for example, as an excuse to station troops in Manchuria itself as well as to enlarge the forces already assigned to the railway line.

By the turn of the century, therefore, an episode that had begun for Japan as a confrontation with a weak China had developed into a more far-reaching and evenly matched rivalry with a nation that was both an Asian and a European great power. Events since 1895 had driven home the lesson of the Triple Intervention—that it was impossible in the long run for Japan to secure foreign successes without respectable allies. Indeed, Japan's first attempt to act on this experience had been made in the same year, when she began to look to what already seemed a "natural" ally—Britain, who had

abstained from the Triple Intervention. Though nothing came of this, there was no reasonable alternative to a British alliance, from Japan's point of view, except a sound understanding with Russia; and the failure of Japan's 1898 initiative proved that there was little to be expected from that quarter. Britain it had to be; and on the British side too from the turn of the century a Japanese alliance was beginning to look increasingly attractive. Not only was Japan's future potential steadily improving, but Britain herself was beginning to suffer the problems of the nonaligned. This policy of "splendid isolation" was becoming unrealistic for a nation whose imperial commitments were threatening to strain its resources, and whose interests—especially in India, hub of the Empire—were coming under heavier pressure from late-starting rivals.

The two potential partners thus had a certain unmistakable interest in each other, although the alliance that was eventually signed in 1902 came into being only after considerable prevarication on the British side. The reasons for this lay principally in the fact that Britain was a European as well as an Eastern power, while Japan was only the latter. Britain, unlike Japan, had to take into account the rival advantages of possible European pacts—with Germany, perhaps, or (as became the case in 1904) with France; in addition, she had to weigh the likely effect on her fellow powers of an alliance that would lend her little direct advantage in the European field, even if it did help her global position. This disparity of interest between the two alliance partners was reflected in their respective assumptions about the pact once it was signed. For Britain, it was primarily valuable as a contribution to the maintenance of the Far Eastern balance of power, and hence of the global status quo; thus too it was evidence of Britain's increasingly defensive posture in imperial affairs, and a sign more of weakness than of strength. On the other hand, for Japan the alliance was the indispensable diplomatic preliminary to challenging Russian supremacy in the Far East; it was the political weapon she had so disastrously lacked in 1895. So from Japan's point of view the crucial part of the treaty was that by which Britain recognized Japan's right to "safeguard its interests" in Korea if these were threatened by any other power, or by an internal disturbance in China or Korea. In practical terms, this was backed up by Britain's undertaking to observe neutrality in the event of a Russo-Japanese war—realistically speaking, a position that would insure her benevolent neutrality vis-à-vis Japan. The alliance was thus the kingpin of Japan's politico-military standing.

The final build-up to the war that eventually broke out between this newly strengthened Japan and Russia was the concomitant of a sudden intensification of Russia's expansionist policy—an episode of crass intervention in Korea, an apt monument to Russia's crumbling governmental structure and will. Although Russia's ministers—Count Sergei Witte (finance) and Count Vladimir Lamsdorff (foreign) in particular—favored a policy of careful penetration in the Far East, in 1901 Tsar Nicholas fell under the unhappy influence of an unscrupulous adventurer named Alexander Bezobrazov. This ambitious former cavalry officer encouraged Nicholas in wild Far Eastern schemes of more personal than national benefit. Ministerial denunciation of Bezobrazov was to no avail; and the Tsar was also receiving sly encouragement from Wilhelm II of Germany, who was eager to see Russia entangled in the East rather than the West.

Complex diplomatic gyrations preceded the outbreak of war, as all the world powers attempted to strike some balance between the safeguarding of their interests and the preservation of the peace. Between Russia and Japan there grew an impenetrable wall of noncommunication, with Russia again, in 1903, refusing renewed Japanese proposals for a mutual recognition of interests, Russia's in Manchuria, Japan's in Korea. In August, 1903, shortly before Russia committed herself to this rejection of Japanese overtures, the reasonable and cautious Witte was dismissed from office; this left as the dominant voice in the government the interior minister Vyacheslav Pleve, who was said to favor a war as a means of diverting "the revolutionary tide." Final efforts at a mediated settlement took up the winter of 1903–1904, but by February Japan had had enough. She broke off negotiations, and diplomatic relations, on February 5; and followed this three days later with her naval initiative.

Russia's foreign policy since 1901 had been less than realistic as far as the Far East situation was concerned: she was driving toward a war for which she was militarily unprepared. In sheer numbers, her troops were impressive enough: a million regulars, and three and a half million reservists. Yet many of these would have to remain in the west, to guard the frontiers there and keep a careful watch on potentially rebellious national minorities—Poles in particular—to say nothing of the Russian populace itself. Moreover, when the war broke out, fewer than 150,000 troops were in the war theater itself; in the course of the conflict, many thousands would have to be transported from metropolitan Russia across a 5,000-mile rail route which was itself incomplete. In quality, too, the Russian army was less than perfect. Among the regiments left behind in the west were some of the most reliable troops. Of the reservists summoned to the colors, there were many who had had no training since the 1880s, and who were unfamiliar with modern weapons. By contrast, the Japanese army, though relatively small in numbers, was generally better equipped and trained. Again, though a maximum of 800,000 troops, regular and reserve, may have seemed puny by comparison with Russia's huge resources of manpower, there was some compensation for this in the Japanese soldiers' superior dedication to the war. Such psychological commitment is of course intangible, yet in Japan as a whole the war was a popular enterprise; it was undertaken with eagerness, and morale was sustained at a high level by

Japanese troops moving toward the southern front—Port Arthur. Within three months of the outbreak of war the Japanese were dominating both the northern and southern fronts.

the consistent success of the Japanese armed forces. In Russia, on the other hand, the opposite was true: among both the public at large and the troops, the war evoked resentment and opposition, to be joined by a progressive demoralization as reverse succeeded reverse. Finally, in the question of supply Japan was at an overwhelming advantage; her supply lines were in any case far shorter than Russia's, and her early establishment of naval superiority meant that she was almost always able to land men and matériel unhindered.

The war itself was, as one historian has bluntly put it, "a series of Russian disasters." Russian troops had crossed the Yalu River frontier between Manchuria and Korea on February 6, and Japan made her first major landing in Korea, at Chemulpo, on February 8, the day of her Port Arthur attack and the effective opening of hostilities. The Japanese army then quickly occupied the Korean capital, Seoul, though nothing more than a series of minor skirmishes occurred until the end of April, when Japanese troops under General Tamemoto Kuroki bridged the Yalu and drove the Russians back into Manchuria, capturing great quantities of equipment in the process. Following this undoubted victory, a second Japanese army under generals Maresuke Nogi and Yasukata Oku was landed at several points on the Liaotung peninsula, on May 5. From now on the Japanese dominated both of the land fronts, pressing their offensive against the increasingly embattled Russians. The larger of the Japanese forces, the armies of Kuroki and Michitsura Nodzu, concentrated on breaking Russia's road and rail supply routes between Mukden, in the north, and the two southern ports of Dalny and Port Arthur; meanwhile smaller forces under Nogi and Oku, together with Admiral Heihachiro Togo's naval squadrons, kept Port Arthur under siege. By August the northern armies had forced the Russians back to Mukden, and the Russians' autumn counteroffensive was beaten back at the

Shaho River, not far from Mukden, in October and November. Mukden itself, however, stood until March, 1905, when it was evacuated by the Russians in the face of a formidable Japanese attack. On the southern front, meanwhile, Port Arthur had capitulated in January, 1905, after an epic siege. Indeed, the major engagements of the war were battles on an enormous scale. In the final capture of Mukden, for example, something like 750,000 men were involved on both sides, while Japanese casualties amounted to 40,000 men. At the Shaho, Japan admitted nearly 16,000 killed and wounded, and claimed to have counted over 13,000 Russian dead on the field of battle. The Port Arthur siege cost the Japanese 60,000 casualties in all; when the city was taken the equipment that fell into Japanese hands included 546 artillery pieces, 35,252 rifles, 30,000 kilos (some 66,000 pounds) of gunpowder, and 2,266,800 rifle cartridges.

At sea the story was a similar tale of Japanese success, though here the Russian discomfiture was even more complete. Japan organized from the first a skillful cooperation between her naval and land forces—naval supremacy being in fact as crucial to the outcome of the war as air supremacy was to be in Europe between 1939 and 1945. The brilliant tactics of Japan's Admiral Togo had by mid-1904 destroyed all Russian hopes of recovering her naval strength through her Pacific fleet and so Russia faced the necessity of bringing up reinforcements from outside the theater of war. The use of the Black Sea fleet—geographically the nearest at hand—was impossible, for an international convention prevented the passage of Russian warships through the strait and into the Mediterranean. In October, 1904, therefore, it was decided to send the Baltic fleet, under Admiral Zinovi Rozhdestvenski, into the distant Chinese waters—a decision that marked the extreme degree of Russian desperation.

Almost at the outset of its 18,000-mile voyage to Japan, Rozhdestvenski's fleet was involved in what

could have become a major clash with Britain, the "Dogger Bank incident." Even before embarkation Rozhdestvenski and his colleagues had become convinced—though their fears were in fact unjustified—that Japanese ships were operating in northern waters under disguise, ready to harass the Baltic fleet on its long journey. On October 21, a series of errors and alarms—involving false signals, a drunken Russian commander and a strayed Russian ship—led to the mistaken identification of a group of British trawlers as a Japanese squadron. Some of Rozhdestvenski's ships opened fire. Two of the fishing vessels were sunk, and several crewmen killed. Too late the Russians realized their error; the damage was done. Popular feeling in Britain ran high; in London there were protest demonstrations and deputations, and the Russian ambassador was jeered. The British government of course made its official protest to Russia in the strongest terms; yet it had no intention of bowing to any public pressure for retaliation. Officially, both the British and Russian governments were less mutually belligerent than their peoples, and were reasonably willing to seek conciliation. Eventually the matter was submitted to an international commission of inquiry, under the Hague Convention; and in March, 1905, the Russians paid the British £65,000 in compensation.

In the meantime, Rozhdestvenski's fleet had continued on its passage, though observed from a less than respectful distance by a squadron of the Royal Navy, which remained with the Russians till Tangier, shaming them by its demonstrations of superior seamanship. So the Russians steamed slowly toward the fate that met them at the end of May, 1905, having won nothing by their great enterprise except a momentary raising of morale as the Japanese were forced to face the last effort of the supposedly beaten enemy. After the catastrophic encounter at Tsushima, both sides felt the need to make peace. Russia, it was true, still had immense numbers of troops in reserve, plus an obvious motive to stay in the war and recover her position; but popular resentment at the war was ripening into open hostility, and so a prudent retreat on all fronts was hardly to be avoided. As for Japan, although her successes had been overwhelming, she now risked overstraining both her economy and her manpower, and in fact had already considered the need for peace as early as March, 1905. In view of this Japan had already approached President Theodore Roosevelt of the United States as a possible mediator, a move of great perspicacity; and on May 31, within a week of Tsushima, he was formally asked by Japan to take up this role as peacemaker.

Negotiations between the two belligerents opened at Portsmouth, New Hampshire, on August 10, 1905. The atmosphere was predictably tough, but the skillful Witte managed to secure both a reasonable compromise for Russia and a certain restoration of Russia's reputation. The lease of the Liaotung peninsula, including of course Port Arthur and Dalny, was assigned to Japan, as also was the railway concession for the line that linked Port Arthur with southern Manchuria, reaching well beyond Mukden as far as the central Manchurian city of Changchun. Russia recognized Japan's "paramount political, military and economical interests" in Korea; both parties agreed to evacuate Manchuria, although in practice Russia's interests in northern Manchuria, beyond Changchun, remained strong. In addition, Russia ceded to Japan the southern part of the island of Sakhalin, together with certain fishing rights along the Russian littoral from the Japan Sea to the Bering Sea. Japan's claim to an indemnity was dropped.

From Japan's point of view, these gains seemed less than consistent with her splendid performance on the battlefield—or so it appeared to the Japanese public, who rioted in protest when the terms were published, and had to be warned by the Emperor against "manifestations of vainglorious pride." Nevertheless, Japan was in no position to give any more military support to higher demands; and in any case the war had already given her something less tangible than territorial concessions but perhaps no less valuable in the long run. What the Japanese military victories amounted to was a confirmation that great-power status no longer belonged to European nations alone. Japan was now involving herself in European-style politics in two ways. First, Japan's attitude to mainland China and Korea was just like that of any imperialist European power, in that she was interested in these territories as sources of political and economic profit, and not as partners. Secondly, through the conflict with Russia, Japan was reaching through the limitations of geography to appear on a stage hitherto the exclusive province of the European powers, with their own choreography of political movement.

For Japan, then, the war and its outcome confirmed both the nation's claim to power and its interests on the mainland—two preoccupations

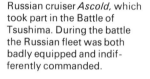

Russian cruiser *Ascold,* which took part in the Battle of Tsushima. During the battle the Russian fleet was both badly equipped and indifferently commanded.

that were to remain paramount in Japan's national life until the disastrous end of World War II. In Russia, the effects of the war were in many ways no less striking, though here they were the reverse of welcome. The Tsar had helped bring about the confrontation against the express wishes of his more sober ministers, and in defiance of popular sentiment. Hence, although there was a certain rallying to the flag in the first months of the conflict, there was never the deep faith in it that was to mark the Japanese people's attitudes. The war was itself a symbol of the Russian ruling regime's inability to deal effectively with the political tensions that were threatening to explode the nation. Accordingly, the government was incapable of a rational pursuit of its chosen policy. Afraid, for instance, of *zemstvo* (local self-government) tendencies toward independent action, it suppressed an initiative from this quarter to organize a system of aid for the wounded, and this forfeited the support even of patriots. Each defeat did indeed release a little more of the popular pressure against the government, to culminate in the 1905 Revolution in January of that year.

The Japanese war had of course been brought to an end before these events, which were also themselves part of a longer process of political development within Russia. Nevertheless, the war had played a crucial role in helping to crystallize the opposition at this moment; indeed, the whole relationship between war and rebellion in 1904–1905 foreshadowed the more decisive causes that led to the Revolution of 1917. This connection with future events was, moreover, not confined to the internal Russian situation alone. In military terms, too, the war was of immediate interest to the European powers. It presented an opportunity to see new tactics and new weaponry in action in the largest field engagements since the far-off days of the Napoleonic Wars. The lessons of insuring that even huge numbers of troops could be kept mobile and properly supplied were brought home to Western observers; the value of searchlights, in use for the first time, and machine guns was proved. As for the naval side, the Tsushima battle immediately became known as Japan's Trafalgar, and Admiral Togo as a second Nelson—not out of mere romanticism, but because the two engagements were of comparable scope and significance.

In all these ways, a war that might at first sight seem remote and relatively inconsequential can be seen as a striking signpost of the future. For Russia, there was a foretaste of the inexorable link between a bankrupt autocracy, a misguided war and bitter national upheaval. For Japan, the war was a whirlwind success which, as well as establishing the new world power, also encouraged her in her vigorous nationalism and embarked her on the troubled path to 1945. For the European powers—in effect, the political world—Japan's performance in 1904–1905 was evidence of a new level of international competition that has since finally shattered Europe's world supremacy.

JANE CAPLAN

Russia's 1905 Revolution unleashes a

Japan

Success in the war of 1894 against China had led the Western powers to recognize that Japan could not be treated as another backward state. The defeat of Russia established Japan as a power in her own right. Korea had already become a protectorate, and Japanese pressure on China mounted steadily, particularly after the collapse of the Manchu dynasty, six years after the Russo-Japanese War. Although the major colonial countries were a little disturbed by the rapidly growing power of Japan, they preferred to see a strong counterbalance to what would otherwise have been complete Russian domination of east Asia. Internally, Japan's new-found international strength and confidence encouraged investment and economic growth. By the beginning of World War I, Japan had already laid the foundations of her later industrial strength.

While Japan's new confidence was apparent to all, the situation in Russia after its defeat in the war of 1904–1905 was very different.

Russia

The results of the disastrous defeats suffered in the war with Japan increased the discontent in Russia, and on January 22, 1905, the inevitable explosion took place. In the middle of a wave of strikes, the workers of St. Petersburg's great Pulitov factory marched in an orderly and peaceful fashion—more a procession than a demonstration—to the Winter Palace, where a petition was to be presented to the Tsar. Singing hymns and carrying pictures of the Tsar, the marchers were met by bullets fired by the Tsar's troops. In Trotsky's words: "The soldiers fired all day long. The dead were counted in hundreds, the wounded in thousands." Such was "Bloody Sunday," the first step in what became the 1905 Revolution, and a day on which, according to Lenin, the Russian working class made more progress in evolving a political consciousness than in all its previous history. After this event, strike followed strike; proletarian organization became more sophisticated; and there was more effective cooperation with the liberal bour-

The battleship *Potemkin* on which the crew mutinied during the 1905 Revolution in Russia.

geoisie. In October the irresistible political momentum forced the Tsar to concede the famous "October Manifesto," promising an elected assembly and a form of cabinet government.

In many ways that revolt was a dress rehearsal for 1917, for although the abortive coup of 1905 had no formal connection with the successful Revolution of 1917, it was an indication of the acute revolutionary situation in tsarist Russia. The events of 1905 had revealed the massive discontent of the Russian people; and the Second Congress guaranteed that there would ultimately be a party ruthless enough to exploit that discontent.

Further reports of catastrophic military defeats, such as the annihilation of the Baltic fleet at Tsushima, soon forced the Tsar to make concessions to his people. A constitution was promised, and a

parliament, the Duma, was set up. But Nicholas' move came too late. Workers in St. Petersburg spontaneously created their own councils (soviets) and under the leadership of a young Social Democrat, Leon Trotsky, the soviets became the real power in the land. Blind fear of the proletariat caused the middle classes to panic. They rallied to the government, and the Tsar was able to suppress the soviets. The powerless Duma remained in existence—a pathetic façade of democracy without a champion. Lenin said that supporting the Duma "was haggling with tsarism over the dead bodies of the workers."

One of the more serious consequences of the 1905 Revolution was Russia's growing introspection. Modernizers, of whom the most prominent was Count Sergei Witte, were swept aside. Had Witte's proposed industrial and constitutional reforms been accepted,

Russia might have been dragged into the twentieth century before World War I. As it was, Russia's path to modernization was to lie through the violence of the Bolshevik Revolution.

The 1905 Revolution was dead, but its consequences were incalculable. The Bolsheviks learned from their mistakes, and in 1917 they did not hesitate to lead the people. "All power to the soviets!" they cried.

Reverberations from the experiences of the soviets were not confined to Russia alone. Through-

Count Sergei Witte, who advocated industrial and constitutional reform in Russia.

out Asia and the Arab world—where the Russo-Japanese War symbolized the struggle between oppressed nations and European imperialists—the 1905 Revolution was seen as part of the struggle against tyranny. It unleashed a wave of unrest that spread from the Middle East to Vietnam.

India

India, too, suffered grave disturbances in 1905. There were agricultural riots in the Punjab and terrorist outbreaks in Bengal as popular opinion turned against British imperialism. In order to run their vast and profitable Indian Empire, the British had been forced to educate many Indians, and by 1900 there were five universities in India. An educated middle class emerged that was aware of the significance of the French and American Revolutions and of Western democratic ideals. They wanted

Ceremonial opening of the Duma in St. Petersburg in 1906. Elected by universal suffrage, this first representative assembly ended in deadlock.

to know why India could not be self-governing like Canada and Australia. The British tried to stem the tide by instituting reforms in 1909 that were aimed at creating "a class of persons, Indian in blood and colour, but English in taste, in opinion, in morals and in intellect." The creation of these Westernized Oriental Gentlemen (or "wogs" as they were derisively known) was a temporary measure. In the long run British rule was doomed. These developments in China, Japan, Russia and India were the first signs that the balance of world power was to shift dramatically as the twentieth century progressed.

Morocco

Despite the difficulties of the British in India, however, the tide of colonialism had not yet ended. On the southern coast of the Mediterranean, the powers competed to establish a presence that would help them in a European war. While some areas of influence—the British in Egypt and the French in Algeria—were clearly established and de-

with Gibraltar, it controlled access to the Mediterranean from the Atlantic. The traditionally close relationship between Spain and North Africa—geographically, culturally and politically—combined with anger at the continued British occupation of Gibraltar to excite Spanish ambitions for the two hundred and twenty thousand square miles of Morocco. France saw Morocco as the natural extension of its colony in Algeria, and wanted to complete the occupation of a North African empire bordered on every side by water or desert. Germany's ambitions were slightly different: Morocco offered the possibility of establishing a useful base from which to extend its rapidly developing trading interests. British interest was more purely strategic than colonial and seemed to be best served by supporting Spain, a support that helped to defuse demands for the return of Gibraltar.

It was only in 1903, however, that Morocco's internal situation allowed European ambitions to take a practical direction. Privileged foreign economic penetration had already reduced tax re-

Bertrand Russell, British philosopher and mathematician.

The signing of the 1912 convention by which Spain recognized France's right to assume a protectorate over Morocco.

fined, relationships elsewhere were less clearly defined. Italian ambitions were already apparent in Libya (Tripolitania, Cyrenaica, Fezzan and Senussi), and by the 1912 Treaty of Lausanne, the Turks acknowledged Italian sovereignty there.

Far more serious was the situation in Morocco, which had considerable strategic significance because,

ceipts, and Morocco was forced to borrow large sums from French bankers to quiet trouble among the border tribes. Three years later European hegemony was effectively established by the Algeciras Conference, although Morocco remained formally independent. This averted a very real possibility of war between France and Germany, but it provided only a temporary

solution to the Moroccan problem. Over the next five years several incidents threatened the peace of Europe. It was not until 1912 that Germany finally acknowledged what had by then become French sovereignty. Spain was given the northern tip of the country. By that time the Moroccan crisis had shown how easily international accord could be threatened, and had played an important part in the long drift to war.

Scientific developments

The early twentieth century saw a host of developments that rapidly transformed the face of science. The year 1900 was something of a watershed in the history of science as it saw the publication of Sigmund Freud's *The Interpretation of Dreams*. A few years before, man's ability to study himself and his world was enlarged by the discovery of x-rays. Radioactivity, too, was discovered in the last years of the nineteenth century.

The scientists of the early twentieth century saw themselves as more than mere fact finders: their work had important philo-

sophical implications, and it is no accident that leading philosophers such as Bertrand Russell (1872–1970) and Alfred North Whitehead (1861–1947) were brilliant mathematicians, while scientists such as Albert Einstein (1879–1955) and Ernst Mach (1838–1916) were well aware that their work would have an influence on the way in which men regarded the universe.

The most influential of these scientist-philosophers in the years before the publication of Einstein's special and general theories of relativity was Max Planck (1858–1947), formerly professor of theoretical physics at the University of Berlin. In 1900 Planck attacked Newton's laws on dynamics—the basis of orthodox contemporary views on physics. Planck, like many of his contemporaries, had been puzzled by the radiation from a "black body" (a body whose surface absorbs all the radiation that falls on it), and his work convinced him that the Newtonian laws were incorrect. Although Planck's quantum theory had a revolutionary effect on physics and on philosophical ideas, Einstein's theory of relativity was to prove even more revolutionary.

E = Mc²

At the beginning of the twentieth century scientists viewed the physical world according to the principles laid down by Sir Isaac Newton two centuries before, and believed that there was nothing new left to discover. Yet "anomalies" persisted—phenomena that could not adequately be explained. Then Albert Einstein, an obscure civil servant in Switzerland, published a paper on the electrodynamics of moving bodies—and totally revolutionized the science of physics, with implications that are still not fully understood today.

At the end of the nineteenth century physicists were complacently confident that they knew the physical picture of the universe at least in broad outline and that only details remained to be filled in. Then, in 1905, Albert Einstein published his first theory of relativity and this picture was ironically turned upside down (if only because the theory said that "upside down" had no absolute meaning). The consequences of the theory, and its more general formulation, which Einstein produced a decade later, kept physicists busy from then on. And even in the 1970s the full ramifications of the theory had not been worked out.

One of the great historical triumphs of physics was the development of Newtonian mechanics toward the end of the seventeenth century. Sir Isaac Newton's monumental works included not only a law of gravitation, but also the spatial framework in which the world of physics exists. It was this framework that was undermined by Einstein's work. However, by working on the basis provided by Newton, physicists for two centuries had developed a description of the universe that gradually seemed to be approaching completion. It was even suggested by some noted scientists that the only task left for physics in the twentieth century would be to measure various known phenomena to ever greater degrees of accuracy. Clearly, this was not to be the case.

Newton had based his postulates on a belief in the absoluteness of time: "Absolute true and mathematical time," he said, "of itself and from its own nature, flows equally without relation to anything external." And on a similar belief in absolute space, that is, a belief in the existence of a fixed standard of reference against which one can define both absolute position and absolute motion: "Absolute space, in its own nature, without relation to anything external, remains always similar and immovable." Thus, while in the Newtonian system

it was possible to accept not only that the Earth is in motion around the Sun but also that the Sun may be in motion, it was believed that there was some fixed standard against which all their motions could be judged absolutely.

With the development, during the second half of the nineteenth century, of theories of electromagnetic radiation (light and all other forms of radiation—such as radio waves—that travel at the speed of light), it seemed that this absolute frame of reference might be provided by a hypothetical material called the "lumeniferous ether," or ether for short. It was well known, by this time, that waves require a medium in which to travel. Thus, without water, there are no water waves. Similarly, without air, there is no sound: a bell ringing in a vacuum makes no noise. Scientists at the time believed that light was a form of wave; consequently, there must be some medium through which it traveled. As light traveled from distant stars, it seemed probable that this medium permeated the whole of space. Hence, it might provide a frame of reference by which all measurements of position and motion could be made.

In 1881, the American scientist A. A. Michelson attempted to measure the speed of the Earth through the ether; six years later, he attempted the experiment again in a more refined version, with a colleague, E. W. Morley. The so-called Michelson-Morley experiment is one of the most famous in the history of physics. Although it was only one of several experiments pointing to a failure of the Newtonian system to provide a comprehensive explanation of the world, it was possibly the most significant.

If two objects, such as boats, make round-trip journeys of exactly the same distance at exactly the same speed, both covering the same route, they will both return to base at exactly the same time. However, if the journeys do not cover the same route, and one boat goes, for example, across a river, while the other goes directly upstream and

Albert Einstein, the obscure civil servant who revolutionized the science of physics.

Opposite The laboratory in the Zurich Federal Institute of Technology where Einstein carried out his first experiments.

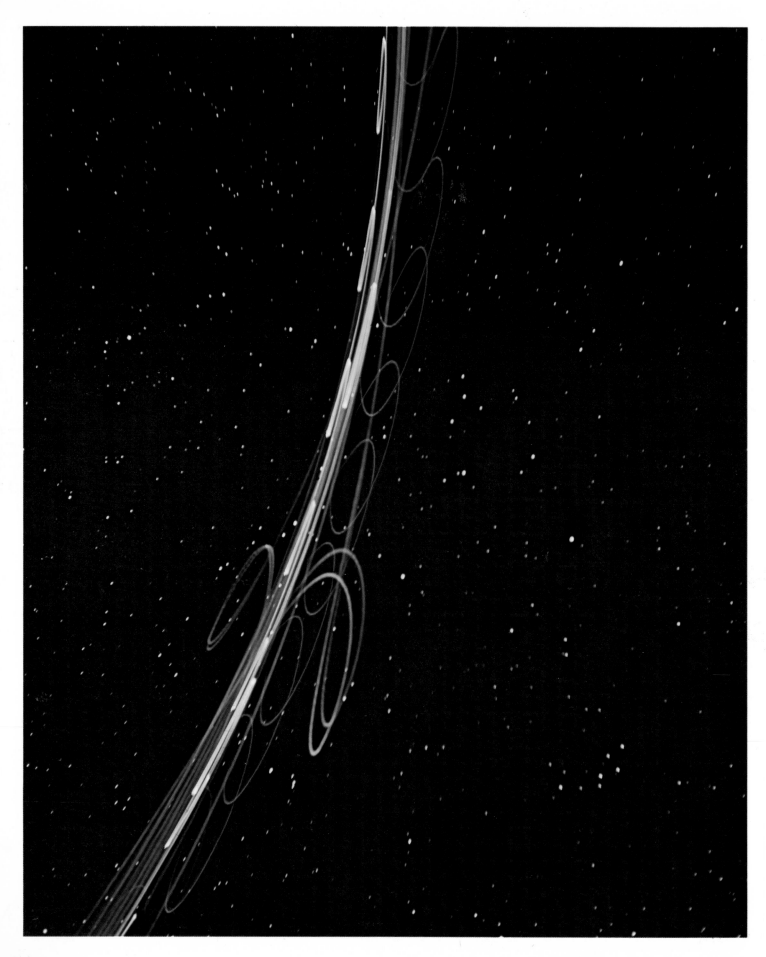

downstream, it can be shown mathematically that they will not complete the journey in the same time as each other, and that the difference in journey time will be related to the speed at which the river flows downstream.

In essence, the Michelson-Morley experiment sent light waves out on journeys of identical length, but at right angles to each other. Using a phenomenon called interference, it should have been possible to measure the difference in time taken for the two journeys, and from this the speed at which the Earth was moving through the ether. Although the apparatus was sufficiently sensitive to measure a movement of one kilometer per second (later refined to one fifth of this value), no difference between the journey times of the two light beams was ever detected.

Many physicists tried to find explanations for such a result. The most important, discovered independently by the Irishman G. F. Fitzgerald in 1893, and the Dutchman Hendrik Lorentz in 1896, and known either as the Fitzgerald or Lorentz contraction, proposed that when an object is in motion, it shrinks in the direction of its motion, but not in the perpendicular direction. Consequently, the lengths of the two journeys in the Michelson-Morley experiment had not been identical (although it would never be possible to measure the differences, as any measuring instrument would also be subject to the "shrinking" phenomenon).

This provided an answer to the puzzle set by the Michelson-Morley experiment, but the whole atmosphere had changed; was it never going to be possible for physicists to detect the ether in any way? Other experiments were devised; none produced evidence for the existence of the ether. Some, however, threw doubt on the correctness of the Fitzgerald-Lorentz hypothesis.

In 1905, in the German scientific journal *Annalen der Physik*, Albert Einstein, then aged twenty-six, published a paper entitled *On the electrodynamics of moving bodies*. Einstein was not, as one might have imagined, an experimental physicist, but a patents examiner. Born in 1879, in Ulm, Germany, he had grown up in Munich, and completed his education in Switzerland. It was here, in Berne, that he took a job in the Patent Office because he could not find a better one. As early as 1902, he had worked out a new analysis of the phenomenon known as Brownian motion, which played an important role in persuading doubters (and there were, at that time, doubters even among leading members of the scientific community) of the existence of atoms.

What Einstein said in his 1905 paper, which embodies the special theory of relativity, appears at first unexceptionable. There were two basic statements:

1. That every inertial observer may regard himself as at rest.
2. That the speed of light is always the same in all directions, regardless of the state of the body from which it originates.

The first statement is the "special principle of

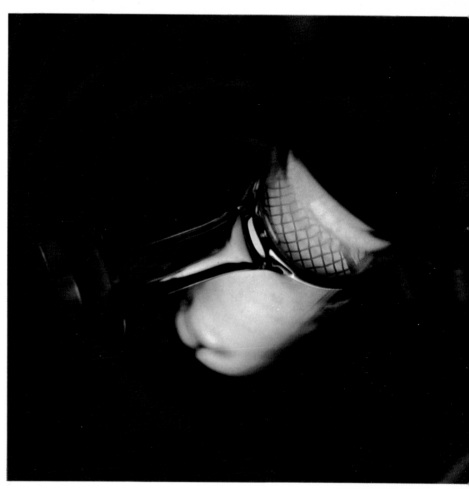

relativity" which explains why the Michelson-Morley experiment did not work. What it says is that it is not possible to detect uniform motion through the "ether." For a person moving at constant velocity (the "inertial observer"), there is no way of telling whether he is moving or not. While this appears to contradict common sense, it is possible to give an example of the relativity of motion which most people have experienced.

Assume you are sitting in a train that is stopped at a station and, rather than looking at the platform, you look at another train, standing beside yours on the track. One of the trains begins to move slowly. For a brief moment, you may not be able to tell whether your train is still at rest and the other moving past it, or vice versa. You can solve this paradox simply by looking the other way and seeing if you are moving relative to the station platform, or are still stationary with respect to it. What Einstein's postulate says is that, on a cosmic scale, there is no platform for you to look at and check whether you are moving or stationary. So, whether you are moving or not, you can assume that you are at rest—just as we do when we stand still on Earth, although we may know that the Earth itself is racing around the Sun.

The second postulate is the one that really appears to contradict common sense, for it undermines the basis of the Newtonian system that time is an ever-flowing stream in which nothing can produce even

Above A plasma (or very hot stream of ionized atoms). According to the Einsteinian relationship $E = Mc^2$, when the nuclei of small atoms, such as hydrogen, fuse together, some of the matter is converted into energy. All the energy from the Sun comes from such fusion reactions.

Opposite The loops of Venus, Mars and Mercury and the retracting motion of Jupiter and Saturn, recorded in the Munich Planetarium. Copernicus had explained the planets' movements by placing the Sun at the center of the planetary system, but it was not until Einstein's theory of relativity that anomalies such as Mercury's movement were accounted for.

the smallest ripple. What it means is that, if one has two systems moving with respect to one another, and they both measure the speed of light from an external source, both will get the same answer. A closer examination of this appears to indicate logical inconsistencies. For example, if in one system two experimenters send light waves to one another over a very large distance, then if they know the speed of light (*c.* 300,000 km/sec) and the distance between them (say, 450,000 km), they can calculate that a ray of light will reach the second experimenter 1.5 seconds after transmission by the first experimenter. If the second experimenter now reflects that light ray back, it will reach the first experimenter's laboratory three seconds later than he transmitted it —at least, three seconds later by his clock.

If these events could be seen by an observer in the second system, would he see them the same? According to Einstein's first postulate, people in either system can imagine themselves at rest. Therefore, let us assume that the observer in the second system sees the first system moving past him at very high speed—say, eighty percent of the speed

of light (as will be seen later, there are "systems" that move at even greater speeds than this). For simplicity's sake, we assume that the two experimenters in the first system are separated by a distance at right angles to the direction in which the system is moving with respect to the external observer. Because he considers himself at rest, he does not see the two experimenters send a light beam 450,000 km, but a larger distance for, in the time taken for the light to reach the second observer, the system which they are in has moved with respect to the outside observer. Diagramatically the light travels along the hypotenuse of a triangle, the other sides of which are the distance traveled by one system relative to the other and the distance between the two points in one of the systems. Using simple geometry, it can be shown that, under these conditions, according to the outside observer, the light takes 2.5 seconds to go from one experimenter to the other. To make the round trip takes five seconds. This disparity in time results from the second postulate of relativity—the nondependence of the speed of light on the relative motion of its source.

What follows is that time is no more an absolute than space. The idea that events follow one another sequentially need not be true if they are in different frames of reference. For example, in the year 1054, Chinese astronomers noted the appearance of a very bright new star in the constellation of Taurus. It is now known that this event was a supernova (stellar explosion) that produced the Crab Nebula. This event according to Earth time occurred twelve years before the Battle of Hastings. Yet, in many other places in the Universe, it would have seemed to occur long before, or even long after the Battle of Hastings, had observers been able to see both events.

Three years after Einstein had published his theory, Hermann Minkowski, a German mathematician, put a geometrical interpretation on it, which showed how time can be seen as a "fourth dimension." Minkowski's contribution is important; it was not just a mathematical formulation of Einstein's principles, it was a formulation done in such a way that it guided Einstein on toward his general theory of relativity.

In addition to making time another dimension of space (Minkowski said, "Space in itself and time in itself sink to mere shadows and only a kind of union of the two retains an independent existence"), the Einstein-Minkowski formulation made matter a property of space-time. Following work by James Clerk Maxwell and by Lorentz (whose contributions to modern physics should not be underestimated; Einstein wrote that Lorentz' work was "of such consistency, lucidity and beauty as has only rarely been attained in an empirical science"), Einstein was able to show that matter and energy can be interrelated (through what is probably the world's most famous equation, $E = Mc^2$). He was also able to subsume the three basic conservation laws of physics, those of conservation of mass, energy and momentum into a single conservation law.

The general theory of relativity differs from the special theory in that it deals with systems that are accelerating or decelerating, while the special theory deals only with those that are at rest or moving with constant velocity. In simple terms,

Part of the intricate engineering of a particle accelerator. These machines, used by physicists studying the basic structure of matter, accelerate subatomic particles to such high speeds that Einstein's relativity equations are important in their design.

the general theory states that acceleration and gravitation are, under certain conditions, indistinguishable. The force of gravity thus becomes a natural outcome of the behavior of space-time. From this theory came the prediction that light rays can be bent by gravity, because Einstein had by then reinstated the view that light was not just a wave like other waves, but also had a particulate nature.

Theories are only useful in science if they explain observed phenomena. (This does not mean they are right; the phlogiston theory in the eighteenth century explained many chemical observations, but was still wrong.) For one theory to supersede another, it should not only explain adequately all the phenomena explained by the older theory, but also take into account phenomena that, in terms of

the older theory, are "anomalous." Why, then, do physicists accept Einstein rather than Newton?

One of the major vindications of Newtonian theory was that it accounted well for the observed motions of the planets. In fact, on the basis of Newtonian theory, it was predicted that irregularities in the motion of the planet Uranus were caused by the presence of another, undiscovered planet. Further, the theory enabled scientists to postulate where one should look for this planet—and when astronomers looked in the predicted direction, they found the planet Neptune. Similar irregularities were observed in the motion of the planet Mercury, and some astronomers predicted the existence of a hitherto undiscovered planet, which they named Vulcan. But Vulcan does not exist. For, when Einsteinian theory was applied to

planetary movements, it was found that the observed irregularities of the motion of Mercury were exactly as the theory predicted.

A second vindication for relativity is the behavior of certain particles with respect to time. Atoms vibrate with specific frequencies, which can be measured on Earth as they occur on Earth, or as they occur in distant stars. According to Einstein's predictions, an intense gravitational field should affect the vibration time, causing a change in the observed wavelength of the spectral lines. Such Einsteinian shifts have been observed in the light from white-dwarf stars. Another example of temporal relativity occurs in cosmic ray showers. These can contain particles called mu-mesons. On Earth, mu-mesons have a life of about one and a half millionths of a second; in cosmic ray showers, this lifetime is extended a hundredfold because the particles are moving at speeds close to the speed of light. (We, as external observers, see the lifetime of the particles extended; if an observer were traveling on the mu-meson, he would still measure its lifetime as one and a half millionths of a second.)

Einstein's predictions that light rays bend when passing through a gravitational field was confirmed during the total eclipse of the Sun in 1919. His relationship between mass and energy was most dramatically demonstrated at Alamagordo on July 16, 1945, when the first atomic bomb exploded. Einsteinian physics is used to calculate the design of cyclotrons, in which physicists accelerate fundamental particles to speeds that are significant fractions of the speed of light. The cyclotrons that have been designed on this basis operate effectively, which would not have been possible if they had been designed on orthodox Newtonian principles.

However, the story of Einstein's theory of relativity is not complete. One of its most elegant experimental verifications occurred in 1960, when Rudolf Mössbauer showed with great exactness that a beam of gamma rays falling downward gains energy as it falls with gravity—one of the requirements of the general theory. And, in the early 1970s, radio-astronomers at Cambridge, England, measured the bending of light from recently discovered quasars and found that the amount of bending agreed accurately with Einstein's predictions.

In addition to the physicists' use of Einsteinian theory, there have been endless philosophical debates about the principle of relativity. Does the principle of cause and effect still hold, if before and after can be changed about, according to where an observer is placed? Is everything relative, and nothing ultimately real? These debates tend to be largely (possibly wholly) timewasting, because we live in what is essentially still a Newtonian world. Where objects move very slowly by comparison with the speed of light, Newtonian equations and explanations suffice. It was not the world as we know it that was changed by Einstein's theory of relativity, but the world as we understand it. The effects of Einstein's theories are felt directly only by high energy physicists and cosmologists. However, the renaissance of physics which occurred as a result of Max Planck's expounding of the quantum theory and Einstein's relativity equations clearly shows the dangers of believing that our scientific understanding of the universe is ever nearing completion.   MARTIN SHERWOOD

Above Einstein (bareheaded) on Christmas Island in the Indian Ocean, where he went in 1919 to confirm his theory of relativity.

Above left Hendrik Lorentz, whose work on the phenomena of moving bodies led to the promulgation of the theory of relativity.

New techniques and approaches

Scientific developments

The years between Einstein's publication of his special law of relativity and the outbreak of World War II saw rapid scientific advance. Einstein broadened the scope of his relativity theory in 1915 by the publication of his general law, and by 1920 his ideas had largely been accepted by most of the scientific community. Anxious to avoid the danger that his theories, which he regarded as merely the best hypotheses available at the time, would become as stereotyped an orthodoxy as those of Newton, he continued to express his belief that there was as yet no theory available that provided a complete logical basis for physics. Yet despite his modesty, Einstein's fame spread rapidly and after his emigration from Nazi Germany to the United States in 1933 he helped to create the reputation of the newly formed Institute of Advanced Studies at Princeton, New Jersey.

Ernest Rutherford's room in the Cavendish Laboratory, Cambridge, England.

Einstein's genius was quickly recognized, but quantum physics had a wider impact through the study of the structure of the atom. Throughout the early years of the century work on atomic physics advanced rapidly, particularly in England at the Cavendish Laboratory, Cambridge, where J. J. Thomson (1856–1940), Ernest Rutherford (1871–1937) and James Chadwick (1891–1974) worked, and in Germany, when Arnold Sommerfeld (1868–1951), Werner Heisenberg (1901–) and Erwin Schrödinger

(1887–1961) made important discoveries. By the end of the 1930s it had become clear from the work of the Joliot-Curies in Paris that disintegrating a uranium nucleus would cause others to disintegrate also—the basis of the use of atomic energy, whether in peace or war. By 1942 Enrico Fermi (1901–54) had set up the first nuclear pile, and only three years later the first atomic bomb was detonated.

Biology and medicine

No less profound were developments in biological sciences. These sprang largely from the work of the nineteenth-century Czech abbot of Brno, Gregor Mendel (1822–84), whose work on the fertilization of sweet peas forms the basis of modern genetic studies. It was not until the early twentieth century that the significance of Mendel's work was recognized. It led ultimately to a modification of Darwinian ideas of evolution.

Of more immediate impact than genetics in the early twentieth century was the application of science to medicine. Many previously incurable and unavoidable diseases, such as the mosquito-borne malaria and yellow fever, were brought under control, and as a result of immunization typhoid and tetanus ceased to be a menace to Western society. As a result of the research of Clement Pirquet (1874–1929), it became possible to diagnose tuberculosis at an early stage. Other serious diseases and complaints for which prevention or

Sir Alexander Fleming, whose discovery of penicillin made possible the control of bacteria.

cure became possible were syphilis and diphtheria, and the discovery of insulin made diabetes a manageable disease. Perhaps more important than the cure of any disease was the discovery of penicillin by Sir Alexander Fleming (1881–1955) as it made possible the control of bacteria.

Dietary habits were changed by research on vitamins. Little less significant for the future was the pioneering work of Clarence Birdseye (1886–1956) in deepfreezing food. Clothing too was affected by science, as the development of artificial fabrics such as nylon began to make itself felt in the 1930s. But not all scientific work proved to be of such value: in 1912 the scientific community was forced to rethink many of its ideas by the "discovery" of humanoid skull fossils in an excavation in Piltdown, England, together with animal bones of great antiquity. "Piltdown Man" was thus dated from 200,000 to 1,000,000 years ago, far earlier than previous evidence had suggested. It was not until forty years later that it was proved to be a fake.

Psychology

The early years of the century saw an enormous increase in interest in the study of the human mind. Initially this was dominated by Middle Europeans, of whom Sigmund Freud was the most influential. The development of psychoanalysis found competition in *Gestalt* psychology, which was also largely Viennese. Unlike psy-

choanalysts, who sought to analyze consciousness in its constituent parts, *Gestalt* psychology saw experience as a whole and held that it could not be broken down. In the 1920s the development of behaviorism in America led to a concentration on behavior patterns, which were seen as reactions to particular external stimuli, rather than on consciousness. This approach found much in common with the work of the Russian psychologist Ivan Petrovich Pavlov (1849–1936), who experimented on conditioned reflexes in dogs.

Other influential schools developed largely as Freudian "heresies." Alfred Adler (1870–1937), for example, stressed the importance of man's aggressiveness and power lust, while Carl Jung (1875–1961) developed an elaborate system based on archetypes and a belief in a collective unconscious, and William Reich (1897–1957) produced a synthesis of Marxist and psychological ideas notable chiefly for its eccentricity.

The arts

In the arts the prevailing mood was violent. The Futurists advocated movement and violence as ends in themselves, and their paintings were obsessively concerned with racing cars and speedboats. In music the mood was, perhaps, less obvious but nonetheless significant. The savage, tramping rhythms of the Sixth Symphony of Gustav Mahler (1860–1911), published in 1904, were strangely prophetic of the political and social horrors to

Gustav Mahler, whose Sixth Symphony was prophetic of the social and political horrors to come.

revolutionize music, literature and the visual arts

come. Equally ominous themes were to be found in such musical landmarks of the prewar period as *Rite of Spring* by Igor Stravinsky (1882–1971), in which savage and primeval rhythms abound, and the Fourth Symphony of Jean Sibelius (1865–1957), in which the prevailing mood is one of desolation. But perhaps the most prophetic musical utterance of all, in the summer of 1914, was *Planets Suite* by Gustav Holst (1874–1934). A section called *Mars* seemed a bleak and relentless assertion of war's cruel brutalities.

Violence was not, however, the only characteristic of art in the period before World War I and in the interwar period. The period was no less significant for the birth and acceptance of modernism in all the arts.

Literature

Writing, like music, was revolutionized by new techniques and new approaches. Most influential were an Irishman, James Joyce (1882–1941), and a Frenchman, Marcel Proust (1871–1922), who charted a new passage for the novel. Although the traditional novel, with its essentially external, social view of human character, continued to be read, Proust and Joyce concentrated rather on portraying the inner personality of their characters. Proust's twelve-volume *A la Recherche du Temps Perdu* (*Remembrance of Things Past*), which was published between 1913 and 1928, was not unusual in its subject matter—the relationships between members of the decaying French aristocracy and *haute bourgeoisie* in his youth—but was revolutionary in approach, describing all that happened in his life through the impact that it had on him.

Joyce, too, adopted a highly subjective approach, and his novel *Ulysses* (1922) was a highly personalized account of a single day—June 16, 1904—in the lives of a group of Dubliners. In it he adopted a stream-of-consciousness technique which, in a forty-page monologue, showed a woman's thoughts as a continuous process by dispensing with punctuation so that one idea rolls into the next. Even more striking than *Ulysses* was Joyce's later novel *Finnegans Wake* (1939), in which vocabulary and syntax were treated in the same cavalier fashion as grammar,

F. Scott Fitzgerald with his wife Zelda and daughter "Scottie" in Annecy, France, 1931.

making the book one of the most remarkable—if least readable—masterpieces of English literature.

Joyce and Proust were merely the most exceptional of many literary innovators, another of whom was the Paris-based American Gertrude Stein (1874–1946) whose explorations of the meaning of words and phrases had a certain influence. Like Stein, other Americans found a more congenial working atmosphere in Europe than in the United States. Until his death in 1916, Henry James was the most influential of the expatriate writers, but in the 1920s the younger novelists, F. Scott Fitzgerald (1896–1940) and Ernest Hemingway (1899–1961), showed that talented American authors still looked to Europe for inspiration. Thomas Stearns Eliot (1888–1965), the outstanding poet of his generation, found the pull of Europe irresistible and emigrated to London. The American poet Ezra Pound (1885–1972), the leader of the imagist movement and mentor of Eliot and

Joyce, also lived in Europe.

It was not hard to see the attraction of Europe for American writers. The intellectual climate was far more receptive to new ideas. In England, for example, the Blooms-

Virginia Woolf, novelist and member of the Bloomsbury Group.

bury Group followed Lytton Strachey (1880–1932) in debunking what they saw as the pompous, self-righteous attitudes of the Victorian era. But the Bloomsbury Group sought to replace Victorian values with their own "advanced" ideas about sex, society, politics and above all, literature and art. The perceptive, poetic novels of Virginia Woolf (1882–1941), the forceful economic writings of John Maynard Keynes (1883–1946) and the lyric joyousness of the paintings of Duncan Grant (1885–   ) show how catholic were the talents of this group.

Music

Music, like literature, developed in revolutionary directions. The key figure in the breakdown of established musical tradition was the Viennese composer Arnold Schoenberg (1874–1951). He was chiefly responsible for the abandonment of the classical tonal system as the structural basis of musical composition. In the late nineteenth century, Wagner had shown a certain acceptance of dissonance, and although largely self-taught, Schoenberg was much influenced by Wagner's music. Believing that "order, which we describe as artistic form, is not an aim in itself but merely an expedient," he adopted an atonal system based on a twelve-note scale.

In America there was a musical revolution of a different kind. In New Orleans and other Southern cities a new form of popular music, based on songs, marches and dances, developed in the first two decades of the century among the Negro population. Jazz, which gave musicians the chance to bring out the full potential of a limited range of instruments and also gave opportunities for improvisation, was to have a wide influence.

Architecture, too, developed in new and radical directions in the twentieth century. The revival of defunct styles was largely abandoned and architects such as Walter Gropius (1883–1969) and Le Corbusier (1887–1965) saw the need for new styles that would have some relevance for the contemporary society and would utilize advanced construction techniques to their full advantage. Painting did not escape this revolution in the other arts, as the birth of Cubism was to show.

Picasso Revolutionizes Art   1907

As the twentieth century opened, the Renaissance ideal of beauty was under wide attack. Vlaminck and Derain were calling attention to the unfamiliar splendors of the art of tribal Africa and the theories—and paintings—of Paul Cézanne had aroused widespread excitement. It remained for Picasso to take the revolutionary step. With Les Demoiselles d'Avignon *he totally renounced Renaissance beauty, jettisoned such concepts as traditional perspective, and instead of painting what he saw was there, painted what he knew was there. Modern art, as we know it, was born.*

Les Demoiselles d'Avignon is considered by many to be the beginning of modern art. While this is an oversimplification it is sufficiently true for the painting to be legitimately regarded as a symbol of the revolutionary changes in art that took place in the early years of this century. This pictorial revolution was due in large part to Pablo Picasso, and *Les Demoiselles d'Avignon* bears witness to the struggle he underwent in his formulation of the new approach. In it he consciously rejected the Classical ideal of beauty that had by and large been recognized by artists since the Renaissance, five hundred years earlier. In addition Picasso abandoned completely all traditional methods of perspective, thus heightening the expressive power achieved through his deliberate distortion of the figures. The prime importance of the picture, however, does not lie so much in these negative values as in the revolutionary and positive step that Picasso took in representing what he knew existed—as opposed to what he saw existing—from a single static position. This combination of different viewpoints in a single figure, shown in its crudest form in *Les Demoiselles*, provided the basic starting point for the whole of the Cubist movement. Furthermore, in a wider sense, this shift from perceptual to conceptual methods of vision is fundamental to the majority of the ensuing developments in art, during the first half of this century.

Picasso, who had moved to Paris from his native Spain in 1903 when he was twenty-two, began work on *Les Demoiselles* at the end of 1906. By this time he was already acknowledged as a gifted and original artist, who was even beginning to reap some commercial reward for his success. Some of the most important collectors had already begun to buy his work and he was living in a state of relative prosperity compared to his poverty-stricken student days in Barcelona. The world of art in Paris, at the end of 1906, was still dominated by the Fauves (a group of artists centered in France whose works were characterized by vivid colors in immediate juxtaposition). Their brilliantly colored canvases overshadowed all others at the annual exhibitions of the Salon d'Automne, which had been founded as a reaction against the academic sterility of the established Salon and was the focal point of the avant-garde. In the autumn of 1906 Henri Matisse, the Fauves' acknowledged leader, exhibited his large-scale work *Le Joie de Vivre*, which caused a sensation as it represented a considerable departure from his earlier style. Apart from Matisse, however, it was becoming apparent that the original energy of the Fauves was dwindling. The time was ripe for further developments within the avant-garde, a situation of which Picasso must have been aware. Up till this date, however, Picasso's art had been noted for its emotional and symbolic content rather than any innovation in formal terms. The cold tonality and poignant atmosphere of his Blue Period paintings had begun to be replaced in 1904 by softer pinks and grays and a general lightening of mood, culminating in his series of circus and harlequin themes. In 1905 he visited Holland where some of his work was characterized by a new solidity and fullness of form. This awareness of three-dimensional volume led him to produce some sculpture, for example his bust of a harlequin, which was cast in bronze. He almost certainly studied Classical sculpture about this time, as can be seen from the famous figure of the boy leading a horse, which has a striking resemblance to a certain Greek *Kouros* in the Louvre. In the following year, however, he returned home to Spain and again saw the Romanesque and Gothic sculpture that is reflected so strongly in *Les Demoiselles*. Some reliefs from Osuna in southern Spain were exhibited at the Louvre in 1906, and Picasso himself acquired two Iberian stone heads in 1907.

Les Demoiselles is essentially a strikingly new and

West African wooden mask. The influence of African art on Picasso is evident in *Les Demoiselles,* particularly in the extraordinary resemblance of the two right-hand heads to Gold Coast masks.

Opposite Les Demoiselles d'Avignon. Taken to date the beginning of the Cubist movement, this work laid the foundation upon which abstract art has been built.

Les Grandes Baigneuses II, by
Paul Cézanne. Picasso's early
sketches for Les Demoiselles
reveal that, in the early stages
of the work's conception,
Picasso had some of
Cézanne's bather composi-
tions in mind.

original painting, but no great work of art has ever appeared in a vacuum. Picasso, in particular, never attempted to disguise his sources, preferring to acknowledge them freely, secure in the conviction of his power to revitalize even the greatest images. The grand figure of Paul Cézanne hovers over *Les Demoiselles*, although little specific evidence of any relationship remained in the final painting. In retrospect, however, in his fundamental concern with the three-dimensional actuality of ordinary objects, Cézanne appears as the natural precursor of Cubism. Cézanne's belief in the value of the eye and the brain working together was logically developed by Georges Braque and Picasso into the formal movement of Cubism. There are, however, several important differences between the art of Picasso and that of Cézanne. Their attitude to color is fundamentally different; Cézanne used color to demonstrate volume whereas color was never a primary consideration of Picasso's, which is also a basic difference between his art and that of Matisse. The extensive series of early sketches for *Les Demoiselles* reveals that, in the early stages of its conception, Picasso almost certainly did have some of Cézanne's bather compositions in mind. They show that Picasso originally intended the picture to contain seven figures, five women and two men, grouped around a central still life. Picasso himself later explained that the central figure was a sailor, surrounded by naked women. The painting was initially referred to as *Le Bordel Philosophique* by friends and associates of Picasso such as the writer and art critic Guillaume Apollinaire. One of the figures in the early sketches carries an object,

apparently a skull, thereby suggesting that the whole work was conceived as a kind of moral allegory. The present title of the painting refers to a street in the prostitutes' quarter in Barcelona, thus retaining its erotic implications, albeit in a somewhat obscure form.

Picasso spent several months working on the studies before painting the final canvas, which is unusually large, measuring eight feet by eight feet. In the spring of 1907 he invited some of his friends to come and see it. Without exception they were aghast. Even Georges Braque, who had recently become a friend of Picasso, was initially scandalized. The Russian collector Sergei Shchukin was moved to exclaim: "What a loss to French art!" Their reaction is not difficult to understand, even today when the painting's historical value has been so consistently emphasized. It must have come as a real shock to his friends, who only knew the elegant and accomplished style of his earlier work. This group of hieratic women staring ahead with opaque black eyes presented the greatest possible contrast to the poignant charm of such paintings as the *Woman in a Chemise* two years earlier. It is also immediately apparent that the style is full of willful inconsistencies. It is almost certain that the two central figures were painted first, as they relate most closely to his earlier work, particularly in the awareness they show of primitive sculpture. Picasso had for some time been familiar with the work of Paul Gauguin, who had drawn attention to the power of primitive art. Picasso later told Christian Zervos, who was to draw up a monumental catalog of Picasso's works, that he had been studying Iberian sculpture while he was working on *Les Demoiselles*. In these two figures its impact is very pronounced. The heads are simplified, producing enormous dramatic effect, while the bodies have been flattened into angular shapes, represented without any attempt at modeling. The pink flesh is opaque and harshly treated, compared to the atmospheric fluidity of Picasso's earlier work. The figure on the extreme left is treated in a similar way, but the darker pigment of the head emphasizes the hieratic solemnity of the profile, which is reminiscent of an Egyptian frieze.

Whether Picasso repainted this head or not is a subject of debate among art historians, but it is almost certain that he did repaint the two right-hand figures. It is undeniable that they are painted in a completely different style from the rest of the picture, and it is within their creation that the radical transformation of style took place. The savage distortion of their masklike faces is quite unlike anything that Picasso had painted previously. The explanation lies in his sudden discovery of African art. Maurice de Vlaminck and André Derain had been enthusiastic about African art as far back as 1904, and Picasso must almost certainly have seen some before painting *Les Demoiselles*. It seems, however, that he was suddenly struck by the expressive significance of African art during a visit to the Museum of Historic Sculpture at the Trocadero. Whatever the precise details of his revelation, the two right-hand heads bear an extraordinary resemblance to Gold Coast masks, as the component parts share almost exactly the same simplifications of form. The significance of the use of primitive art is twofold. First, it results in an extraordinary and expressive brutality (which is quite foreign to Picasso's earlier work and also to his subsequent analytical Cubism). Second, it engenders a basically conceptual method of approach. The Negro artists consciously simplified their forms for a particular expressive purpose, instead of imitating reality. Picasso has extended this approach in a revolutionary manner, in the bodies of the two figures. In the squatting figure he has consciously violated all the rules of traditional perspective. The limbs have been pulled around so that the figure is seen from the front and back simultaneously. This combination of viewpoints is a basic feature of later Cubist art, and as such marked a new era in the history of European art.

Picasso did not show the picture to the public for thirty years—it remained rolled up in his studio until it was finally exhibited at the Petit Palais in Paris in 1937, before being bought by the Museum of Modern Art in New York. Its impact in artistic terms was, however, enormous. Picasso himself did not choose to develop the Cubist implications immediately, so much as to explore the expressive effects of the massive volumes of African sculpture. Once freed from the European tradition of illusionism he proceeded to explore these paths in a series of paintings usually referred to as belonging to his Negro period. Works such as *The Dancer* of 1907 are

crudely experimental, but they succeed in generating the potent energy of tribal art.

The following year Picasso spent the summer at La Rue-des-Bois, near Creil, north of Paris, where he painted a series of landscapes. When he returned he discovered that Braque had been painting some remarkably similar landscapes at L'Estaques in southern France. Both artists had been concentrating on the geometric simplification of the landscape forms, with each element treated in terms of its volume. This procedure derived directly from Cézanne and, although these paintings are usually referred to as the first Cubist pictures, it would be more accurate to call them post-Cézanne works. In fact the term Cubist was first used by Louis Vauxcelles, the critic who had already christened Fauvism. He wrote of Braque in 1908: "He mistakes form, reduces everything sited, faces and houses, to geometrical schemas, to cubes."

During the following summer at Horta de Ebro in northern Spain, Picasso developed the principle of geometricization even further. As he came to

Self-portrait, by Picasso. This work predates *Les Demoiselles*. The masklike quality of the head reflects Picasso's growing interest in African art.

45

terms with the perspectival ambiguities implicit in the opaque planes of Cézanne, his paintings were forced into becoming more ruthlessly logical. On his return he began working in close association with Braque. The two artists set out together to clarify and systematize their new conception of vision, whereby form is not seen as a finite characteristic of an object. They saw an object in terms of planes that indicate the various aspects of its reality, so that the relationships between the planes gave the object a new, individual reality. In order to clarify this they limited their palettes severely; restricting color largely to sepia and gray. Instead of using color to render the visible form of an object as Cézanne had done, they used it to strengthen the architectonic unity of the work as a whole. They also began to diverge from Cézanne in their stress on the contours of the planes, as they opened out the volumes instead of concentrating them. They also began to moderate the tipping of the planes into depth, so that soon they had both progressed far beyond Cézanne's famous injunction to treat nature in terms of the sphere, cylinder and cone.

The shifting relationships between the interpenetrating planes resulted in a restless, dynamic quality quite different from the volumetric grandeur of Cézanne. Their work became increasingly formalized and purely conceptual. For a while they even preferred not to sign their works, in order to emphasize their purely objective creation. Although the paintings became increasingly abstract in appearance, they were all still based on a real object. There are always clues to their discovery—the curl of a moustache or the parallels of guitar strings. The point of looking at a Cubist painting, however, is not to reconstruct reality but rather to observe the new configuration of the planes brought about through the artist's internal vision. The totality of the object is expressed in a way that gives it an autonomy of its own.

In the summer of 1911, Picasso and Braque visited Ceret, a village in the French Pyrenees. It is only just possible to decipher Braque's view of the rooftops and chimney stacks. Braque later explained that he used fragmentation to establish space as he was unable to introduce objects until after he had

Below right The Acrobats, by Picasso ; a typical example of Picasso's pre-Cubist paintings. In the light of this early naturalistic work it is easy to understand the shock caused by *Les Demoiselles.*

Below The Violin. An example of Picasso's *papiers collés ;* the more lighthearted side of Cubism.

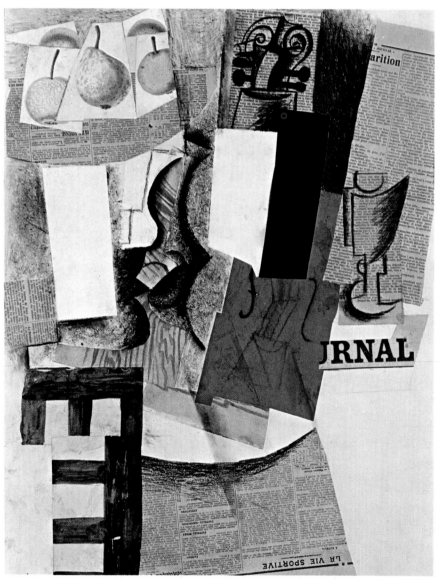

46

created space. Together with Picasso's *The Accordionist*, Braque's *The Portuguese* may be taken to represent the high point of analytical Cubism. Both take the human figure as the starting point but suggest rather than describe the volumes. The essence of this phase of Cubism is summed up in Picasso's famous remark that he painted the forms as he thought them rather than as he saw them. By the end of 1911, however, it was becoming clear that the Cubists were producing an art of an intellectual purity so great that it was becoming completely self-contained. (It is usually described as "hermetic.") They therefore recognized a need to provide some new kind of link with reality.

As early as 1910 Braque had introduced a *trompe l'oeil* (visual deception) nail into one of his best-known paintings, the *Violin and Palette*. In *The Portuguese* Braque added the letters "BAL" and the number 10:40 in order to get as close as possible to reality. In addition the letters were

... forms that could not be distorted in any way, being themselves flat, these letters were not in space, and thus, by contrast, their presence in the picture made it possible

to distinguish between objects situated in space and those which were not.

Picasso also started to incorporate letters, usually in the form of references to his current girl friend, Eva. Braque, however, soon went one stage further toward the real world by developing *trompe l'oeil* techniques. He had been trained by his father as a painter-decorator and knew the techniques of imitating marble and wood graining. He also mixed paint with materials such as sand and sawdust in order to give actual texture to the surface of the canvas. From there it was but a short jump to the pasting on of other materials altogether. Picasso was the first to take this step with his *Still Life with Chair*. In this he glued on a piece of oilcloth printed with a caning design. This added a completely new dimension to the work, as suddenly that part of the canvas upon which the oilcloth was glued was rendered more real than the rest of the work, which remained illusory. Picasso had imitated reality by using a material—oilcloth—created for a different purpose and not normally associated with art. Braque soon followed with his *Fruit Dish and Glass*,

The Portuguese, by Georges Braque. Together with Picasso's *The Accordionist* this painting is taken to represent the high point of analytical Cubism.

Headline from the Chicago *American*. Even Picasso's artistic friends were aghast when he first showed them *Les Demoiselles* in 1907; public taste was outraged.

Three Musicians, by Picasso; monumental example of synthetic Cubism.

the first of his *papiers collés*, which used three pieces of wood-grained wallpaper in conjunction with a charcoal drawing. This process initiated a significant change in the development of Cubism. Instead of using an objective intellectual process to achieve an analytical fragmentation of the forms, Picasso and Braque were beginning to construct or "synthesize" forms. Their transformation of the material that they incorporated often resulted in a kind of visual pun, producing a much more lighthearted atmosphere. At the same time both Braque and Picasso started using stronger color, principally in order to give a sensation of depth. Thus they created a new system of perspective quite different from the crystalline facets of analytical Cubism. The development of synthetic Cubism, however, marked a divergence between the styles of Braque and Picasso. Braque used the flat colored shapes of his *papiers collés* to make designs of elegant accomplishment, while Picasso ignored decorative considerations in

order to communicate his actual experience of reality. In his *Woman in an Armchair* the large flat areas are combined in an image of utmost gravity, the power of which was later acknowledged by the Surrealists. The monumental example of this synthetic Cubism is the *Three Musicians* of 1921. Again, despite the gay subject the whole picture is tinged with mysterious and threatening implications.

At the same time Picasso was also developing his ideas in three-dimensional terms. From 1912 his collages became increasingly varied and soon he was producing constructions in bas-relief, half way between painting and sculpture. His use of ready-made objects anticipated the Dada movement, although they were never simply anti-art statements.

From 1909 onward a number of other talented artists flocked to join the Cubist movement. The most important of the early recruits were Robert Delaunay, Albert Gleizes, Auguste Herbin, Henri Le Fauconnier, André Lhote, Jean Metzinger and

Portrait of Picasso, by Juan Gris. In one sense the most intellectual of the Cubists, Gris developed the abstract elements of his composition into pictorial forms related to the natural world.

the sculptor Alexander Archipenko. In 1912 Gleizes and Metzinger published *Du Cubisme*, which expressed the tendency toward autonomous construction in their work which later led to the development of nonfigurative art. In one sense the most supremely intellectual of all the Cubist painters was another Spaniard, Juan Gris. He described his own work as an art of synthesis or deduction. He planned the structures of his paintings and then developed the abstract elements of the composition into pictorial forms related to the natural world. This system of construction was also extremely important for the development of nonfigurative art. The other major Cubist artist was Fernand Léger who, in contrast to Gris, always proceeded from visual experience, which is sometimes a little difficult to appreciate. His work prior to World War I is very close to abstraction, but his experience of the war made a profound impact on him and he determined to create an art for the people he had come

into contact with during it. Léger found a kind of elemental purity in the form of machinery and his work has provided a unique interpretation of our mechanized society.

It was therefore the intellectual bias of Cubism that led indirectly to abstraction. Picasso himself seldom, if ever, created a purely abstract work, or one that has no reference whatever to any object outside itself. Although he continued to extend the boundaries of Cubism after World War I, his work had always remained fundamentally concerned with the appearance of the natural world. But for the first time a movement set out to create nonrepresentational art. The foundation upon which abstract art would be built was laid and although Cubism would go out of vogue and Picasso's art would develop in other directions, the step Picasso took in 1907 by painting *Les Demoiselles d'Avignon* remained of paramount importance in the development of twentieth-century art. FENELLA CRICHTON

Painting

In retrospect it becomes clear that Picasso's *Les Demoiselles d'Avignon* can be seen as the source of much of abstract art. However, abstraction is far from the whole story of twentieth-century art. The other side of the coin is figuration, and in the early part of this century almost all the important figurative artists were either directly concerned with or affiliated in some way with the Expressionist movement. Expressionism can be defined loosely as an art that is fundamentally concerned with the artist's deepest personal feelings, in contrast to the objective and intellectual art of the Constructivists. By and large, Expressionist artists painted the real world in a recognizable way, although they may have distorted or exaggerated the elements in order to heighten the emotional impact of their painting.

Although Vincent van Gogh (1853–90) is truly regarded as the father of Expressionism, the first coherent group of artists that relied solely on the truth of their own subjective experiences were the Fauves, of whom the principal artists were Henri Matisse (1869–1954), Maurice de Vlaminck (1876–1958) and André Derain (1880–1954). (The name Fauve, literally "wild beast," was first used contemptuously by the art critic Louis Vauxcelles and was cheerfully adopted by the artists he was attacking.) Following on from Edvard Munch (1863–1944) and Paul Gauguin (1848–1903), the Fauves developed the expressive possibilities of violent color in paintings that horrified the contemporary French public. Their subject-matter, however, was principally decorative. Georges Rouault (1871–1958) was the first French artist to develop the new style in order to convey an intensely emotional message—in his case religious. Other important European artists of this period whose work is characterized above all by its passion, included Amedeo Modigliani (1884–1920), Chaim Soutine (1894–1944), and Marc Chagall (1887–). The Expressionist movement proper, however, may be said to have originated in Germany, initially with the formation of *Die Brücke* (The Bridge) group of artists, out of which the famous *Blaue Reiter* (Blue Rider) movement developed.

The Drinker, self-portrait by Ernst Kirchner, co-founder of *Die Brücke* (The Bridge), a group of artists who sought an expressionistic rather than academic impressionism.

Among the artists related to this movement were Emil Nolde (1867–1956), who shared Rouault's predilection for religious themes, and Oskar Kokoschka (1886–) who came from Vienna, but arrived in Berlin in 1910. One of the most brutal and horrifying manifestations of Expressionism can be found in the work of the German artist Max Beckmann (1884–1950), who used his art to convey his fundamental despair with human civilization.

All these artists worked in a largely figurative idiom. Vasili Kandinsky (1866–1944) and Paul Klee (1879–1940) were the first artists who managed to break away from the confines of figuration, while still managing to express their innermost and deepest feelings. Their art conveyed Expressionist ideas through an abstract style and as a result they are regarded as two of the major artists of the century. This synthesis between the two styles was not really fully developed until after World

War II by the great school of American artists, led by Jackson Pollock (1912–56) and Arshile Gorky (1904–48) and known as the Abstract Expressionists.

The Surrealist movement can be related to the Expressionists, insofar as the Surrealists also relied on the validity of subjective experience. It originated in 1924 when André Breton (1896–1966) published the *Surrealist Manifesto*, in which he defined Surrealism as "pure psychic automatism through which it is proposed to express either verbally, in writing or in any other manner, the real functioning of thought." The first Surrealists, Man Ray (1890–), Jean Arp (1887–1966), Paul Eluard (1895–1952), Joan Miró (1893–) and Louis Aragon (1897–), had originally been associated with the Dada movement, which had established a spirit of complete revolt against all moral and spiritual order. The first Surrealist exhibition also included the work of Giorgio de Chirico (1888–), who had

invented Metaphysical painting. His weird architectural settings filled with an irrational collection of objects, all depicted with meticulous realism, can be seen as the direct precursors of the strange dream-world of the Surrealists. The three most important Surrealists were probably Max Ernst (1891–), Salvador Dali (1904–) and René Magritte (1898–1967), all of whose work constitutes profoundly disturbing comment on the nature of reality.

Meanwhile in Paris in the years immediately preceding World War I, Cubism had led to a number of interesting developments. Raymond Duchamp-Villon (1876–1918) and Alexander Archipenko (1887–1964) developed Cubist sculpture, different aspects of which were also investigated by Henri Laurens (1885–1954), Jacques Lipchitz (1891–) and the Russian Ossip Zadkine (1890–1967). Robert Delaunay (1885–1941) and Jacques Villon (1875–1963) took Cubist fragmentation and through it reexamined the color theories of the nineteenth century in order to create a new study of color known as Orphism. Criticism by Amédée Ozenfant (1886–1966) and Le Corbusier (Charles Jeanneret, 1887–1965) of the decorative aspects of Picasso's work led to the creation

Weeping Women, by Max Beckmann.

of Purism, which aimed to restore the supreme order of the machine age to art. Their belief in the relevance of modern technology in art was shared by the Futurists, led by the Italian poet Emilio Marinetti (1876–1944). Although they intended to revolutionize the whole of art, the Futurists' greatest actual contribution was their concept of simultaneity, by which a work of art is not static but records a whole existence.

bourgeois society gives birth to Expressionism

At the same time as the Futurists were making their flamboyant declarations, however, a true revolutionary art was being created in Russia. In 1912 Mikhail Larionov (1881–1964) had taken the first steps toward abstraction in his Rayonnist paintings and in 1913 Kazimir Malevich (1878–1935) produced his first Suprematist works. He defined Suprematism as "the supremacy of pure emotion in art" and to achieve this he used the simplest possible elements, such as a black square on a white ground. Malevich's ideas became the foundation of Constructivism but Vladimir Tatlin (1885–1953), the originator of the movement, believed that art had a social purpose and that the artist should subordinate all individuality for the common good. Although the Constructivist movement was subsequently crushed by official government opposition, its achievements were a vitally important factor in the development of much in European art. One of the most important of the Constructivist theoreticians was the Hungarian sculptor László Moholy-Nagy (1895–1946), who taught at the Bauhaus for several years before founding the Institute of Design in Chicago. His theories about light, movement and space remain the basis of much of contemporary art. In Holland the very important periodical *De Stijl* had been founded by Piet Mondrian (Pieter Cornelis Mondriaan, 1872–1944) and Theo van Doesburg (1883–1931) in 1917. Their ideas were not confined to pictorial art but aimed at creating an inclusive modern style embracing furniture, architecture and all kinds of design. The new aesthetic of a totally functional design, from which ornament as such was rigorously excluded, made an important contribution to the teachings of the Bauhaus.

Mondrian eventually split with van Doesburg as he considered his Elementarism, in which he employed diagonal lines as well as horizontal and vertical, heretical. He moved to Paris and his studio became an important meeting place for artists such as Moholy-Nagy, Arp, Antoine Pevsner (1886–1962), Walter Gropius (1883–1969) and Naum Gabo (1890–   ). Mondrian is regarded as the most single-minded exponent of pure abstract art. In 1940 he moved to New York, where he spent the last four years of his life. With him the center of interest shifted from the European scene to America and the stage was set for the great paintings of the New York School.

Rebellion in China

The decline in China's strength during the late nineteenth century was dramatic, and the ruling Manchu dynasty was blamed for it. The death in 1908 of the Dowager Empress Tzu Hsi, whose long rule, though disastrous, had at least been firm, further weakened the dynasty. In 1910, when a provisional national assembly was summoned, popular resentment at last found a means of expression, and a group of plotters planned an uprising in Wuchang.

Actual rebellion, however, began almost by accident. A series of explosions in Hankow in October, 1911, led police to the conspirators and forced them to advance the date of the rebellion. The rebels set up a provisional government in Nanking. The civil war that followed soon reached an impasse, but the deadlock was broken when the cynical politician and military commander Yüan Shih-kai, who had designs on the imperial throne himself, procured the abdication of the five-year-old Emperor in return for being made president of the new Republic. Sun Yat-sen had been appointed provisional president, but recognized that he could not argue against Yüan's military strength. The Son of Heaven had abdicated, and 2,132 years of imperial rule had been brought to an end. Although Yüan had made himself the leader of the revolution he was deeply conservative and distrusted the notion of representative government, which brought him more and more into conflict with the newly founded Kuomintang (Nationalist) Party and its military backers. At the same time he was confronted by Japanese aggressiveness. The Chinese revolution had not ended; it had scarcely begun.

Central and South America

China was not alone in facing the problems of rebellion. In the perennially politically unstable former colonies of Spain and Portugal in America, violence and disorder were normal. Although politically free, most Latin American states were economically dependent on European traders and bankers and had little cultural independence. In the wake of the Venezuelan border dispute of 1897 and the 1898 war with Spain, the United States was beginning to adopt an imperialist attitude not dissimilar to that which it criticized so vigorously in the European powers, and this added further uncertainty to the future of Latin America.

Although there had been earlier risings and coups d'état, the most significant change in Latin America was the Mexican Revolution of 1910. The government of the dictator Porfirio Diaz (1830–1911) was fairly efficient but highly conservative. The tiny landed aristocracy and a few foreign investors flourished, while the standard of living of the Indian and *Mestizo* (half-breed) majority fell. Despite expensive showpiece schools in many towns, the level of illiteracy remained high. As a consequence of Diaz' wooing of foreign states, and particularly of the United States, a wave of xenophobia swept the country. A popular rising took place in a successful effort to prevent Diaz' reelection, and a liberal, Francisco Madero (1873–1913), was elected President. But Madero's ineffectual government led to counterrevolution, and for ten years civil war raged. While the war still continued, a new constitution was passed in 1917, and this reversed Diaz' generous investment incentives for foreigners entirely and gave back much land to the peasants.

U.S. technological achievements

Under the presidency of the cautious William Howard Taft (1857–1930) momentous changes occurred in America's way of life. Scientific and technological advances began to make a real impact on the lives of the masses. Phonographs and refrigerators were becoming common, and Henry Ford's new automobile offered mobility to the average wage-earner.

President Diaz and Japan's ambassador attend a Japanese exhibition in Mexico.

The Emperor Kuang-hsu (right) with his brother. When Kuang-hsu attempted to introduce reforms in 1898, Tzu Hsi resumed power intending to close China to the world.

An Automobile for the Masses

"History is bunk," Henry Ford asserted—even as the company he founded made automotive history year after year. In 1908 the first Model T rolled out of Ford's Detroit plant; in the next two decades Ford would produce some 15 million nearly identical Model Ts by his refined assembly-line process. Those boxy, spartan, economical automobiles were to revolutionize American life, bringing low-cost locomotion to rural regions, mobility to the middle class, and privacy to courting couples. Equally important, Ford's landmark decision to institute voluntarily an eight-hour, five-dollar day for his employees inaugurated a new era of labor-management relations. By 1923, Ford's loyal employees were turning out more than 2 million Model Ts a year, and it could truly be said that Henry Ford had put America on wheels.

"I will build a motor car for the great multitude," Henry Ford once said. "It will be constructed of the best materials, by the best men to be hired, after the simplest designs that modern engineering can devise. But it will be so low in price that no man making a good salary will be unable to own one."

Such heady promises were foreign to the American Gothic temperament of the former Michigan farm boy whose fascination with engines had drawn him into the business of building automobiles. But Henry Ford kept his word, and in October, 1908, his first Model T—an oblong, boxlike machine that bespoke not beauty but stark utility—rolled out of the Piquette Avenue Ford plant in Detroit and, after vigorous hand cranking, sputtered to life.

"The way to make automobiles is to make one automobile like another automobile," Ford once said, "to make them all alike ... just as one pin is like another pin when it comes from a pin factory, or one match is like another match." His philosophy was soon put to the test, for with Model T production under way, the building of other Ford models was abruptly suspended. Model T and Ford became synonymous, and not only were all Ford cars alike in late 1908, but they changed very little over the next nineteen years. Except for technical modifications and an occasional face-lifting, the first car to be affectionately dubbed the Tin Lizzie was very much kin to the car being sold in 1927 (when, after exceeding 15 million in number, the Model T was finally retired).

What made the car so popular? For one thing, it was inexpensive. Automobiles were still considered rich men's toys in the first decade of the twentieth century. Most cars cost well over one thousand dollars and fully half were priced above two thousand. Stripped of accessories—which was how it left the factory—the first Model T Runabout, a two-passenger roadster, could be purchased for eight hundred and fifty dollars. The Model T's high performance and appealing homeliness transcended the bounds of trade, profession or status. It was comparatively simple to operate, and for a man with a slight mechanical bent, easy to maintain. It had been the dream of an unprepossessing machinist, a man whose patchy education and apparent disregard for scholarship could prompt him to say, "History is bunk," even though the company he had founded made history year after year.

Henry Ford had been born in 1863 on a forty-acre farm in Dearborn township, two miles east of Michigan's Rouge River. Although an indifferent student, he was an impassioned tinkerer. He helped his father with the farm work—not by plowing or reaping, but by hammering out hinges on a forge and fixing wagons, farm implements and harnesses. "My toys were all tools," he wrote in *My Life and Work*, one of two autobiographical books that bear Ford's name.

At seventeen, Ford left the family farm and took the first of a series of factory jobs in Detroit. During his early years in that city he repaired and operated a number of steam engines and, according to his memoirs, even "built a steam engine that ran." Through the English and American mechanics' magazines that came into shops where he worked, Ford followed some of the progress being made toward development of the internal combustion engine. It was only a matter of time before he would abandon the idea of steam in favor of this more promising means of power.

Shortly after his marriage to twenty-one-year-old Clara Bryant in April, 1888, he began talking of the feasibility of building a "horseless carriage." He was not alone, of course. Almost three hundred American inventors were striving to put self-propelled, wheeled vehicles in operation in the waning years of the nineteenth century. Very few of these

Henry Ford, photographed in 1909—one year after the appearance of the first Model T.

Opposite The first mass-production line in America: the Ford plant at Highland Park, Michigan. (*Top*) Magneto assembly workers; (*bottom*) dropping the engine onto the chassis.

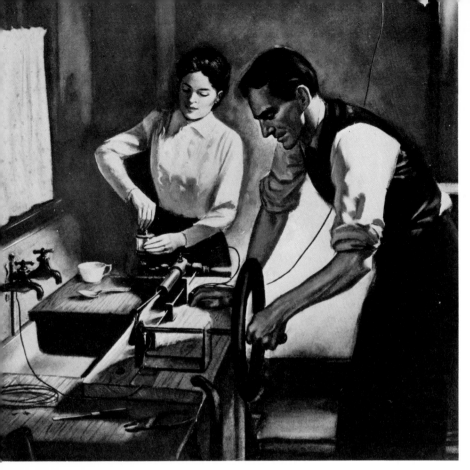

men were aware of the work being done in Europe—specifically by Gottlieb Daimler and Karl Benz, who both took out individual German patents on self-propelled vehicles within six months of one another in the mid-1880s.

Henry Ford began building a gasoline engine in his workshop behind the house on Bagley Street, Detroit, that he shared with his wife and infant son Edsel. His first engine was a simple one-cylinder contraption that he tried out in his wife's kitchen on Christmas Eve, 1893. Soon he was at work on a two-cylinder version, which he eventually mounted in a small carriage that rode on four bicycle wheels. This quadricycle was the first of a series of experimental vehicles conceived and built by Ford—cars whose performance on the road and in competition brought him the recognition, and much of the financial backing, that he needed to begin manufacturing automobiles. The Ford Motor Company, formed in 1903, produced eight different models before the Model T came along. There were two- and four-cylinder cars and a six-cylinder luxury vehicle that weighed one ton, cost twenty-five hundred dollars and could go fifty miles per hour. It was the last high-priced Ford to be built until 1922, when the company acquired Lincoln.

The Model T, introduced when the Ford Motor Company was only five years old, was no radical piece of auto engineering. Almost its only unique aspect was the way it seized and held a special place in American life. In 1908 Ford built 6,000 cars; in

Above A fanciful painting of the young Henry Ford building the engine for his quadricycle in the kitchen of his Detroit home.

Below The first gas station in Ohio—and possibly in America. Motorists drove their cars in the front door and out the back.

1909, the first full year of Model T production, the output rose to 10,000. From then on, production figures showed a rarely interrupted rise each year (some years they actually doubled) until they reached their peak of 2 million in 1923.

Preceding the production boom—and possibly anticipating it—Ford had sought a place to build a new and bigger factory. In 1906 the company purchased sixty acres in an area called Highland Park at the north end of Detroit. Construction had progressed far enough for the company to begin moving in on New Year's Day, 1910. Over the next four years, as facilities were being completed, a staggering array of the latest precision machinery appeared in the plant: 3 million dollars' worth of lathes, planers, milling machines, drill presses, borers and grinding machines.

The presence of this equipment signaled the development of new methods for putting vehicles together. Previously, the men who built cars had been mechanical jacks-of-all-trades. They moved about the factory—to the parts bins or the tool cribs—and worked on a car from bare frame to finished product. As output increased, however, this leisurely and somewhat disorganized method of assembly proved inefficient. By 1908, line production, which already was in use in other industries, was being tried out by auto manufacturers, and most earnestly by Ford.

The idea was simply to save time and motion. Gravity slides and conveyor belts made it possible to move the work from man to man and machine to machine, keeping each man virtually in one spot. Various Model T components—engine, radiator, chassis, steering gear—were put together this way in individual subassemblies. But final assembly of all the components was accomplished pretty much as it had always been—by many hands doing many jobs to produce a finished car.

Line production was only partly successful because, like lanes of irregularly flowing traffic, some lines were fast and others slow. Cars were assembled in spurts, and much of the time that was gained along the line was lost in the chaos of final assembly. But during 1912 and 1913 the company thoroughly refined its assembly-line procedure, and Ford became the first auto manufacturer to turn entirely to mass production. In place of the various sub-assemblies, a continuously moving assembly line was installed. It started at one end of the factory and moved along at an even pace as one component after another was fed into the line and then added in sequence—until a completed car could be rolled away. A second assembly line was in operation by the end of 1913, and a few months later four lines were functioning.

The results were almost unbelievable. Whereas in August, 1913, it had taken twelve and a half hours to assemble a Model T chassis, the time span had shrunk to an hour and thirty-three minutes by the following January. And mass-production techniques continued to improve.

Despite its efficiency, the Ford Motor Company

The automobile rapidly gained acceptance throughout the world. King George V of England with his Daimler at military exercises in 1914.

was producing almost more cars than it could handle, and, as a result, labor was becoming demoralized. As pressure for greater output increased, working conditions grew steadily worse. Workers had to function in cramped spaces and remain in uncomfortable positions for long stretches of time. Machines were placed so close together that Ford himself later recalled that they appeared to have been "piled right on top of one another."

Worst of all was the dull and stultifying routine that factory work had assumed. Instead of helping to complete one car at a time, a skilled mechanic was now required to work on a great many cars doing only one job, the same job, with maddening repetition. The monotony of the work and the continual emphasis on speed sparked simmering resentment among Ford workers. Their bitterness reached a peak in the summer of 1913 when the company ended its policy of rewarding individual initiative with bonuses. Now the average worker knew that no matter how much he applied himself, he could earn no more than the standard wage: $2.34 a day. Disillusioned, a great many Ford workers began drifting to other jobs.

Clearly, a new labor policy was needed. Factory jobs could not be made more interesting. Moreover, because teamwork and precision had taken precedence over individual initiative, job satisfaction was no longer a factor in cementing company loyalty. Henry Ford, accustomed to pouring much of his profit back into the business, decided to invest some capital in a most important resource: manpower. On January 5, 1914, he announced that the Ford workday would shrink from nine to eight hours and the minimum wage would rise to five dollars a day.

The response to this surprise announcement was

A 1919 Model T Ford. The body style is somewhat different from that of the 1915 model, but the concept remains the same.

A 1913 British Daimler, which cost ten times as much as a Model T Ford.

immediate and galvanic. The next morning 10,000 job applicants appeared outside the factory and, in their passion, threatened to storm the gates. They came again, day after day, huddling together in the near-zero weather. They were a hungry, sorry lot, and most of them were doomed to disappointment, for only a handful could be hired. But their presence was viable proof that, in terms of the workingman, Ford's labor policy was a triumphant success.

The business community reacted adversely. Its mouthpiece, the *Wall Street Journal*, called the five-dollar day an "economic crime," and influential bankers denounced Henry Ford as a traitor to his class. They were wrong, of course, at least as far as his company's fortunes were concerned. Buoyed by higher wages, Ford employees were working faster, more efficiently and, considering the cost of assembling each car, for less money. The increased output more than offset the wage hike, and not only did the turnover of personnel diminish, but absenteeism was also markedly cut.

Despite grave predictions, the five-dollar day did not prove injurious to industry in general. Henry Ford recalled that it had had little effect at first, though he would have been delighted if other firms had been compelled to raise wages to the level he had set. Hadn't he promised to build a car for the "great multitude"? The more money workingmen earned, he reasoned, the more Model Ts he could expect to sell. To add impetus to mass sales, he periodically reduced prices. And he once promised that if he could sell 300,000 cars in a given twelve-month period, each purchaser would get fifty dollars back.

In the second decade of the century, the Model T's success seemed unassailable. The car had crotchets and failings, but once a part of the American scene it was as firmly entrenched as folklore. And the jokes and jests made at the car's expense worked like free advertising to further the legend.

The first attempt at streamlining the Model T took place in 1917 as graceful curves replaced some of the clumsy, squarish design that had been its hallmark. That year more than three-quarters of a million Model Ts were built. The next year production dipped somewhat when the company turned over some of its facilities to the manufacture of ambulances, trucks, aircraft engines, caissons and steel helmets during the period America participated in World War I. However, within three weeks of the armistice, civilian auto production had resumed, and by early December, 1918, the daily output of Model Ts had reached one thousand vehicles and was still climbing.

On January 2, 1919, Henry Ford announced another corporate milestone. Henceforth, he said, the Ford Motor Company would pay a daily wage of six dollars. This was not quite the windfall for workers it may have seemed, for the cost of living had more than doubled in five years. Still, the rise was significant. Other employers had matched Ford's wage scale, but none had exceeded it.

Ford's success spiral—higher and higher wages, lower and lower prices—was contingent on an always-expanding market. Thus when a depression hit the country in 1920 and caused a general drop in auto sales, the effect on the Ford Motor Company

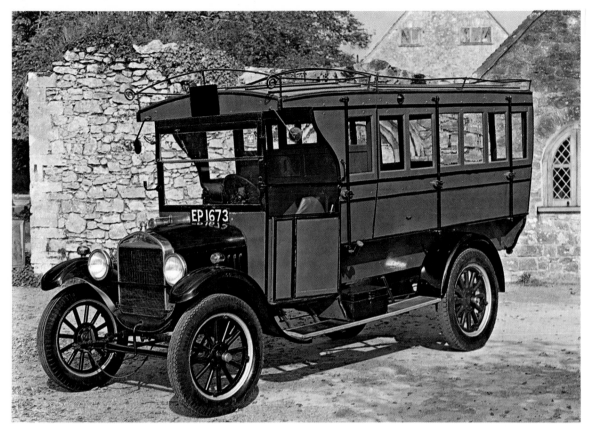

A 1921 bus based on the Model T Ford: the Model T was used as the basis for many types of vehicles.

was nearly devastating. Henry Ford had been borrowing huge sums of money to buy out his minority stockholders. And during the previous three years the company had spent nearly 100 million dollars on an expansion program that included construction of a new factory on the Rouge River near Springwells, Michigan.

When another price cut failed to produce enough of a sales spurt, Ford performed a financial coup that made him few friends but won him everlasting respect as a canny and crafty businessman. In mid-1921 he had 93,000 surplus cars assembled and shipped—cash on delivery—to dealers across the country. By this bold action he successfully divided his financial burden among a large group of men who dared not refuse to shoulder it, since a dealer's refusal would risk the possibility of having to forfeit his franchise.

Thus Henry Ford and the Model T survived. But many Ford executives and a number of farsighted dealers began to be aware of a shift in the public taste. They realized that with the growing prosperity of the 1920s, the spartan, inelegant Model T would soon cease to satisfy the great multitude for whom it had been created. Henry Ford at age sixty seemed more conciliatory than ever, yet in matters affecting the Model T, which had long since become his alter ego, he was more unyielding than ever. He dismissed requests for a wholesale redesigning of the car by insisting that "so far as I can see, the only trouble with the Ford car is that we can't make it fast enough."

In 1926 the Model T chassis was lowered, the radiator was raised, and for the first time since 1913 the car came in a choice of colors: fawn gray, gunmetal blue, phoenix brown or highland green. But only a modest increase in sales resulted. Another price cut was instituted, but this failed to alter the sales trend at all. In 1926 Ford's share of the market fell below 40 percent for the first time since 1918; it threatened to drop to 25 percent in 1927.

It was widely rumored that the long-lived Tin Lizzie would be discontinued, but Henry Ford kept insisting that "the Ford car will continue to be made in the same way." A few months later, however, the company announced that production of the car would cease. The last of 15,007,033 Model Ts came off the line on May 26, 1927. Nine months later the more contemporary, but otherwise conservative, Model A was introduced with enormous marketing fanfare.

"The Model T was a pioneer," Henry Ford said in retrospect. "There was no conscious public need of motor cars when we first made it. There were few good roads. This car blazed the way for the motor industry and started the movement for good roads everywhere."

In his history of the Ford Motor Company, Alan Nevins summed up the Model T's myriad virtues this way: "No other single machine, in all probability, did so much to induce people of provincial mind to begin thinking in regional and national terms; none did so much to knit together different parts of the county, the state and the country; none did more to create the sense of a freer and more spacious life." MERVYN KAUFMAN

A 1915 Model T Ford.

Public order comes under attack as

Petroleum

By 1912 there were over a million automobiles on the road in the United States and by 1920 there were nearly nine million. The rapid spread of the automobile had an enormous social effect. As an anonymous British versifier put it in 1902:

'Twas said by a Whig
That a man with a gig
Enjoyed a clear claim to gentility,
But a man who would now win a
    parvenu's bow
Must belong to the automobility.

If Henry Ford brought the possibility of automobile ownership to hundreds of thousands, the great race of 1908 from New York to Paris via Moscow vicariously brought the excitement of driving to millions, and created the mass market. From the first the automobile made an enormous demand on resources: roads had to be built and improved and high-grade gasoline had to be readily available.

Contemporaneous developments in industry and the changeover from coal to oil as a source of power for ships still further increased the demand for oil. Despite the decline in the use of oil for lighting, due to the spread of electricity and gas, oil production and consumption soared. In the United States, for example, petroleum production rose from under ten million barrels in 1873 to nearly ninety million barrels in 1903. Thereafter production rose still more rapidly, reaching two hundred million barrels in 1911, more than three hundred million in 1916, and

nearly four hundred million by 1920. Outside the United States, too, oil production was growing rapidly. The British and the Dutch saw the potential of oil and started operations in Russia and Asia.

Standard Oil was the main beneficiary of the American growth in demand: by 1911 it controlled two-thirds of the nation's oil production, refining and marketing, and had assets of over $860 million. But it had only achieved this monopolistic position by a disregard of the federal and local laws and a total contempt for the rights of its smaller competitors. The consequence of this was that there was continual litigation and in 1911 the Supreme Court of the United States obliged the combine to divest itself of most of its subsidiaries.

War fever

Giddy visions of war dominated the imaginations of statesmen and citizens alike as Europe approached the brink of World War 1. Excited throngs jammed the streets of every major European capital to cheer declarations of war; other world events were diminished by comparison. Socialist parties in France and Germany ignored their commitment to the universal brotherhood of man and voted war credits with enthusiasm; in London, large crowds sang "God Save the King" outside Buckingham Palace. For many, war promised relief from the dreary sameness of their everyday lives, for the war was viewed on a grand and heroic scale.

Georges Sorel, advocate of revolutionary syndicalism.

In a more tragic vein, the conflict also served as a safety valve for civil violence. Long before the war, most European countries had been torn by internal struggles, and these upheavals contributed as much to the crisis of 1914 as did the folly of the statesmen, soldiers and diplomats.

The years preceding the outbreak of hostilities saw violence on a scale never previously witnessed in peacetime. Bomb throwing and assassinations were commonplace, and in 1908, Georges Sorel's handbook of political violence, *Réflexions sur la Violence*, appeared. Sorel's work, which was swiftly adopted by the working-class movement, asserted that violence had a valuable moral and political function. Throughout Europe, workers turned to the doctrine of revolution known as anarcho-syndicalism, which advocated the strike as labor's chief weapon. A series of strikes followed, which culminated in the general strike that sparked the Russian Revolution.

Unrest in France

Most of Europe was affected by the growth of irrationalism and violence. In France, the main workers' union, the *Confédération Général du Travail*, wholeheartedly adopted anarcho-syndicalism in response to rising prices. A series of strikes, including one by civil servants, kept France in a state of almost perpetual unrest. This social crisis was not confined to the working classes. Political scandals

were frequent, although none had as much impact as the Dreyfus affair in 1899. In that controversy a young Jewish army officer, Captain Alfred Dreyfus, was accused, on evidence later shown to be forged, of treason and imprisoned at Devil's Island. Although later vindicated, his ordeal polarized French society and almost destroyed it. The anti-Semitism the case awoke gave rise to a rabidly nationalist organization, *Action Française*, whose street gangs, the shock troops of the radical right, attacked Jews and workers. Perhaps the strongest indication of the state of tension was to come in 1914 when Madame Caillaux, the wife of the ex-Premier, murdered the editor of the newspaper *Le Figaro* in retaliation for a press campaign against her husband.

David Lloyd George, Liberal statesman and Prime Minister 1916–22.

Unrest in England

The problems faced by France, however, seemed mild in comparison with those of Britain. There, giant strikes and a British army mutiny rocked the complacency of the Liberals. All over Europe, governments faced the problems of mass politics. The tempers of the ill-educated masses could easily be aroused by the new pulp press, and appeals to this audience were increasingly made in violent or spectacular terms. Everywhere rabble-rousing replaced the select and

Oil derricks on Signal Hill, Long Beach, California.

socialists and suffragettes agitate for reform

Soldiers escorting a traction engine during the railwaymen's strike in England in 1911.

dignified politics of the previous century. In England issues arose that were to involve the masses and bring the threat of civil war.

The existing social order came under attack from every direction. In a population of thirty-four million, only five million owned half of the nation's wealth. Upper-class opulence contrasted sharply with working-class slums. Liberal Chancellor David Lloyd George tried to redress the balance in 1909 with his People's Budget, which was designed to tax unearned income and to raise government income to meet increased expenditure on defense and old-age pensions; but the House of Lords, sensing a challenge to aristocratic privilege, rejected the budget. A struggle ensued, and, after the Prime Minister had threatened to flood the House of Lords with newly created peers, victory finally went to the Liberals, but not before fist-fighting erupted in Parliament. Die-hard Conservatives did not surrender. They had been forced to give way over the budget, but they were determined to fight again over the Irish demand for Home Rule. When Orangemen (Northern Irish Protestants) formed the Ulster Volunteer Force to resist Home Rule, they were egged on by the Conservatives. "We strongly challenge the government to interfere with us if they dare," said Sir Edward Carson, a Conservative leader. While the government stood helplessly by, private armies drilled in Ireland. The Ulster Volunteer Force squared off against the fanatical Irish Republican Brotherhood, and every time the

government passed the Home Rule Bill in the House of Commons, it was stopped in the House of Lords.

The suffragettes

The Liberals were faced with another threat to public order. Emmeline Pankhurst's "suffragettes" had begun to rebel against the smothering repressions of contemporary values. Revealing her

Suicide of suffragette Emily Davison.

sympathy with the trends of the times, Mrs. Pankhurst declared "the argument of the broken pane is the most valuable argument in modern politics." The government failed to respond to suffragette demands, and on November 18, 1910, a group of women marchers were assaulted by police and onlookers. The suffragettes replied with extreme militancy. Emily Davison threw herself under the King's horse in a race at Epsom Downs, and in March of 1912 plate

glass windows were smashed all over the West End of London. Imprisoned suffragette crusaders went on a hunger strike, only to be force-fed with great brutality.

The Liberal bureaucracy could not cope with the situation; violence was answered with violence. Some militant trade-union leaders such as Arthur J. Cook adopted anarcho-syndicalist tactics, and strikes became a regular event. The great days of the Liberal Party were numbered, as public opinion became increasingly polarized between the Conservative and Labour parties.

All over Europe the story was the same. In Spain, the central government in Madrid could think of no better way to deal with regionalism in Catalonia than to hire professional gunmen whose task was to stir up violence and provide the government with an excuse for suspending constitutional guarantees. Portugal too was afflicted by political troubles.

Crisis in Serbia

The most dangerous outbursts of violence took place in the chaos of the Balkans, where a series of assassinations were attempted by a Serbian nationalist secret society known as the Black Hand. During this same period, the decay of the Turkish Empire and the weaknesses of Austria-Hungary tempted various Balkan groups to fight for national self-determination. Ethnic and political barriers rarely coincided in the Balkans, and consequently various minorities frequently found themselves looking across their borders to compatriots who might liberate them. Serbs and Croats in Austria looked to Serbia, and Rumanians in Hungarian Transylvania looked to Rumania. Slavs throughout the Balkans were determined to break free of Hapsburg domination. "Better a terrible end than an endless terror," Slav leaders said.

These Slavic groups were tied by race and religion to Russia, which kept a perpetual eye on Slav affairs, and that special relationship posed a serious dilemma for Austria. To reunite the Slavic peoples, Austria would either have to conquer the Slavs who had gained independence as a result of the decline of Turkey—and in so doing risk war with Russia—or release those Slavs still under

Austrian rule and thereby shatter the integrity of the Hapsburg Empire.

In Austria, as in other European countries, men of violence were coming to the fore. The military party under Count Conrad von Hötzendorf wanted to eliminate the problem by destroying Serbia. The Austrian Foreign Minister, Alois Lexa Aehrenthal, sought to solve the problem with a dazzling display of diplomatic virtuosity. Anxious to seize Bosnia-Herzegovina and extend the Austrian threat to Serbia, Aehrenthal made a shady deal with the Russian Foreign Minister, Alexander Izvolsky, whereby Austria would annex

Count Conrad von Hötzendorf, Austrian field marshal.

Bosnia and Russia would seize the Dardanelles. Austria promptly moved into Bosnia, while Russia, unable to seize the Dardanelles without Austrian support—which was not forthcoming—was thwarted. Following her diplomatic humiliation, Russia determined not to back down again. "Mark my words," said Izvolsky, "the Eastern Question is now insoluble without a conflict."

Antarctic exploration

A legend dating from Greek antiquity and supported by Ptolemy spoke of the existence of a land in the southern hemisphere. The world's one remaining uncharted continent, too, would become a forum for international competition. Norway would win the race to the South Pole but the success would be marred by the death there of the English polar party.

"Do or Die"

Only one major area of the earth's surface was left uncharted—Antarctica—and more than five major nations were urging the conquest of the South Pole as a national priority. In Britain, an expedition was organized under Robert Falcon Scott, who had scouted the area in 1902, but had not tried to reach the Pole. Gathering scientific data as he proceeded on his torturous journey, Scott with three companions finally reached the Pole—only to find that the Norwegians under Roald Amundsen had been there the previous month. On the return journey, Scott and his companions suffered unusually hard weather conditions—and they all perished. Although the last terrestrial voyage of discovery ended on a tragic note, it provided the impetus for Antarctic research that still continues in the various geophysical stations there.

A cartoon of Robert Falcon Scott as a London socialite. On returning from his 1901–1904 expedition Scott found himself a celebrity and for a while led a very busy social life.

Opposite Watercolor of open leads in new ice and Mount Discovery in the background, by Edward Wilson.

Since ancient times, man had speculated about the possible existence of a *Terra Australis Incognita*—an unknown southern land, mirroring the presumed Arctic continent. The Greeks gave this supposed region the name, *Antarktos*, or "opposite the Bear" (the northern constellation of stars). During the great age of discovery, from the fifteenth to the seventeenth centuries, several expeditions set out in search of the Antarctic—among them from colonial Peru—and a Dutch vessel was forced in a storm as far south as 64°, but no voyager was to set foot upon the mainland until the nineteenth century. The French navigator Kerguelen-Trémarec discovered Kerguelen (also called Desolation) Island in 1772, proclaiming it part of Antarctica, even though it lies, at 49°s., almost as far from the South Pole as England from the North. Kerguelen conjectured that the continent offered, "wood, minerals, diamonds . . . people living in their primitive manner . . . knowing nothing of the artifices of civilized society." He was confident that trading relations could be opened with these mythical tribes. Every first sighting of land in the southern hemisphere, including that of New Zealand and Australia, was hailed as the discovery of the Antarctica mainland, and disproved only when circumnavigation showed that these lands and many lesser islands were unconnected with the supposed southern land mass.

It was not until the late eighteenth century that a sailing vessel first crossed the Antarctic Circle (66° 30's.), when Captain James Cook, on a British naval expedition crossed the circle, reached 71° 10's., circumnavigated the continent, and discovered several outlying islands—though never sighting the mainland. Throughout the early nineteenth century, sealers and formal expeditions from Russia, the United States, Britain and France probed into the cold seas and began brief landings on the mainland. A British expedition under Captain James

Clark Ross in 1840–41 discovered and named Victoria Land and the Great (originally, Ross) Ice Barrier. In 1874, the British ship *Challenger* became the first steam vessel to cross the Antarctic Circle. The end of the nineteenth and beginning of the twentieth centuries saw a proliferation of Antarctic expeditions and the emergence of a number of notable Antarctic explorers. One of these was Robert Falcon Scott.

"Scott of the Antarctic," the son of a brewer, was born on June 6, 1868, near Devonport, England. He was remembered by those who knew him in his youth as a dreamy, moody, and occasionally violent-tempered boy—but one who was nevertheless popular. At the age of thirteen he became a naval cadet on H.M.S. *Britannia*, and, later, a midshipman on H.M.S. *Boadicea*. In 1887, aged 18, he met the man who was to be a major influence in shaping his future career—Clements Markham, an explorer and Secretary of the Royal Geographical Society. Markham was immediately struck by his "intelligence, information, and the charm of his manner."

Scott served as a lieutenant, and studied torpedo warfare, serving on the newly commissioned battleship, H.M.S. *Majestic*. In 1899, he again met Markham —now Sir Clements—and heard of his plans for an Antarctic expedition. Scott promptly applied for the post of leader. Unknown to him, he had already been placed at the head of a list of prospective leaders by his Captain, Sir George Egerton. In June, 1900, by which time—though after much difficulty—sufficient funds had been raised to finance the proposed expedition, Scott was appointed Commander of the National Antarctic Expedition, and promoted to the rank of naval commander.

Lacking any experience of work in cold lands, Scott sought the expert advice of the Norwegian Arctic explorer, Fridtjof Nansen, who was especially helpful in providing information on sled-making.

The expedition ship, specially built to withstand the effects of pack ice, was named *Discovery* and launched in 1901, crewed by a team of selected officers, men and scientists, including the young Ernest Shackleton, as well as several men who were to accompany Scott on his last expedition. Their average age was a mere twenty-five years. Crossing the Antarctic Circle on January 3, 1902, they landed briefly at Cape Adare and visited the grave of an earlier explorer, Nicolai Hanson—until then the only man buried on the continent. The *Discovery* struggled on through heavy pack ice and was often endangered by huge icebergs. At their ultimate landing place, Scott became the first man to make a balloon ascent in the Antarctic. A number of setbacks marred the overall success of the expedition—mostly caused by the almost total inexperience of the crew in working in subzero temperatures. One life was lost, several members of the party were stranded in blizzards and rescued badly frostbitten. The sled dogs, poorly fed and ill-trained, grew vicious or lethargic, and either died or killed each other or had to be killed by the crew. Meanwhile the *Discovery* lay locked in the grip of ice. Many of the crew suffered from scurvy—the existence of vitamins was not known at this time, and the expedition diet was lacking in properly nutritious food. Scott was convinced that scurvy was actually caused by poisoned meat. Scott, with Shackleton and Edward A. Wilson, a physician and zoologist, marched south and crossed the 82nd parallel, within 420 miles of the South Pole, but encountering a

great crevasse, and suffering from sickness and exhaustion, a contemplated "dash for the Pole" was not undertaken, and the team returned to base. Scott also made a westward trek across the Polar Plateau with Edgar Evans and William Lashly, and made numerous important geological and meteorological observations. Upon his return, the relief vessels, *Morning* and *Terra Nova*, appeared, bearing instructions that Scott and his companions should return in the *Discovery*, or, if she were still icebound, in one of the relief ships. The *Discovery* was eventually freed and able to sail in February, 1904. Scott returned to England with an immense amount of experience behind him, and lectured and wrote extensively on the successes and problems of the expedition.

In the ensuing years, the South Pole became a much discussed goal for explorers from many countries. Scott was committed to his naval duties, and it seemed unlikely that he would command another British expedition. Meanwhile, in 1909, Shackleton revisited the Antarctic and marched to within 113 miles of the Pole. An intense rivalry developed between Scott and Shackleton, and the quest for the South Pole became a hotly debated and patriotic subject. The United States, Germany, Japan, Belgium and France also all urged the conquest of the Pole as a national priority.

The British Antarctic Expedition was organized in 1910 after considerable financial difficulties had been overcome. Due largely to the persistence of Sir Clements Markham, Scott was appointed its leader,

Stacking up supplies at Cape Evans with Mount Erebus in the background.

Scott (center) with the officers and crew of the *Discovery* photographed on deck before sailing. Several members of this party, including the young Ernest Shackleton (bottom row fifth from left), would accompany Scott on his last expedition.

Deflating the first balloon to ascend from a field of ice, 1902. Owing to Antarctica's atmospheric conditions, the balloon required an extra 1000 cubic feet of hydrogen which had been brought from England on the *Discovery*.

Sea-Leopard
chasing Emperor Penguins.

S. P. Times. May. 1902.

with Edgar Evans as second-in-command. The avowed aim of the expedition was "to reach the South Pole, and to secure for the British Empire the honour of this achievement." Its other motives were geographical exploration, and research in many scientific fields, including zoology, geology, meteorology and terrestrial magnetism. The financial problems that hindered the expedition's organizers were not fully resolved until after it returned to England. Public enthusiasm was lacking, and funds were slow in arriving. Scott was compelled personally to appeal to businessmen and organizations for every penny of the £40,000 required before the expedition could begin. There was, however, sufficient interest in the aims of the expedition for several thousand men to volunteer to join it, and many schools raised money for sleeping bags, sleds and ponies (the latter, with newly invented motor sleds were to replace some of the functions of the troublesome dog teams), and the bulk of the provisions and equipment were donated by a number of leading manufacturers.

One of the ships that had sailed to relieve Scott on his previous expedition, the *Terra Nova*, a 744-ton ex-Dundee whaler, was chosen for this, the last major terrestrial voyage of discovery. Scott remarked in an article written before the *Terra Nova* set sail in June, 1910, that their primary aim was to reach the Pole. The secondary scientific intentions and the exploration of King Edward's Land and the Great Ice Barrier probably carried much less weight with the expedition's sponsors than the hint that they would also be looking for valuable minerals, including radium-bearing pitchblende. On the eve of their departure, the President of the Royal Geographical Society stated, prophetically: "They mean to do or die—that is the spirit in which they are going to the Antarctic."

This spirit of enthusiasm received a blow when, upon their arrival at Melbourne, Scott learned that the Norwegian explorer, Roald Amundsen, had joined in the race to the South Pole.

After weathering a tremendous storm, the *Terra Nova* arrived at McMurdo Sound in January, 1911. A setback occurred almost immediately when one of the three motor sleds fell through the ice during unloading, and was lost in a hundred fathoms of water. A camp was established at Cape Evans, and scientific research and exploration begun. The ship and shore parties separated on January 25 and, a reserve store—"Safety Camp"—having been set up inland, the *Terra Nova* sailed away, rather than risk becoming icebound in the approaching Antarctic winter.

Scott's first exploratory journey was a sortie across the Barrier with ponies, which were found to be as unreliable as the dogs had been on his first expedition. Several were shot and fed to the dogs—much to Scott's regret, as he was relying on them as pack animals. He was still, however, not convinced that dogs were the ideal form of transport, and made arrangements for Indian mules to be sent to the Antarctic as soon as the *Terra Nova* returned and

could transmit his request to the Indian army. On his first journey, Scott came up against severe weather conditions that made his progress exhausting. On some days he covered a bare six miles after a fatiguing day's man-hauling a laden sled. At 79° 29′ s. he established a food dump containing over a ton of provisions, which he named "One Ton Depot." It was situated at about 670 miles from the Pole, and was to be used by the returning polar party. Returning to his base at Cape Evans, Scott was almost killed when his dog sled team plunged into an immense crevasse, but was miraculously rescued. Back at Safety Camp, Scott learned that Amundsen had arrived and had set up a base in the Bay of Whales. Scott was annoyed, but made no change of plans, despite the fact that he knew Amundsen had no scientific objectives—his only intention was to win the South Pole for Norway.

While Scott's scientific work continued, he began to observe his colleagues closely, assessing their potential as possible companions for an assault on the Pole. By the latter months of 1911, his plans for such a venture were complete. His intention was to march the 1,800 miles to the Pole and back, traversing the four-hundred-mile Great Ice Barrier with motor, pony, dog and man-hauled sled teams that would transport supplies to be laid in depots for the returning parties, climb the Beardmore Glacier (discovered by Shackleton in 1903), cross the Queen Alexandra Mountains on to the ten-thousand-foot Polar Plateau, and reach the Pole. He would take a party of three with him on the final stage of the journey, and would complete the mission during the Antarctic summer, which, in theory, should provide relatively mild weather.

An advance party set out on October 24, 1911, using the two remaining motor sleds, drawing a train of heavily laden ordinary sleds at about one mile per hour. Scott and a party of nine followed on November 1. The motor sleds soon broke down, due to overheating, and were abandoned—although one attained a distance of fifty miles which, in the first decade of this century, was a creditable performance. Meanwhile, Amundsen and a team of four expert skiers and dogs had reached beyond 80° s. and were making rapid progress toward the Pole.

Scott's surviving ponies proved as unsuitable on the treacherous surface as those taken on his earlier journey, and had eventually to be killed at a place Scott named "Shambles Camp." The main party caught up with the motor party on November 21, and two members were sent back to base. An advance party of four of those remaining proceeded at a fifteen-mile distance from the rest, establishing camps and undertaking scientific work. The newly formed main party continued, marching at night when the air temperature dropped, and sleeping during the warmer daylight hours. This party was followed by dog teams laying food stores every sixty-five miles, with sufficient provisions for one week for each returning party. At the foot of the Beardmore Glacier, a blizzard kept Scott and his party in their tent for four days, while precious food was

Opposite above Watercolor of the *Discovery*, the 1901–1904 expedition ship, by Edward Wilson. The ship was specially built to withstand the effects of pack ice.

Opposite below Leopard seal chasing Emperor penguins; watercolor by Wilson for the May, 1902, edition of *The South Polar Times*.

Below left Dr. Edward Wilson, the physician, zoologist and artist to whom Antarctica proved a rich source of inspiration.

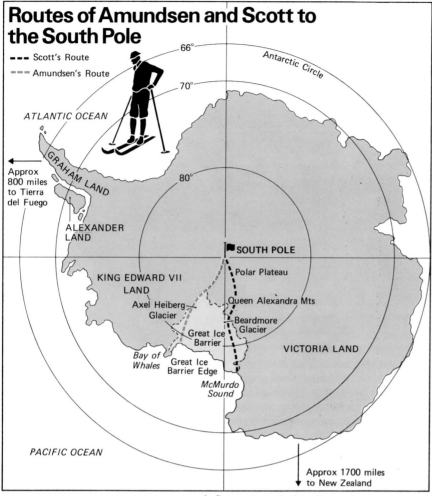

Routes of Amundsen and Scott to the South Pole

- - - Scott's Route
- - - Amundsen's Route

ATLANTIC OCEAN

66°

70°

Antarctic Circle

GRAHAM LAND

←
Approx
800 miles
to Tierra
del Fuego

ALEXANDER
LAND

80°

KING EDWARD VII
LAND

Axel Heiberg
Glacier

Great Ice
Barrier

Bay of
Whales

Great Ice
Barrier Edge

McMurdo
Sound

SOUTH POLE

Polar Plateau

Queen Alexandra Mts

Beardmore
Glacier

VICTORIA LAND

PACIFIC OCEAN

↓
Approx 1700 miles
to New Zealand

consumed. Scott wrote in his diary:

Resignation to misfortune is the only attitude, but not an easy one to adopt. It seems undeserved when plans were well laid and so nearly crowned with success . . . . It is very evil to lie here in a wet sleeping bag and think of the pity of it, whilst with no break in the overcast sky things go steadily from bad to worse.

After the blizzard, a sudden thaw produced eighteen inches of slush that soaked men, animals and equipment. On December 14, as they wrestled with these conditions, Amundsen reached the Pole. He actually passed within a hundred miles of Scott on his return journey, while Scott was still heading south.

Scott, with eleven companions, made slow progress across the Beardmore Glacier. On December 21, at 85° 7′ s., four men were sent back. The last supporting party turned back from 86° 56′ s. on January 4, 1912, leaving Scott with the team he had chosen to accompany him to the Pole. This consisted of four men—although he had originally planned to take only three; the extra man was Lieutenant Henry R. Bowers, the others, Captain Lawrence G. Oates, Petty Officer Edgar Evans and his companion of 1902, Dr. Edward Wilson.

On January 16, in the distance, they spotted a tiny speck:

We marched on, found that it was a black flag tied to a sledge bearer; nearby the remains of a camp, sledge

tracks and ski tracks going and coming and the clear trace of dogs' paws—many dogs. This told us the whole story. The Norwegians have forestalled us and are first at the Pole. It is a terrible disappointment, and I am very sorry for my loyal companions.

They reached the Pole two days later, on January 18. The forlorn photograph they took of themselves, blistered and weatherbeaten after sixty-nine days on the march, conveys better than any words the intense disappointment that Scott and his men must have felt. He wrote:

The Pole. Yes, but under very different circumstances from those expected. . . . Great God! this is an awful place and terrible enough for us to have laboured to it without the reward of priority. . . . Amundsen has done his work, and done it well.

By this time Amundsen was already back on the Great Ice Barrier and only eight days away from his base in the Bay of Whales.

Scott's saddened party began its gruelling return journey on January 18. Scott wrote, "Well, we have turned our backs now on the goal of our ambition and must face our nine hundred miles of solid dragging—and goodbye to most of the daydreams!" Frostbite, hunger, exhaustion and injuries resulting from falls on the icy surface made every step torturous. On February 7 they were again back on intermittently rocky surfaces, after fourteen weeks of nothing but snow and ice. On the Beardmore Glacier, Evans had fallen and injured his head. Probably suffering from brain damage, he began to show signs of physical and mental deterioration, and on February 17, collapsed and died. At the depots along their route they found less fuel than they had anticipated owing to serious leakage caused by faulty seals in the oil cans. Amundsen had returned to his ship by February and had sailed to New Zealand, from where, in March, his conquest of the South Pole was announced to the world.

At the same time, Scott, Oates, Wilson and Bowers were still struggling homeward, though now at a rate of under ten miles a day. At 79° 50′ s. Oates, suffering from severe frostbite and leg injuries, and not wishing to become a burden on his failing companions, took a course of self-sacrifice that has become famous. Remarking to the others that he was ". . . just going outside, and might be some time," he walked into a blizzard and was never seen again—an act that Scott described as that "of a brave man and an English gentleman." The three survivors made very little more progress, and were compelled to remain in their tent for their last days during a blizzard that showed no signs of abating. The blizzard lasted nine days, and they had food for only two and fuel for just one hot meal—One Ton Depot with ample supplies of food and fuel lay a mere eleven miles away, but they were unable to reach it. Accepting their defeat, Scott wrote a number of letters to his family and friends, and a "message to the public" in which he commented:

Had we lived, I should have had a tale to tell of the hardihood, endurance, and courage of my companions which would have stirred the heart of every Englishman.

we shall stick it out to the end but we are getting weaker of course and the end cannot be far. It seems a pity but I do not think I can write more —

R Scott

Last Entry —

For God's sake look after our people

These rough notes and our dead bodies must tell the tale . . . .

He ended his diary on March 29, later adding the final words, "For God's sake look after our people."

It was not until the following November that a search party found the bodies of Scott, Wilson and Bowers. They were left in their tent, and a huge cairn was built above it as a memorial. Today the tomb must be covered by many feet of snow and ice. A memorial to Oates, whose body was never found, read: "Hereabouts died a very gallant gentleman." The news of the fate of Scott's last expedition did not reach England until February 12, 1913. When Amundsen heard the report, he remarked: "I would forgo honor—everything—to bring him back to life. My own triumph is marred by the haunting thought of the tragedy."

Why did Scott fail? In his journal, he himself blamed the late start caused by the depletion of his pony transport, the weather, and the soft surface which made man-hauling immensely tiring. There were undoubtedly many factors involved. The psychological effect of their being beaten to the Pole, and the shock of the death of Evans, who was regarded as the strong man of the team, certainly offered no encouragement, and the return journey was overshadowed by a feeling of despondency. The weather was unexpectedly severe—constant headwinds and blizzards on the Great Ice Barrier,

with night temperatures of $-47°$F. had a deleterious effect—in contrast to the lowest temperature recorded by Amundsen, $-24°$. The lack of knowledge of dietary requirements—particularly the need for vitamins—and the loss of fuel oil for heating the food contributed to the physical and nervous breakdown of the party; over four months is in excess of the period during which men could undertake arduous work at low temperatures on Scott's sort of diet. The average age of the polar party was thirty-six years. It has been suggested that a younger team might have succeeded—but it appears that Scott, at forty-three the oldest of the group, was the last to die. The fact that Scott took four companions, instead of three as planned, probably put a heavy strain on their rations and cramped their sleeping accommodation in a tent designed for four. Several explanations for this course have been proposed— that Scott was unable to decide whom to leave behind, that he wanted as many as possible to share the honor of reaching the Pole, and that he believed that the inclusion of Bowers would give the extra manpower required on a long haul. Concomitantly, the loss of Evans robbed the team of essential hauling power, and slowed their progress. Scott was on the march for 140 days before being halted by the final blizzard; Amundsen achieved his dash to the Pole and back in ninety-nine days. Amundsen was amazed by the fact that Scott had used man-haulage over the large part of the journey (Scott had even hauled thirty-five pounds of rock samples as far as his last camp). Amundsen relied entirely on his dogs for haulage, and as a mobile larder— each of his fifty or more dogs represented fifty pounds of food he did not need to carry. Scott's party, on the other hand, was not only distrustful of the use of dog-power, but undoubtedly squeamish about eating the dogs under any circumstances—on Scott's earlier expedition, he had carried sick dogs on his sleds rather than kill them, and to eat them would have been unthinkable.

When the news of Scott's valiant but thwarted effort reached the world, an appeal fund was launched and raised eventually over £84,000— contrasting with the slow response to Scott's initial appeal for funds for the expedition. In 1921, the Scott Polar Research Institute was established at Cambridge. Numerous memorials were erected to Scott (one sculpted by his widow) and his companions throughout the British Empire.

The British Antarctic Expedition of 1910 was not only the last journey undertaken by Scott, but also the last real voyage of discovery undertaken on the globe. Until then, Antarctica was the only major area of the Earth's surface about which almost nothing was known. Scott's scientific data and geographical exploration filled many gaps in man's knowledge of what, at the end of the nineteenth century, was still a *Terra Australis Incognita*. After the conquest of the South Pole, only space travel could expand man's horizons and offer new worlds to conquer.

RUSSELL ASH

The Balkans provide the tinder

Roosevelt's administration

Russia's defeat in 1904–1905 had turned her away from the Far East and toward the Balkans. Her withdrawal from the Far East removed many points of dispute with Britain, but the renewed interest in the Balkans inevitably led to conflict with Austria. Anxious to remove dissension in central Asia, the British agreed in 1907 to a convention with Russia that would deal with Persia, Afghanistan and Tibet. Germany, which had begun to feel intensely claustrophobic, tried to bully England out of its new alliances. The Kaiser's tactics only served to crystallize Europe into two armed camps—one, on the periphery, held together by German threats; the other, on the inside, desperate to break out.

While Europe prepared for war, America slipped quietly into a period of prosperity. During the presidency (1901–1909) of Theodore Roosevelt, industry surged ahead and foreign negotiations brought significant financial gains. The key to Roosevelt's foreign policy was his determination to "speak softly and carry a big stick." The most significant application of his statement came in 1903, when he asked Colombia for a lease on the Isthmus of Panama, the narrowest point between the Atlantic and Pacific Oceans, so that the United States might build an interocean canal. Colombia refused, and the Panamanians rebelled against their colonial governors. The new independent republic thereby created was immediately granted the beneficent protection of the United States—and the land needed for the canal was leased forthwith to the United States.

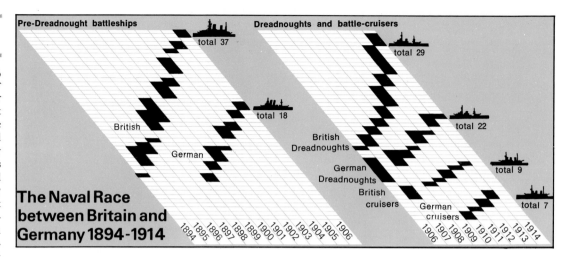

The Naval Race between Britain and Germany 1894-1914

Pre-Dreadnought battleships — British, German — total 37, total 18

Dreadnoughts and battle-cruisers — British Dreadnoughts, German Dreadnoughts, British cruisers, German cruisers — total 29, total 22, total 9, total 7

Roosevelt did not stand for re-election in 1908, but he secured the election of William Howard Taft. However, Roosevelt, dissatisfied with Taft's policies, withdrew his support and organized the Progressive Party and was its candidate for president in 1912. Taft was renominated by the Republican Party. Both Roosevelt and Taft were defeated and Woodrow Wilson was elected.

An age of alliances

At the same time, European diplomacy was elaborating a system of increasingly rigid alliances. The first was formed in 1879, when Bismarck concluded the Dual Alliance with Austria-Hungary. This agreement enabled the German Chancellor to have a say in Austrian policy—and thereby prevent an Austro-Russian war over the Balkans. In later years, however, with less experienced statesmen at the helm of German policy, this agreement meant that Germany was committed to supporting Austrian adventures.

The Dual Alliance soon generated others. France, still smarting from the blows Germany had inflicted upon her in 1870, concluded a formal alliance with Russia in 1894. Henceforth, German military thinking revolved around the problem of how to defeat both France and Russia simultaneously. The solution hit upon by General Alfred von Schlieffen (1833–1913), the German Chief of Staff, was to knock France out in a lightning thrust and then to wage a longer campaign against Russia.

At this time, the Franco-Russian alliance might have been countered by an Anglo-German understanding, but several factors made such an arrangement impossible. Germany was seen as the cause of Britain's deteriorating position in world trade, and allegations were made that the Germans were selling shoddy goods using the trademarks of respected British firms. The German monarch's Wagnerian conception of Germany's role in world politics did not help matters. Through such reckless gestures as sending a telegram of support to the Boer leader, Paul Kruger (1825–1904), the touchy and tactless Kaiser effectively eliminated all chances for amicable Anglo-German negotiations.

Britain's realization that an alliance with Germany was impossible paved the way for a rapprochement with France. Such a detente was indeed necessary, for years of Anglo-French quarreling over Egypt had come to a head in 1898 at Fashoda, when a small French expedition led by the explorer Jean Baptiste Marchand (1863–1934) was confronted by the forces of General Horatio Kitchener (1850–1916) on the Upper Nile. The confrontation almost

precipitated a war, but France recognized England's superior naval power and withdrew. The incident served as a necessary purgative in Anglo-French relations; France finally recognized that she could do nothing about the British in Egypt. Edward VII's triumphant visit to Paris in 1903 soothed the memories of Fashoda, and in 1904 the prospect of the Russo-Japanese War expedited the conclusion of the Anglo-French detente. In an extensive treaty the Entente Cordiale was concluded. Britain's Egyptian claims were recognized in return for the acceptance of French ambitions in Morocco. During the next decade British and French interests were increasingly united, mainly as a result of the threat of German expansionism.

Arms race

"A state that has oceanic, or—an equivalent term—world interests must be able to uphold them and make its power felt beyond its own territorial waters. National world commerce, world industry . . . world intercourse and colonies, are impossible without a fleet capable of taking the initiative." The new aggressive naval stance taken by Germany—with its now-massive naval strike power—after the appointment of Alfred von Tirpitz (1849–1930) as Germany's naval minister in 1898, caused considerable disquiet in Britain and in 1906 the *Dreadnought*, with more than twice the firepower of the largest existing battleship, was launched at Britain's vast naval base at Portsmouth. Germany's determination to keep up with Britain in the race for naval superiority

Blowing up the Gamboa Dike which allowed the Atlantic and Pacific Oceans to join in the Panama Canal.

to set Europe alight

meant that the Kiel Canal linking the North Sea with Germany's vast Baltic seaport and naval base of Kiel had to be widened in order to accommodate dreadnought-type ships. As Britain determined to retain its lead at least in building the heavier type of ship such as dreadnoughts and battle cruisers, a new and far more expensive naval race was soon under way. On land, too, there was a race to build up well-equipped armies. By 1914 the defense budgets of the great powers had risen to unprecedented levels: in that year Germany spent $539 million, Russia $432 million, Britain $343 million, France $284 million and Austria-Hungary $274 million. Due to the enormous rise in state expenditure generally, however, there was very little public outcry against this. In Britain for example, government expenditure rose from about seven percent of the national income in 1873 to about fourteen percent in 1914, while during the same period—despite the increasing cost of defense—the military budget fell from thirty-four percent to twenty-five percent of government expenditure. Huge arms firms such as Krupp in Germany and Vickers in Britain expanded rapidly, and smaller ones like Bofors in Sweden found their factories inadequate to meet the demand. Arms salesmen, of whom the most notorious was Sir Basil Zaharoff (1850–1936), grew immensely rich. Technical developments in the manufacture of guns followed rapidly. Efficient machine guns—most of them designed by Americans—replaced the old-fashioned Gatling gun, and such

German cartoon (1909) on the race for naval superiority.

guns were to be responsible for the vast majority of the battle casualties in World War I. Artillery range and caliber was also being increased rapidly. Scientists were making a still more frightening contribution to the horrors of war by working on gases to blind or burn the enemy.

Despite—or because of—the development of sophisticated equipment, the military machine grew increasingly dependent on manpower. Only two men were needed to operate a machine gun, but those two men could kill and wound hundreds in a few minutes. Periods of compulsory military service were extended to provide suitably trained gun fodder; in France, for example, the period of compulsory service was extended from two years to three in 1913. But it was in Germany, the original home of the modern mass army—which

Kaiser Wilhelm II; an intelligent and idealistic but impulsive and headstrong ruler.

had played such havoc with the French in 1870—that the army was strongest. This was partly due to political considerations; the army with its strong Junker officer tradition was for all practical purposes an independent estate. Through such commanders as Schlieffen and Helmuth von Moltke (1848–1916) the German army became the most efficient in Europe. Schlieffen had developed the original plan for an attack on France through Belgium, although it was much modified by Moltke. But elaborate war plans, even if they were "academic" as Schlieffen had claimed, required large armies. By 1914 Germany was capable of mobilizing more than four million men, France more than three and a half million and Russia more than one million; the other powers had smaller armies.

Although this escalation in arms and armories did not inevitably lead to war, it made the consideration of war inevitable. The increasing rigidity of the system of alliances made the danger of war more serious. Austria-Hungary and the Prussian establishment, natural enemies for so much of the nineteenth century as a result of the power-conflict in Germany, could now find common ground. Ironically, too, the Ottoman Empire, for so long the rival of Austria-Hungary in the Balkans, was drawn into the alliance. Britain stood outside the Franco-Russian alliance, but was increasingly drawn toward it by the Entente Cordiale.

As Russia and Austria glared at each other across the Balkans, their allies, Britain and Germany, were drawing further apart. The British

Foreign Office had come to the conclusion that the only interpretation of German policy that fitted the known facts was that Germany wanted war. Germany, rapidly becoming more assertive in European politics, offended and disturbed the British with its well-publicized effort to outbuild the Royal Navy. As the world's naval power, the British concluded that this German expansion was directed at them. Therefore in addition to building dreadnoughts, the British began to concentrate their strength in the North Sea, leaving the Mediterranean more to the French (a division of labor that further committed the British to the French alliance).

Fanned by a sensational press, the arms race soon polarized existing antagonisms. The newspapers discovered that blood and thunder created readers—and revenue. Diplomacy came to be followed as avidly as a national sport. In England the *Daily Express* and *Daily Mail* became jingoistic guardians of national honor, and even *The Times* selected its information

Balkan rats attacking an inert Austria.

to stress the German menace. The German press was, if anything, more rabid. Both the *Neue Prüssiche Zeitung* and the *Deutsche Zeitung* demanded the creation of a navy able to wrest maritime supremacy from the British. Sensible diplomats were helpless. The times demanded excitement, and international affairs provided it; national honor had become everything.

The Balkans were to provide the cause for which all Europe seemed to be searching. But initially none of the European great powers—Britain, Germany, or France—was involved. The Balkans, a power vacuum because of Turkish weakness, provided the tinder to set Europe alight.

Launching a dreadnought at Portsmouth, England.

Assassination Sparks the Great War

By the spring of 1914, imperial Germany was spoiling for war. Germany's leaders were determined to break up the Triple Entente of Britain, France and Russia that had isolated Germany in Europe and thwarted its territorial ambitions. And when a young Bosnian nationalist assassinated Archduke Franz Ferdinand, heir to the throne of Germany's lone ally, Austria-Hungary, the Kaiser had the "incident" he had been looking for. In the diplomatic controversy growing out of the assassination, the Kaiser threw his full support behind Austria-Hungary and against Russia. This set in motion a series of political and military maneuvers that made a full-scale continental war virtually inevitable. The scope and inflexibility of Germany's master plan for mobilization—the infamous Schlieffen Plan—necessarily involved both England and France in any conflict between the Kaiser and the Tsar. And thus when Germany declared war on Russia on August 1, World War I was launched.

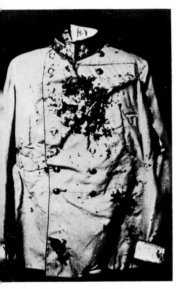

The blood-stained uniform of Archduke Franz Ferdinand, heir to the Austro-Hungarian Empire, after his assassination on June 28, 1914.

Opposite Kaiser Wilhelm II of Germany with his commander in chief, Helmuth von Moltke, on the Western Front at the beginning of World War I.

On June 28, 1914, in a narrow street in Sarajevo, the capital of Bosnia, two shots were fired setting off the train of events that culminated in the start of World War I six weeks later. Those two shots were fired by a Bosnian student, Gavrilo Princip, one of three young Bosnian nationalists who had traveled to Sarajevo on the instructions of a Serbian secret organization known as the Black Hand. The shots were fired at the Archduke Franz Ferdinand, the heir-presumptive to the throne of Austria-Hungary.

Why did this particular event lead to war? In 1912, all the Balkan states with the exception of Rumania had attacked Turkey—a crisis considerably more serious than a single assassination—yet there had been no wider repercussions. And since that time the ambassadors of the Great Powers had met regularly in London under the chairmanship of Sir Edward Grey, the British Foreign Secretary, to ensure that their countries were not dragged into war by the deeds of the belligerents.

Outwardly, the international situation in 1914 was much more settled than it had been in 1912. Indeed, one of the major antagonisms of international relations—the rivalry between Britain and Germany—seemed to be dying down. Britain had met some of Germany's colonial grievances; Britain's objections to German penetration of the Turkish Empire had finally been overcome in early 1914; and a contingent agreement for the division of the Portuguese colonies between Germany and England had also been concluded at that time. Moreover, each nation had seemed to accept the existence of the other's navy.

But this was only the surface reality. The division of the world into two power blocs was largely a result of German policy, a policy that concentrated on raising Germany from a continental to a world power. Its basis was Germany's economic expansion, which had succeeded in radically transforming its social, political and economic structure during the preceding generation. This rapid expansion in all spheres of economic life only heightened the Germans' awareness of the inadequacy of the country's sources of raw materials and created the general conviction, reinforced by nationwide propaganda, that Germany's frontiers had become too narrow. Germany's territorial ambitions ran counter to the designs of the other imperialist powers, and those powers were provoked into a policy of containment.

Germany's diplomacy never waivered in its ultimate objective—the expansion of Germany's power—although it vacillated in its methods. (At one time that policy emphasized rapprochement; at another, it aggressively insisted on Germany's claims.) Between 1912 and early 1914, Germany attempted to reach an understanding—which, it was hoped, would lead ultimately to an alliance—with Britain. But its efforts in this direction left it clearly subordinate to Britain and made it apparent that its objectives were not to be attained without a fundamental restructuring of the relations between Britain, France and Russia. This Germany had manifestly failed to do by peaceful means; the only alternative was preventive war against any nation that thwarted Germany's efforts to achieve its territorial objectives. But why did Sarajevo provide the opportunity for such a preventive war, and, more importantly, why did the assassination of Franz Ferdinand lead to the outbreak of a more horrific general war?

It is easy enough to see how the assassination at Sarajevo could lead to a localized conflict in the Balkans. After all, Franz Ferdinand had come to

Franz Ferdinand. His death sparked the war that ended an epoch.

Right The arrest of Gavrilo Princip after the assassination at Sarajevo.

Bosnia to attend Austro-Hungarian army maneuvers that were nothing more than a gesture to remind the Balkan Slavs of Austria-Hungary's power. The Hapsburg monarchy had been rocked in the 1860s by the secession of its Italian and German members, and had only prevented the same thing from happening to its Hungarian domains by taking the Magyar aristocracy into partnership.

By 1914 the existence of the Austro-Hungarian Empire was being threatened by a movement of Slav nationalism. Partnership with the Slavs was out of the question because the Magyars would not tolerate a further dilution of their power, and consequently the only road open to the Hapsburgs was to bring the Slavs to heel. There were those in Vienna who felt that the crime committed against Austria at Sarajevo provided an excellent opportunity to teach the Slavs a lesson. Both Count Franz Conrad von Hötzendorf, the Chief of Staff, and Count Leopold von Berchtold, the Foreign Minister, felt that a demonstration against Serbia (which was suspected of being behind the assassination) would be a good way to reassert Austria's prestige.

At this point, the issue became considerably more complicated. An operation to humiliate the Slavs could well rouse Russia, the protector of the Slav nations, and the Austrians needed to be reassured that they had the support of their German allies before making their move against Serbia. Yet for seven days they did nothing. The immediate indignation arising from the assassination was allowed to evaporate, and Austria's subsequent action appeared to be concerned less with avenging an insult than with crushing the Serbs. On July 4, a full week after the assassination, the Austrians sent a letter to Kaiser Wilhelm II, asking for his support.

The Germans, who were so conscious of being isolated by the Triple Entente of Britain, France and Russia that they were prepared to do almost anything for their only certain ally, Austria-Hungary, readily pledged their support. The Kaiser, who was the decisive factor, became violently excited, gave the Austrians the go-ahead, and promised German support in case of Russian intervention. In doing so, the Kaiser sided with the generals who opined that, if preventive war against Russia was inevitable, it ought to come before Russian industrialization made it a more formidable enemy. In any case, the Kaiser was convinced that the Russians would back down, and he therefore made a chivalrous gesture that he felt was unlikely to be put to the test. This gesture strengthened the Austrians' resolve to be firm.

Nevertheless, the Austrians still hesitated. At the best of times Austrian policy was dilatory and hesitant; now it was held back by the knowledge that French President Raymond Poincaré was visiting St. Petersburg. Strong immediate action therefore could not be taken against Serbia—on the chance that the fire-eating Poincaré might encourage the Russians to take a pro-Slav stand.

Almost a month passed and nothing happened: Europe breathed a sigh of relief. Perhaps Sarajevo had just been one of those minor events in the Balkans.

But on July 23, Poincaré left St. Petersburg, and the diplomatic log jam began to break. At 6 P.M. on July 24, Austria-Hungary presented a provocative ultimatum to Serbia, one that was tantamount to an Austrian takeover of Serbia's internal policies. That ultimatum had a forty-eight-hour time limit. When it was presented, Serbia's Prime Minister Nikola Pašic was away, and he did not return until 5 A.M. on July 25. By that time eleven hours of the forty-eight had expired. That day, Sir Edward Grey suggested to Lichnowsky, the German ambassador in London, that Britain and Germany ask Austria to extend its time limit or accept mediations by France, Italy, Britain and Germany. Grey's move convinced the Germans that Britain was so anxious to avoid trouble that it would not intervene. Feeling free to encourage their Austrian allies, the Germans did not pass on Grey's message until after the ultimatum had expired. In fact, Theobald von Bethmann-Hollweg, the German Chancellor, seems to have had war with Russia and France as his main objective at this time. And he was apparently prepared to gamble on the possibility of Britain's entry into that war. If war had not ensued, Germany's diplomatic victory would have been sizable nonetheless. France's failure to support the Russians—and Russia's failure to support the Serbs—could quite easily have called the whole alliance system into question.

On July 24, the Germans notified the other powers that they felt that the Austrian ultimatum was reasonable and, attempting to create a peaceable impression, urged the powers to localize any conflict. The Russians stated that they could not acquiesce in the demise of Serbia, and the French announced that they would meet their obligations to Russia. This encouraged the Serbs to reject the Austrian ultimatum completely, although their reply was conciliatory. The Serbs refused to accept

unconditional surrender, and the Austrians immediately broke off diplomatic relations. Yet when the Kaiser saw the Serbian reply to the Austrian ultimatum, he said, "All reason for war has gone."

It was a reasonable conclusion, drawn by an intelligent and reasonable—if excitable—man. But the Kaiser had not reckoned with two forces, and these were the factors that transformed the small-scale local disagreement between Austria and Serbia into a continental and then into a world war. One factor was the determination of Chancellor Bethmann-Hollweg and the German Chief of Staff, Helmuth von Moltke—and the interests they represented—to have their preventive war. The other was the rigidity of the Germans' military plans. By July 28, the Kaiser was genuinely afraid of the possibility of a European war, and he suggested that the Austrians save their honor by a token occupation of Belgrade, the Serbian capital. Bethmann-Hollweg held back the Kaiser's sane proposals until after Austria had declared war on Serbia. At this point the Russians decided to mobilize as a gesture of support for Serbia, to show that the Russian bear was not sleeping. This might have caused the Austrians to have second thoughts, but they were emboldened by messages telegrammed by Moltke.

Even at this point general war was not inevitable. Bethmann-Hollweg sued for British neutrality, in exchange for which he promised to forego annexation of French and Belgian territory. But the British stood firm, and Bethmann-Hollweg, who knew that the odds on a German victory had been dramatically diminished by Britain's move, lost some of his nerve. He pressed the Austrians to modify their plans in accordance with the earlier British proposals of a "halt in Belgrade." He did not want the Austrians to drop the matter entirely, however. Indeed, he was aware that the Russians would reject the British proposals. He was attempting a sleight of hand, one that was intended to lay the blame for any hostilities on Russia. (He hoped thereby to alter British intentions.) The appearance of Russian aggression would greatly assist him in another objective—the winning over of the German public, especially the Social Democrats.

The Russians held the stage in the next act. A partial mobilization might have balked the Germans, but such a move was impossible. Russia's plans for mobilization were such that, if the country only partially mobilized against Austria, the chaos on the railway system would effectively preclude any wider mobilization. To prevent Russia from being left defenseless in case of German attack, any Russian mobilization had to be total. Yet that massive mobilization was meant only as a diplomatic maneuver, and not a decision for European war.

Russia's mobilization was precisely what Germany had been waiting for. Two ultimatums were immediately dispatched: one to Russia, demanding

A French infantry regiment leaving for the front in 1914. Five million Frenchmen were killed in Flanders during World War I.

German student-conscripts, with flowers in their helmets, at the beginning of the war.

German and British biplanes and triplanes fighting.

Opposite Two World War I posters. Both sides felt that they were fighting a crusade against the forces of evil.

1914 ———— 1917

Zeichnet die Sechste Kriegsanleihe

BRITAIN·NEEDS

YOU·AT·ONCE

demobilization against Germany and Austria, and one to France, demanding that it make explicit its stand in the event of a German attack on Russia. War had become inevitable, primarily because of the nature of Germany's only military plan, the infamous Schlieffen Plan.

Of all the Great Powers, Germany alone had two potential enemies, France and Russia. It therefore faced the special problem of fighting two major wars simultaneously. Because of Russia's enormous size and huge manpower resources (which threatened a long, drawn-out war during which the French could break into Germany from the west), it was necessary to knock out France before Russia could mobilize. That was the battle plan devised by Alfred von Schlieffen, who had been German Chief of Staff before Moltke. Thinking that France's network of frontier fortresses was impregnable, Schlieffen proposed that the German armies outflank the French lines by means of a wheeling movement through Belgium. Such a move involved two problems, the consequences of which seem to have been ignored. First of all, the forcible violation of Belgian territory was likely to arouse the British, for whom the neutrality of the Low Countries was a fundamental policy. Secondly, in purely military terms, the Schlieffen Plan involved pouring four army groups through the railway junction at Aachen. One army would have to be through and on its way before the next one arrived, and that meant incredibly ingenious and intricate synchronization of railway timetables. It also meant that once German mobilization started, it could end only with troops leaving Aachen and violating Belgian neutrality. Thus for Germany mobilization meant war, and war on both France and Russia.

The part played by this plan in escalating the war and in ensuring that one particular interest prevailed in the German ruling class was enormous. Even as the Kaiser was ordering mobilization, news came of a British offer to guarantee French neutrality—provided Germany would refrain from attacking Russia. The Kaiser thought peace might

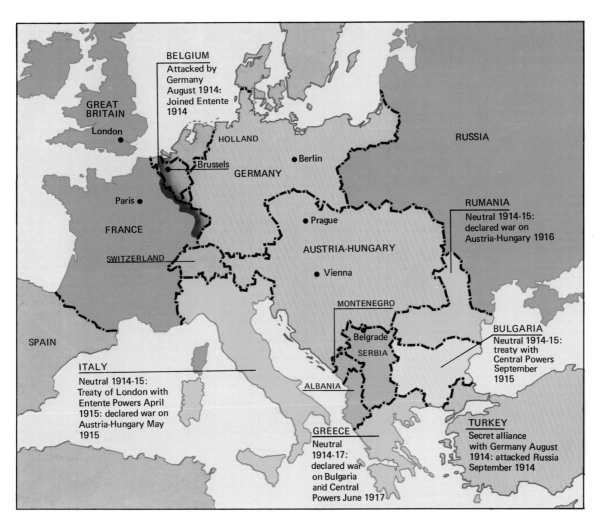

BELGIUM
Attacked by Germany August 1914: Joined Entente 1914

GREAT BRITAIN
London

HOLLAND

Brussels

GERMANY

Berlin

RUSSIA

Prague

Paris

FRANCE

AUSTRIA-HUNGARY

SWITZERLAND

Vienna

RUMANIA
Neutral 1914-15: declared war on Austria-Hungary 1916

SPAIN

MONTENEGRO

Belgrade
SERBIA

BULGARIA
Neutral 1914-15: treaty with Central Powers September 1915

ITALY
Neutral 1914-15: Treaty of London with Entente Powers April 1915: declared war on Austria-Hungary May 1915

ALBANIA

GREECE
Neutral 1914-17: declared war on Bulgaria and Central Powers June 1917

TURKEY
Secret alliance with Germany August 1914: attacked Russia September 1914

- ● Entente Powers
- ◐ Allies of Entente Powers
- ○ Later allies of Entente Powers
- ◑ Central Powers
- ○ Ally of Central Powers but declared neutrality on outbreak of war
- ■ Western Front December 1914

still be saved, but Moltke told him that it would not be possible to stop German mobilization (since doing so would involve the rerouting of 11,000 trains). In any case, Russian mobilization was a threat to Germany's split-second timing. It had to press on —to force Russia to demobilize or to prevent Russia from getting a start and nullifying Germany's advantage of speed.

On August 1, Germany declared war on Russia. Two days later, it declared war on France. By August 3, the Balkan quarrel had been transformed, with the help of the Schlieffen Plan, into a European war involving France, Germany and Russia. So far, the British had managed to stay out, although there was a division of opinion inside the cabinet as to Britain's best course of action. This division of opinion may have been a factor encouraging belligerence on the Continent—encouraging the Germans to bank on British neutrality and the French to count on British support.

At this point, Schlieffen chalked up his greatest posthumous victory: in accordance with an 1839 treaty guaranteeing the independence and neutrality of Belgium, the British asked the Germans to respect that neutrality. The exigencies of the Schlieffen Plan ensured that the Germans could not comply with the British request (which Bethmann-Hollweg described as "stabbing a man from behind, while fighting for his life"). He could not believe that the British would go to war, "all for just a word, neutrality, just for a scrap of paper."

That Bethmann-Hollweg could use such an expression about an international treaty reflects the Germans' cavalier approach to international relations and their willingness to engage in a continental war, even at the risk of making it a world war. The Schlieffen Plan was part and parcel of this approach. Once the tenuous truce had been broken, the scope and inflexibility of the Plan made world war a virtual inevitability.   BRIAN GROGAN

Over the Top. British troops advancing in Flanders.

Idealized concepts of war

The course of war

In October, 1914, barely four months after Sarajevo, the United States Ambassador in London, Walter Hines Page, wrote to President Wilson: "It is not the same world as it was last July." Page's observation was a profoundly accurate one, for the first clashes of World War I had ended an epoch that had begun in the Renaissance. When the war began, Europe dominated the world. The emperors of Germany, Austria, Turkey and Russia ruled the territory between the Rhine and Vladivostok, and Great Britain ruled the seas. When it ended, the four empires were in ruins. Europe was drained and exhausted, and the political structure of the world as we know it today was beginning to emerge.

Both sides believed that the war would quickly be won, and among almost all the combatant countries there was great enthusiasm. Civilians joined up without waiting for their conscription orders, feeling that they were fighting against the forces of evil. In reality, however, World War I was a nationalist and territorial rather than an ideological war. At the beginning of the war Germany was determined to crush opposition in the West as soon as possible in order to make resources available for the struggle against Russia. The French, failing to understand the danger of an attack through Belgium, had only a quarter of a million men defending that frontier, against a German

force almost three times as great. Along the border between France and Germany the two armies were fairly evenly matched, with about three quarters of a million men on each side. The German offensive from Belgium was, however, held up somewhat, mainly due to the good discipline of the heavily outnumbered French and Belgians and to the timely intervention of a British expeditionary force at Mons. After their first surge forward to Meaux, only twenty miles northeast of Paris, the Germans were gradually pushed backward. In an attempt to outflank the French army, which had been reinforced, von Moltke ordered an extension of the front line as far as Ypres.

The failure of the Schlieffen Plan (as modified by Moltke) meant that vital German military resources were held down in the West, and that the army on the Russian front could not be reinforced. The Germans were heavily outnumbered by the Russians, who attacked East Prussia within the first few weeks of the war. The German commander ordered his men to retreat as far as the Vistula River, but his orders were quickly countermanded and he was replaced by the more aggressive combination of generals von Hindenberg and Ludendorff. At the Battles of Tannenberg in August and of the Masurian Lakes in September, the Russian offensive collapsed, and Germany captured or killed over a quarter of a million men. Success at Tannenberg was a massive psychological as well as military victory for Germany,

French soldiers in a trench in 1916.

After the Battle of Tannenberg (1914).

which felt that the shame of the defeat of the Teutonic Knights by the Poles half a millennium before had been wiped out at a blow. (Although Hindenberg and Ludendorff received credit for the victories, the man responsible was more likely the brilliant Colonel, later General, Max Hoffmann, then a staff officer.)

But German successes against Russia lost some of their value because of the poor performance of the Austro-Hungarian army. The Russians were more successful against the Austrians—partly because Slavic officers in the Austrian army had kept the Russians in-

formed of military plans. An Austrian attack toward Lublin in Galicia was speedily halted, and to prevent his army from being encircled, the Emperor ordered it to retreat west of the Carpathians. In 1915, however, the Russian army found the strain too heavy and began to retreat slowly, losing territory both to Germany and to Austria-Hungary. Hundreds of thousands of Russian soldiers were captured by the Central Powers.

In the Balkans—the original excuse for the outbreak of war in 1914—hostilities gradually widened. Serbia was able to defend itself against the attack of the Austro-

Admiral von Tirpitz, German Minister of Marine, during the war years.

perish in the trenches

Hungarian army in 1914. In the following year, however, Bulgaria, previously neutral, joined the Central Powers, and Serbia found itself attacked from the rear. By the time Rumania joined the Allies in 1916 Serbia had fallen—partly as a result of a typhus epidemic that took more than three hundred thousand lives, and the Rumanian army soon collapsed. The Central Powers gained little from this victory, however, as the Black Sea oil wells were destroyed. Italy, which had previously been a noncombatant supporter of the Central Powers, eventually entered the war on the Allied side in 1915, backed by offers of territorial expansion, but failed to play any useful role.

The war at sea

The war at sea was no more decisive, although it was slightly less bloody than the land war. It was also something of an anticlimax after the fierce naval rivalry of the prewar years. The Royal Navy eagerly awaited a second Trafalgar, this time with the much-vaunted German High Seas Fleet as the victim. The Germans wisely stayed in port—excepting a few raiders and a fleet of five cruisers under Admiral Maximilian von Spee (1861–1914), which raided British outposts and shipping in the Pacific until December, 1914, when they were encountered at the Falkland Islands and four of the five sunk. The fifth, the *Dresden*, escaped, only to be trapped in March, 1915, at Juan Fernández and scuttled by her crew. But the rest of the fleet stayed put—at least until May, 1916, when they inaugurated a scheme to entrap isolated British ships. The only major naval battle of the conflict took place off the west coast of Denmark. This naval clash, known as the Battle of Jutland, was indecisive, but it did keep the German fleet in port for the rest of the war. Aside from Jutland, the Royal Navy confined itself to two tasks. The first was participating in the disastrous Allied attacks on Gallipoli and Salonika in an effort to turn the German flank. The second was organizing an economic blockade that cut off Germany's food supply —a crippling blow. Neutral ships were stopped and if there was any possibility of a cargo reaching Germany it was confiscated. The

Women agricultural workers in Britain during the war.

neutral states of Europe complained energetically, as did the United States, which loudly proclaimed "the freedom of the seas."

The German reply to the Royal Navy's blockade led to the great turning point of the war. Unable to combat the British on the seas, the Germans decided to do so *under* the seas, and the first U-boat (submarine) attacks took place in 1915. American complaints about the indiscriminate use of submarines were ineffective. In May of that year the British passenger liner *Lusitania* (which may also have been carrying arms) was sunk; among the 1,200 victims were 139 Americans. There was a huge outcry in America, in part because the Germans had medals struck to commemorate the sinking. But the Germans, who did not have enough

submarines to sustain all-out submarine warfare, soon succumbed to international opinion and called a halt to the attacks.

At this stage, the United States was determined to stay out of the war. It was enjoying a most profitable neutrality, derived in part from the necessity for Britain and France to sell their assets in America to obtain American loans to buy American goods.

By the beginning of 1916 it was clear that neither side could hope for immediate victory. Civilian enthusiasm for the fighting had rapidly evaporated, and politicians had come to see the danger of having too large an army; defects in the supply of food and the manufacture of munitions affected the armies of both sides. The problems of the Central Powers were

smaller than those of the Allies; short, internal lines of communication eased the problem of supply. In addition the most important areas of French heavy industry were in German hands. In other ways, however, the Allies retained the advantage. British control of the seas allowed the importation of food, equipment and, after 1915, of men from the colonies to continue unchecked. Moreover, the combined industrial strength of the Allies was greater than that of the Central Powers. Nor was Germany able to place much reliance on the support of the Turkish and Austro-Hungarian empires—the only real question was whether the Ottoman Empire or the Hapsburg would collapse first—both of which had been given a new but necessarily temporary lease on life by war. No less important for the Allies was the failure of the modified Schlieffen Plan, which left Germany bogged down in a war that had to be fought on two fronts, a situation that German strategists since Bismarck had sought to avoid.

The result of the need for increased industrial output and a large army was that new sources of labor had to be found. The employment of women rose rapidly— an innovation that advanced the cause of female suffrage enormously. State control over industry expanded rapidly in response to the needs of war. In Britain the coal mining and railroad industries came under government control. In addition, the British government bought a half share of British Petroleum (Anglo-Persian Oil Co.), in order to be sure of oil supplies for the Royal Navy. In a more general way civilian liberty had to be restricted, and in Germany constitutional government took decades to recover from the dominance of generals.

The Western Front

By 1916 it was clear that if the deadlock between the Central Powers and the Allies was ever to be broken it could only be done by a change on the Western Front. Germany could not hope to conquer Russia while a million men were held down in the mud of Belgium and France. Nor could naval power break the deadlock. Both sides concentrated their efforts on huge set-piece battles in Belgium and northern France.

Women in a London arms factory operating copper turning machines.

Slaughter at the Somme 1916

By 1916 the fighting had consolidated into trench warfare—each side dug into carefully prepared positions against which attacks were brutal, bloody, and generally unsuccessful. To counter the pressure of the Germans' determined attack on the French at Verdun, the Allies decided to mount an offensive along the Somme—a strategically worthless area. Following an artillery barrage that was supposed to obliterate everything, the Allied forces moved forward—to slaughter. More than 60,000 casualties were sustained by the British in the first day's fighting alone. Although the battle was decided on the first day—perhaps even in the first minutes— fighting continued for four more months. Marred by incompetence and bad generalship on the Allied side, the battle was still a turning point in the war, for the Germans had lost trained men they were never able to replace.

On the morning of July 1, 1916, the Allied armies launched a massive offensive designed to create a breach in the German trench system, pour cavalry through it, and gain victory in a renewed war of movement. At day's end all such hopes had died along with the thousands of men who fell on the sun-warmed slopes below the German trenches. Effectively decided on that first day, the battle dragged on until November. By then a wedge nine miles deep had been driven into the German positions, but neither of the initial objectives of Péronne or Bapaume had been taken.

In the wake of the great battles of 1915 on the British front, in the northern sector of the line that ran from the Channel to the Alps—Neuve Chapelle in March, Second Ypres in April, Aubers Ridge in May and Loos in September—it had been clear that this offensive would be no easy undertaking. After Ypres in the spring of 1915 the Germans had accepted the stalemate on the Western Front and had decided to remain on the defensive. Easily able to hold off French and British attacks they were prepared to wait until something happened: a compromise peace, perhaps, or the collapse of Allied morale. Militarily the Germans held every advantage. Yet the Allied High Command regarded 1916 as the year in which the trench deadlock would be broken.

The French administrative department of the Somme had no strategical advantage such as, for example, Flanders, where a major advance, with naval support, might have penned the Germans up against the sea and the frontier of Holland. Yet the Somme was chosen, probably, because the Allies could go forward together in a concerted attack.

Lord Kitchener, made Secretary of War on the outbreak of hostilities, had been one of the few men in England to see at once that against the organization and spirit of the German army there would be no swift victory. In 1914 the burden of the fighting had been borne by the regular units of the British Expeditionary Force, most of which had been destroyed. In 1915, the battles had been fought by remnants of the regular army, reservists, Territorial units and volunteers. In 1916 it was planned to use the very large volunteer force known as Kitchener's Army. This was, in effect, the first national army of Britain, and in 1915 thousands of men had flocked to the recruiting offices in response to a famous poster appeal: Kitchener's pointing finger and the slogan "Your Country Needs YOU."

The offensive was to be launched in June on a front of nearly forty miles and would be predominantly French (forty French divisions, twenty-five British), but the massive attack made by the Germans against Verdun in February, 1916, necessitated a radical alteration of the plans. The French defended the fortresses of Verdun with the defiant cry of *"Ils ne passeront pas!"* (They shall not pass) but as their casualties mounted it became clear that something had to be done to divert the main German effort. This was another argument for the choice of the Somme area, as a major attack would reduce the German pressure on Verdun.

Thus the Somme offensive was still to be a combined operation but the attack would be reduced to a front of twenty-five miles, the British share being two-thirds of the line, from Gommecourt in the north down to Maricourt, and the French share being the remaining eight miles from just south of Maricourt to Dompierre. Despite the lack of success in 1915 it was proposed to use the same methods, merely applying greater force and thereby, it was hoped, realizing greater efficiency. The task, as visualized by the General Staff, consisted of meeting the requirements of offensive support in the rear areas, collecting huge quantities of guns and ammunition, and arranging full cooperation between the infantry, the artillery and the air force.

In the sphere of high command, much was ex-

Propaganda on postage stamps issued to raise money for the French war effort.

Opposite Hell, by Georges Leroux, *c.* 1916.

Explosion of a mine under the Hawthorn Redoubt, ten minutes before Zero Hour of the assault at Beaumont Hamel, July 1, 1916.

Allied troops advancing through the wire during the Somme offensive.

pected from recent changes. In December, 1915, General Sir William Robertson had become Chief of the Imperial General Staff and General Sir Douglas Haig, a cavalryman, had taken over the appointment of Commander-in-Chief of the British Expeditionary Force in France. Haig, pressed by the French, who told him they could not hold on at Verdun after July 1 unless the German effort was diverted, had made plans for the June offensive even though he felt this was too early to commit the inexperienced troops of Kitchener's Army to what had become a major British, rather than an Allied, design. He seems to have changed his mind about the hoped-for outcome of the battle, for in May he warned his army commanders that the object now was to relieve the French at Verdun, inflict casualties on the Germans and place the Allies in a favorable position for victory in 1917.

General Sir Henry Rawlinson was the commander of the new Fourth Army and responsible for the main attack. He felt that victory could be won in the summer of 1916 only if the entire operation were carried out in a series of limited stages, with advances of about one mile at a time across belts of land which his guns could make uninhabitable for the enemy. In essence, the plan depended on artillery preparation. Rawlinson was convinced he could emulate the German success at Verdun, where bombardment had destroyed the comparatively shallow French front line trenches. These had been occupied by German infantry while the artillery pounded the next defensive line, and the procedure had then been repeated. It all seemed so simple.

The British air force made photographic reconnaissance flights over the enemy positions and came back with pictures showing in great detail the nature of all strongpoints and gun areas. Carefully camouflaged batteries were easily located by the tracks leading to them. All this vital information was given to the Fourth Army staff, yet the guns were merely allocated a sector of enemy front, calculated by dividing the number of guns into the total length of frontage, and each gun was given a width of 100 yards. Gun crews were told to saturate that area, regardless of what was in it.

The Germans, well aware from their own aerial reconnaissance that a major offensive was coming, worked hard to make their already commanding positions impregnable. Their defensive wire, with barbs as thick as a man's thumb and held by stout iron posts, was in some places thirty yards thick. In the chalk hills they burrowed to extraordinary depths, fashioning exceptionally deep dugouts in which they could sit in safety until the shelling was over.

The quality of the nearly two million shells fired during the bombardment before the Battle of the Somme was so poor that premature bursts destroyed guns and their crews; shells bursting short caused casualties among Allied infantry; and many failed to explode. Even worse, no local commander was authorized to switch guns to a particular target.

During the attack the guns lifted from one line of enemy trenches to the next without any regard to the pace of the infantry advance or the problems facing them. The result was that the guns fired far ahead of the infantry who were shot down by machine gunners untouched by the barrage.

The ammunition requirement had been worked out on the basis of the bombardment starting on June 24 and the attack being launched on June 29. But at the last moment, at the request of the French, the latter date was changed to July 1, so the ammunition available for the bombardment had to be spread over an extra two days. On the afternoon of June 30 the units of the eleven assaulting and five close reserve divisions marched out of the villages where they had been billeted. Some of the brigade and divisional commanders turned out to watch the troops march to the trenches that led up to the front line. Everyone radiated confidence. Word of Rawlinson's conviction that nothing could be left alive in the German front line had filtered down to the soldiers. As the men marched up to the front they passed their supporting artillery and saw the sweating, exhausted gunners working the howitzers which had opened the bombardment six days before.

The bombardment seemed to take effect, for the troops holding the front line during the barrage had been able to stand up above their trenches and

French Troops Resting, painted in 1916 by the British war artist C.R.W. Nevinson.

Aerial view of the Somme offensive in the French sector, showing the arrival of Allied reinforcements at captured German trenches during the attack on Vermandovillers, September 17, 1916.

Right Patrol crawling toward the German trenches during the attack on Beaumont Hamel, July 1, 1916.

watch the shells bursting on the enemy lines. Either Rawlinson's confidence was justified or the Germans were being deliberately inactive. But large areas of enemy wire were still intact; enemy troops had been seen repairing it, and trench raids made during lulls in the bombardment had encountered strong resistance. This information, obtained from observation posts, aircraft and ground patrols, was not passed on to the assaulting battalions.

During the final stages of planning there had been considerable discussion on two points: the timing of Zero Hour and the tactics of the assaulting infantry. Many of Rawlinson's subordinate commanders felt success depended not on the effectiveness of the barrage, but on an ability to cross no-man's-land before the survivors—and there might be many—could open fire. The speed of the assault was critical, and so was visibility. The infantry must be up on their first objectives before the enemy machine gunners could see well enough to identify targets. Zero Hour must be just before dawn. Rawlinson and Haig agreed with this, but General Foch, on Rawlinson's right flank, insisted that his gunners be able to observe the effects of the last stage of their bombardment. And so Zero Hour was fixed for 7:30 A.M. at a time of year when the daylight begins before four o'clock.

The normal method of crossing no-man's-land was for assault groups to make their way forward as rapidly as possible, taking advantage of any cover such as shell holes, until they could lob grenades into the enemy trenches and then rush them. Rawlinson, however, issued orders for an orderly advance in waves not more than a hundred yards apart, at walking pace, the men shoulder to shoulder in proper alignment with fixed bayonets on rifles held aslant across the body. One unit was told: "You will not need rifles. You will find the Germans all dead, not even a rat will have survived." As if to make certain no man would be so undignified as to run, the troops were made to carry a minimum load of about seventy pounds.

On the evening of June 30, the exhausted men reached the forward trenches tired by marching, in some cases twelve miles, carrying enormous weights. The trenches were densely packed and many were waterlogged. It was difficult to rest and virtually impossible to sleep. There was still much work to be done in preparation for the next day and the atmosphere was fraught with the tension that precedes a great battle. As darkness fell, ration parties set out to bring up a hot evening meal, but heavy German shelling prevented many units from getting anything at all.

At dawn the next morning the sky was overcast and a light rain began to fall. There was no wind and pockets of mist lay on the low ground. At 4 A.M. it was light enough to see the enemy trenches. Everyone was waiting for the order to advance and tension mounted as the light grew stronger. At half-past four the men were told that Zero Hour would not be until 7:30. The idea of an attack in broad day-

light caused considerable apprehension. Hunger, fatigue and a miserably uncomfortable night in wet trenches had sapped the confidence of many.

By 7:30 the sun was high and hot on the faces of the men in the packed trenches. Exactly at Zero Hour the barrage was lifted from the enemy's forward line to the communication trenches behind, to prevent reinforcement. Eleven mines were exploded at various points along the front, officers blew their whistles, and the men struggled up out of the trenches and began to move forward.

The Germans were ready and waiting. On the previous evening a British staff officer at La Boiselle, afraid that Rawlinson's message wishing all ranks "good luck" for the next day might not reach units if taken by hand through the crowded trenches, had passed it on over the field telephone. It had been picked up by a German listening post.

At the moment when the barrage lifted, the Germans came up from their dugouts to man their machine-gun posts, many of which were hardly damaged at all. On the carefully pinpointed lanes through the British wire they brought down a murderous fire. At Beaumont-Hamel, relieving units coming up later buried lines of corpses immediately in front of the British wire, a clear indication of the Germans' speed in action. It has been said the battle was "lost by three minutes," for greater speed across no-man's-land would have given the Germans no time to man their weapons;

but the assaulting waves of men, laden like pack animals, could barely stagger up the slopes. Out in the open the long, slow lines, shoulder to shoulder, were a gift to the machine gunners.

Nearly 60,000 British officers and men became casualties on the first day of the Battle of the Somme —the equivalent of six complete infantry divisions. In terms of ground gained, three fortified villages were taken and in the south the line moved forward barely a mile. Nowhere had there been any breach of the German second line of defenses.

By the evening of July 1, the British had been repulsed everywhere from Gommecourt to the main Bapaume road by a perfectly sited, overlapping chain of machine guns, many of them concealed in armored emplacements. Rawlinson, despite the appalling losses, proposed to renew the attack at once, all along the front, but Haig, determined to restrict the battle to the area where most damage had been done to the German defenses, intervened. Narrowed to a front of six miles, the battle went on.

On July 14, Rawlinson was almost successful with one of the very few large night attacks of the war. Routes were marked with white tapes, an advance of 1,500 yards in pitch darkness went perfectly, and the German second line was overrun for five miles. In the late afternoon cavalry rode through the standing corn pursuing fleeing Germans, but counterattacks next day won back a mile of ground.

Two months later, on September 15, the Germans were confronted with a secret weapon far more decisive in its influence on the war than either of their main surprises—huge howitzers and poison gas. "Tanks," as they were called—a "cover name" for the canvas-shrouded shapes when they were on railway flats—came into action for the first time. They weighed twenty-seven tons, traveled at three miles an hour and could cross obstacles five feet high or a trench eight and a half feet wide.

The attack on September 15, and another on September 25, both made advances of about one and a half miles on 15,000-yard fronts and created a severe crisis for the Germans, whose fortified zone now was dangerously thin. Rumania's recent entry into the war and her attack on Transylvania had compelled the German Command to send divisions to the East, and their total reserve on the whole of the Western Front had fallen to five divisions. But by the end of September, the German commander of the Western Front, General Erich von Ludendorff, had virtually restored the situation. October brought incessant rain, and the Germans considered that on a battlefield which was a shell-devastated area six miles deep, of almost impassable mud, no more major attacks were feasible. Even so, one last British effort was made in November, and 7,000 German prisoners were taken in an operation against Grandcourt, above the Ancre River, where the ground was still hard.

Thus ended the campaign on the Somme. Whether or not it was a British success is perhaps a matter of opinion. Haig's three aims seemed to have been achieved. The pressure on Verdun had been relieved and the French saved from defeat; but there is evidence that the battle for Verdun was already waning because of the exhaustion of both sides. Casualties had been inflicted on the Germans and the German army never recovered from its loss, at Verdun and on the Somme, of the irreplaceable hard core of experienced troops. Voluntary surrenders had been almost unknown, but the Somme marks the beginning of a steady trickle of German deserters—an ominous sign of sinking morale. The Allied positions on the Pozières Ridge in November were certainly better than the line they had held on June 30; but all the advantages disappeared when the Germans withdrew in the spring.

Despite initial failure, the British army gained experience from the Somme, and this was reflected in the spring attack in front of Arras. The mistakes which led to that failure are obvious now. Too much had been expected from, and depended upon, the preliminary bombardment. Much of the ammunition had been defective. In the timing of the attack, the difference between the half-light of a misty dawn and bright sunshine was measured in thousands of lives. Rawlinson's tactics for the advance had been a reversion to those of Frederick the Great—when the effective range of a musket was barely a hundred yards. Haig, who favored an initial probing forward by strong fighting patrols, using ground and cover as the Germans had at Verdun, and as Foch's troops had in the French sector of the Somme offensive, should probably have overruled him.

The Battle of the Somme was a turning point, toward Allied victory and German defeat, but would not be recognized as such until years afterward. Immediately after the first dreadful day, when the Allies had lost 60,000 and the Germans 8,000 men, there was no talk of light victory. The set battle that so many hoped would end the war was effectively decided on that first day in July, yet dragged on until November. By November the Allied casualty list had risen to over 600,000; the Battle of the Somme was both the glory and the graveyard of Kitchener's Army.   JOCK HASWELL

Paths of Glory, by C. R. W. Nevinson.

Opposite Dead German in a Trench, by Sir William Orpen R.A.

America's entry into the war foreshadows

America goes to war

Despite the massive losses on the Somme, neither side had improved its position by the end of 1916. A new factor in the war from the beginning of 1917 was increasing American involvement. In January of that year the British—who had broken the German codes—revealed to President Woodrow Wilson that the new German Foreign Minister, Arthur Zimmermann (1864–1940), had told his ambassador in Mexico to recruit Mexican assistance should the u.s. enter the war against Germany.

American forces landing in France in 1917.

In return for Mexico's waging war against the u.s., Germany promised financial aid plus the assurance that Mexico would "recover the lost territory in New Mexico, Texas, and Arizona." When the State Department published the "Zimmermann Note" it caused enormous public feeling against Germany in the United States. Much more serious, however, in American eyes was the increasing loss of shipping as a result of submarine attacks. By the end of 1916 the British blockade of Germany was beginning to take effect. Admiral von Tirpitz, who had reluctantly abandoned all-out submarine warfare eighteen months before, was now convinced that Germany's best hope for ending the war quickly lay in starving England into peace talks. Submarine attacks on every ship—belligerent or neutral—entering or

leaving British ports were attempted. Wilson, who had been reelected in 1916 on the platform of continued neutrality, protested, but the Germans ignored his pleas as they hoped to destroy Britain before America could intervene. As the submarine toll grew—540,000 tons of shipping were sunk in February, 600,000 tons in March and 870,000 tons in April—American anger mounted. The United States had severed diplomatic relations with Germany on February 3. On March 8, without Congressional approval, Wilson ordered the arming of American merchant ships. On March 12 an American ship was sunk without warning, followed by three more on March 16, and on April 2, 1917, Wilson asked Congress for a declaration of war on Germany. America, the sleeping giant, had awakened, and its entry into the war foreshadowed the end of Europe's hegemony over the civilized world.

The American declaration of war came none too soon. The submarine attacks had left Britain with no more than six weeks' supply of food, and Germany's fleet of a hundred and forty submarines—of which no more than fifty were usually operational at one time—had proved a far better investment than the huge dreadnoughts that scarcely saw action in the war that they had helped to cause. It was only gradually that effective ways of combatting the submarine menace were developed. The use of aircraft and hydrophone equipment made the destruction of submarines easier, while the practice of convoying ships—inconvenient as it was—made attacks less likely.

Meanwhile on the Western Front the Allies were making progress of sorts, although at immense cost. At Passchendaele in November, 1917, the Canadians and British managed to push the Germans back five miles, and at Cambrai later in the same month four hundred British tanks helped to create a large dent in the German line. But at the end of the year the Allies were faced with a new menace; as a result of the Russian Revolution, which took Russia out of the war, the Germans were able to reinforce their western armies.

War and revolution

One of the greatest changes brought about by the war was in the colonial

sphere. Before the war the challenge to European imperialism was hardly noticed; by 1917, the end of colonialism was a clear possibility. Revolutionary movements in all corners of the globe benefited by the war. Germany supplied the Bolsheviks with cash and shipped the exiled Lenin to Russia in the hope that revolution would destroy the Russian war effort. And German rifles were shipped to Ireland, where war had not blunted the desire for Home Rule. Britain was no less guilty. Anxious to protect their oil interests in Persia and to secure the Suez Canal from Turkey, the British encouraged Arab nationalism against the Turks.

Turkish decline

The decline of Turkey from the height of its power in the seventeenth century had been gradual, but by the middle of the nineteenth century the Ottoman Empire was the "sick man of Europe" instead of a constant threat to Christendom. The early twentieth century had seen a continuation of the decline, caused by the birth of nationalism. Arabs and Slavs showed their discontent with Ottoman domination, and even in Turkey itself there was a powerful movement to modernize the Empire. The failure of a constitutional experiment in 1876 did not end the desire for elective government. In 1908 a group of army officers, the "Young Turks," had seized power. Although they deposed the Sultan in favor of his hapless brother and set up the apparatus of a parliamentary democracy, they remained dependent on military power. But even military power was insufficient to keep order and in 1913 a triumvirate of Young Turk leaders seized power.

Unprepared for war, with little enthusiasm and with still less hope of victory, Turkey was dragged into World War 1. Up to the last moment it was unclear which side Turkey would join, but an impressive display of German naval strength in the Bosphorus finally swung the balance, and Turkey joined the Central Powers.

This decision left Turkey surrounded by enemies, and the Ottoman Empire began to crumble almost at once. But the government was determined not to give in without a fight. The Allies wanted to improve communications between the West and Russia and

made an enormous effort to open the Sea of Marmara, which linked the Black Sea and the Mediterranean. An Anglo-French naval expedition was, however, repulsed from the Dardanelles Strait by Turkish shore batteries in 1915. The British sought to silence the batteries by landing an army in the Gallipoli Peninsula, but gross mismanagement coupled with bad luck made this vastly expensive in men, money and equipment, and the army had to be withdrawn. Against the Russians, too, the Turks put up a good showing, particularly after the Revolution of 1917. Georgia, Armenia and Azerbaijan were captured, although the important Black Sea oilfields of Baku were only briefly occupied by the Turks.

Duplicity in the Middle East

However, what the Russians and British lacked in arms, they made up for in diplomacy. The British had little difficulty in stirring up trouble. As early as 1915, they were negotiating with Husein ibn-Ali (1856–1931), Sharif of Mecca, to stimulate an Arab revolt. In the course of negotiations, the British promised to help in the formation of independent Arab kingdoms in Arabia, Palestine, Iraq and Syria. Operating on that assurance, Husein's son, Faisal (1885–1933), joined with Britain's T. E. Lawrence (1888–1935)—called Lawrence of Arabia—in an Arab war against the German-Turkish lines. But, unbeknown to the Arabs, the British and French at this time had already arranged the Sykes-Picot Agreement—a plan for partitioning the Arab world between Britain and France.

As if this display of bad faith

Lawrence of Arabia.

the end of European hegemony

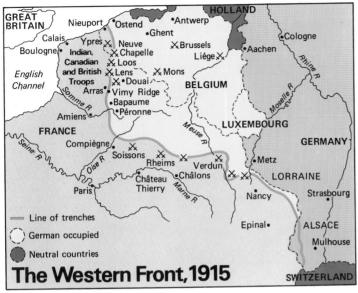

The Western Front, 1915

Map legend:
— Line of trenches
◌ German occupied
● Neutral countries

General Allenby's official entry into Jerusalem.

Troops near Vraignes, 1917.

other British army fought its way up the Tigris Valley from Basra, reaching Kirkuk early in 1918.

Unrest

Colonial unrest was not confined to the Near East during this period. Indeed British problems were brewing in India, where the reforms of 1909 had proven ineffective. The outbreak of war had provoked a display of enthusiastic Indian support for the British government. Hundreds of thousands of Indians had volunteered to serve in the British army, and a million pounds had been contributed to the war effort. But the war had two corrosive effects on the British position. First, it gave Indians an intoxicating glimpse of independence, as the Indian army took over imperial duties to release British units for Europe. In business and administration, Indians had a chance, small though it was, to see what they were capable of. Second, they began to realize how weak their British overlords were.

Revolutionary chaos in Russia left the way open for a German and Turkish advance on India. The British were simply not strong enough to deal with such an attack — especially if they could not guarantee the absolute loyalty of their Indian subjects — and in August, 1917, the British were obliged to issue a declaration promising "increasing association of Indians in every branch of the administration and the gradual development of self-governing institutions." It was just as well they did, for nationalist stalwarts had gained control of the Congress movement. Moreover, India had at last found great leaders capable of mobilizing its vast population. Mohandas K. Gandhi (1869–1948) was a lawyer who had worked in South Africa, where he defended Indians against prejudicial laws. In the course of his work he had discovered the power of the device of civil disobedience. Jawaharlal Nehru (1889–1964) was educated at Harrow and Cambridge, and in England he became aware of Western techniques of political organization. Together, Gandhi and Nehru turned Indian nationalism into a mass phenomenon. It would take years, but they had discovered the key to British withdrawal.

World War I was more of a European than a world war, for it represented the death throes of the old order rather than global conflict. The requirements of total war placed strains on the administrative and organizational skills of governments, and Europe's notions of the functions of government changed. Rationing and control of raw materials laid the basis for planned economies and welfare states. The growth of government propaganda machines—in liberal England as well as in militarist Germany—showed how far the war had forced acceptance of the needs of mass society on Europe. In February, 1917, that strain led to the final collapse of the Russian government. Agonies stifled since 1905 suddenly found their voice, and Russia began a descent into chaos. Governments succeeded one another with terrifying rapidity, and for a while it looked as if reactionary generals might succeed with a counterrevolutionary coup. Then Nikolai Lenin (1870–1924) intervened with a decision that would alter the course of world history.

were not enough, the British also promised Palestine to the Jews. Throughout the war, Zionism had grown in influence, largely through the efforts of the leader of British Zionism, Chaim Weizmann (1874–1952). Weizmann, a Russian-born chemist at the University of Manchester, managed to convert the British cabinet to the idea of a Jewish national state. He accomplished this by emphasizing the usefulness of a Jewish state to the defense of Suez and by shrewdly suggesting that a pro-Jewish gesture was required to offset the unfavorable effect Russian anti-Semitism was having on the Allied cause in America. In a letter from Foreign Secretary Arthur James Balfour to the Jewish financier Lord Rothschild (the letter was later known as the Balfour Declaration) Britain pledged itself to the idea of a Jewish Palestine. The policy of dishonesty paid off. The British found widespread support among the Arabs of the Ottoman Empire, and Jerusalem was captured on December 9, 1917. An-

"Peace, Bread and Land"

St. Petersburg—Peter the Great's glittering capital, his "window on the West"—changed names twice during the first decades of the twentieth century. In 1914, as an expression of wartime patriotism, Peter's city was given the Russian name Petrograd. A decade later, that name was changed to Leningrad, to honor the man who meanwhile had toppled the Russian government. Ironically, it was to Petrograd—the city that would eventually bear his name—that Lenin traveled in 1917. And it was there, on October 23, that he met with the Central Committee of the Bolshevik Party to plot the overthrow of the moderate Provisional Government that had replaced the monarchy the preceding February. A fortnight later, Lenin's followers arrested the entire Provisional Government. A new government, a new state and a new society were proclaimed. Its rallying cry was "Peace, Bread and Land," and its ambition was to transform the world.

Lenin, architect of the Revolution and ruler of Russia.

Opposite: Petrograd, no surrender. A poster dating from the Revolution.

On the evening of October 23, 1917, a number of nondescript, shabby men, some of them in disguise, slipped unobtrusively into a small, middle-class flat in the city of Petrograd (which had been known, until a few years before, as St. Petersburg, and which was soon to be renamed Leningrad). The surroundings were informal. For ten hours the talk concentrated on one topic only: should this group seize control of the government of Russia?

The get-together was, in fact, a full session of the Central Committee of the Bolshevik faction of the Russian Social Democratic Workers' Party. The leader of the group was Vladimir Ilich Ulyanov, better known as Lenin. He was forty-seven years old, tiny and bald, with small, deep-set eyes and high cheekbones. He generally wore a small Vandyke and moustache. For this occasion, however, he had taken the precaution of putting on a wig and shaving off his beard. Also present were Lev Davydovich Bronstein, better known as Leon Trotsky, and Iosif Vissarionovich Dzhugashvili, better known as Stalin. Trotsky was relatively tall, with a shock of bushy hair and a goatee. He had a powerful, musical voice and piercing blue eyes behind spectacles. Stalin was very small, with a slightly withered left arm, pockmarks, yellowish eyes and a heavy moustache.

Lenin had called the Committee together to make a proposal: he had decided it was time for an insurrection. During the ten hours of discussion he swung over to his own view all those who had not already been in agreement with him. Once made, the decision set in motion preparations that a fortnight later were to destroy the Russian government and institute a regime made up of Bolsheviks committed to the novel enterprise of transforming Russia, and indeed the whole world, into a socialist society. This was the first time in history that power was taken by a group of people in a conscious attempt to implement a preconceived theory not merely for personal reasons but to change society as a whole.

The tsarist government had been battered into helplessness by its long and exhausting involvement, during the preceding two and a half years, in World War I. Its resources were drained and its people exasperated by the strains of a war that, while seeming to lead nowhere, was at the same time exacting an immense toll of killed and wounded soldiers. But there was also a political element in the restiveness of the Russian people. The Russian intelligentsia—educated people of all classes who believed in changing things for the better—had given rise to a revolutionary movement in the last third of the nineteenth century. One branch of this movement believed in using the collective traditions of the peasantry to build a new society on the basis of some form of socialism; the other branch pinned its hopes for a socialist transformation of Russia on the industrial working class, or proletariat. This second branch had come to be dominated by the ideas of Karl Marx, whose major work, *Das Kapital*, had been translated from German into Russian before appearing in any other language.

Marx held that the middle classes, while perfecting capitalism, were simultaneously creating an indispensable working class. He thought that as capitalism evolved, it was bound to bring about the polarization of society into a smaller and smaller group getting richer and richer, and a larger and larger group getting poorer and poorer. He predicted that this larger group would ultimately be driven to despair by its misery; then, under the leadership of the proletariat, it would bring about the overthrow of the bourgeoisie through the extinction of capitalism and would install a new society based on socialism.

Russian Marxists thought that Russia would follow these general lines, and that as capitalism sank its roots (a little belatedly) in Russia, it would go through the process of creating the working class that would eventually bring about the destruction of capitalism. Russian Marxists accordingly accepted the development of capitalism as a way of bringing about the general rise in the economic level of the

The abortive Revolution of 1905 ended when troops opened fire on the workers.

country that would ultimately ensure the triumph of the working class. Hence many Marxists worked together with other nonsocialist critics of the tsarist autocracy. In 1905, these critics had staged a dramatic though unsuccessful insurrection against the Tsar. Lenin had called the 1905 Revolution a "dress rehearsal" for the two revolutions of 1917—the February Revolution that undid tsarism and his own Bolshevik insurrection.

Yet when tsarism vanished so quickly, all political groups were unprepared. The concerted attack in 1905 had been beaten back, the revolutionary movement scattered in defeat. Before the outbreak of World War I in 1914, the prospects for a revolution in Russia had in fact been very somber. Still, when tsarism was shattered by the strain of the war, the revolutionary training and political experience of Petrograd intellectuals and workers very naturally produced the Soviet of Workers' Deputies (named after a similar institution that had sprung up and been dissolved in the 1905 Revolution and its aftermath) as one half of the new regime. Since the well-known leaders of the Russian revolutionary movement were all abroad or in exile in February, 1917, the Soviet was organized, more or less spontaneously, by secondary figures and by the rank and file of many parties and organizations. But as the more famous leaders began drifting back to Russia, the Soviet grew more and more powerful.

The link between the Provisional Government and the Soviet of Workers' Deputies was bizarre. The Provisional Government was theoretically sovereign, and acknowledged as such by the Soviet. Yet in practice it could do nothing without the specific permission or authorization of the Soviet. The power of the Soviet rested firmly with workingmen who were indispensable to the performance of the most vital functions—telegraph operators, railway men, printers, factory workers. Hence its agreement was needed before anything could be done. In addition, from the very beginning peasants as well as soldiers were represented in the Soviet; indeed the Soviet represented some 95 percent of the population.

Meanwhile, World War I continued to place an agonizing strain on the country's resources. Russia faced a grave economic crisis. The morale of peasants and soldiers (who were, of course, mostly peasants themselves) continued to fall. More important, the revolution had raised hopes, and the clamor for instant reform grew. Peasants demanded land; workers, better wages and working conditions; the minorities, autonomy. The Provisional Government believed in the war, largely for patriotic reasons, and it tried to soothe all elements of the population with promises of reforms that would take place after the war had been won. Meanwhile, the people were kept locked to the treadmill of the war and its gargantuan demands.

Until Lenin returned to Russia in April, 1917, he had accepted the impossibility of a socialist party's taking power there. He was distinguished from the Mensheviks, a rival faction in the Social Democratic

Party, not so much by his interpretation of Marx as by his differing view of how the revolutionary party should be organized. Lenin believed in restricting the membership of the revolutionary party to full-time professionals; the Mensheviks thought it should be open to all "sympathizers." This difference of approach between Bolsheviks and Mensheviks was rooted in an ambiguity of Marxism itself.

Marx had predicted that the transition from capitalism to socialism was both inevitable and dependent upon the armed proletariat. Abstractly, there was no contradiction between the two points—the proletariat, made "self-conscious" by the increasing misery of its exploitation under capitalism, was to organize itself with the help of the revolutionary party; then it was to arm and to bring about the transition to socialism. In practice, however, the theory was open to two interpretations. One maintained that since the transition to socialism was inevitable, socialist parties needed to do nothing more than quietly educate the proletariat to its future responsibilities. On the other hand, since it was the armed proletariat that was to bring about the transition to socialism, a second view held that the organization of the proletariat—aimed, naturally, at an eventual coup d'état through conspiracy—was the main task of the revolutionary party. Historically, the socialist parties on the Continent, including the Russian Mensheviks, clung to the first view; the Bolsheviks under Lenin took the second.

To be sure, Lenin's views on organization required a theoretical justification in Marxist terms. When he came back to Russia in April, 1917, he had contrived a variation of Marxism that enabled him to give his preoccupation with organization that theoretical justification. This variation was borrowed from Leon Trotsky, a younger Marxist who had been hovering for years outside all partisan affiliations. Trotsky, in collaboration with a cosmopolitan Marxist called Parvus (born Helphand), had worked out a Marxist twist of his own. His version maintained that since the Russian bourgeoisie was too weak to crush tsarism and carry out the requisite perfection of capitalism before the Russian proletariat grew strong enough to oust it, the proletariat would have to take power in order to accomplish a bourgeois revolution. Afterward, on the basis of the accomplishments of a bourgeois revolution, the proletariat would be able to construct socialism.

Lenin adopted this theory to support the streamlined party hierarchy he had created, and he made himself a contender for power. Trotsky, attracted by this combination, gave up his independence and joined the Bolshevik Party a couple of months before the insurrection. Lenin, by accepting Trotsky's theory, and Trotsky, by accepting Lenin's concept of the revolutionary party as a tightly knit caucus of dedicated professionals, made a fusion of theory and practice that enabled the Bolsheviks, by setting a course for the seizure of power, to elude the dilemma of their socialist rivals. In short, Lenin—unlike his rivals—had been flexible enough to change his mind.

Since that time, various Communist historians

Above The Red Guards attacking the Winter Palace during the last days of the Provisional Government.

Below Each factory raised a detachment of Red Guards in preparation for the Revolution.

Marc Chagall's picture entitled *Peace in a Hut, War in a Palace* epitomizes the period.

have attempted to smother Lenin's change of mind underneath a mountain of mythology. It has suited the Soviet regime to pretend that from the time that Lenin was born he had been proceeding stage by stage along the path laid down by the omniscience of Marx. Many enemies of the Soviet regime have, for their own reasons, concurred in this view. Yet it is plain that something special happened when Lenin arrived in Petrograd in April, 1917. His first speech flabbergasted not only his opponents and rivals but his own followers, who had also been clinging to "general Marxist" formulations. When he said that the proletariat—represented, of course, by the Bolsheviks—could and should take power, the Bolsheviks themselves were dumbfounded. His justifying this proposal by a theory borrowed from Trotsky, who was ten years younger and a non-Bolshevik to boot, made it no more palatable. Lenin needed all his personal authority and powers of persuasion to bring his followers around.

The decision made during that fateful ten-hour reunion of the Bolshevik Central Committee in that flat in Petrograd crystallized the program Lenin had announced in April. The decision was all the more momentous because Lenin played a role that in history has been rare: without him no Bolshevik insurrection was conceivable. In view of the consequences of the Bolshevik triumph, Lenin has surely been one of the greatest world-shakers in history.

Lenin's decision was a sine qua non for action. The Bolsheviks had been growing stronger in the Soviet between April and October, so that the relative weight of the Soviet vis-à-vis the Provisional Government had been increasing. After Lenin's arrival the Bolsheviks, no longer hampered by a doctrine that enforced subordination, had tended to be even more independent of the Provisional Government than the Soviet as a whole had been. Thus the rivalry between the Soviet and the Provisional Government was complicated by pressure within the Soviet to eliminate the Provisional Government. But sovereignty could not be sovereignty unless it was proclaimed to be such. The de facto power that had been exercised by the Soviet could not become state power until it was acknowledged—until the legal conception underlying the authority of the Provisional Government was replaced by another conception. Hence Lenin's decision to take power was an indispensable step.

Following the April announcement, Lenin had demonstrated his capacity not merely for theory but for effective politics—organization plus propaganda. He had skillfully harped on the afflictions besetting Russia, on the groaning of the workers, peasants and soldiers. He had also streamlined his own party and had given both its rank and file and its commanders a firm sense of purpose. He had provided the intellectual contingent of his party with "sound Marxist theory" for a daring enterprise, while at the same time carrying on a broad-gauge campaign aimed at the man in the street, a campaign in which the slogan that was to carry the day was the down-to-earth phrase, "Peace, Bread and Land!"—all

quite irrelevant to the ideas of classical Marxism.

During the night of November 6–7, a fortnight after the midnight reunion in the Petrograd flat, the Military Revolutionary Committee commanded by Trotsky arrested the entire Provisional Government. (Shortly before, a handful of party people and a small number of troops had seized the Winter Palace, the seat of the Provisional Government.) With scarcely any hubbub, the Bolshevik militia—the Red Guards—occupied the Tauride Palace, the post offices and the railway stations, the national bank, the telephone exchanges, the power stations and other strategic points. It took only a few hours to obliterate the Provisional Government, and there were virtually no casualties. Though the Bolsheviks had been proclaiming their general intentions for weeks, the confusion and discouragement of their opponents, the support (or apathy) of the military, and the reluctance of the Bolsheviks' socialist rivals to move against their fellow socialists ensured an almost complete lack of resistance.

A new government, a new state and a new society were proclaimed. The overthrow had happened with dreamlike ease, against a background of turbulence, discontent, suffering and futility. The enthusiasm of the Bolsheviks was boundless; they had achieved a titanic victory so effortlessly that they had not even bothered to work out a program. They thought themselves on the verge of a vast ground swell that was about to transform the world; they expected to be caught up at any moment by similar eruptions and similar seizures of power throughout Europe and then the world at large. (It is true that in Russia a movement of resistance sprang up in the wake of the insurrection. A civil war raged for several years with much bloodshed and many atrocities on both sides. But the superior capacities of the Red Army, newly organized and commanded by Leon Trotsky, settled the issue decisively in favor of the Bolsheviks.)

Yet the victory of the Bolsheviks did not spread

A cartoon entitled *The First Coalition* which satirizes the doomed Provisional Government.

92

immediately, and for decades no revolution succeeded anywhere. The Bolsheviks, isolated in an exhausted country, found themselves obliged, in spite of the material difficulties and in the teeth of their traditional theories, to construct something that could be called socialism. They had thought that the élan of the suffering peoples, an élan generated by the tug of history, would be enough to bring about a transition to an ideal society; in fact, it was brute force—as well as a zeal for construction—that was needed for the realization of their large-scale innovations. Indeed, an apparatus of constraint was created that has survived to this day.

As the illusions about world revolution were swept away, the rigors of Soviet life emerged in stark relief. Lenin himself, who clung to his hopes for world revolution until a year before he died in 1924, was deeply disturbed by a feeling that the "machine had gotten out of control." The necessities of administering the vast country that the Bolsheviks had captured turned former writers, speakers and thinkers into a corps of bureaucrats. And as the bureaucracy expanded, the power it symbolized came to be concentrated in the hands of the man who controlled the allocation of personnel—Joseph Stalin, the General Secretary of the Central Committee.

Even before Lenin's death Stalin had become the most important man in the party apparatus; from 1928 to his death in 1953 he was the most important man in the country. He had emerged triumphant from the ferocious infighting that broke out in the Bolshevik Party as it found itself confronting the insoluble problem of creating socialism where none was possible (while at the same time pretending that all had been foreseen by Marxist analysis). Using his growing power within the administration, Stalin outmaneuvered, crushed, and finally exterminated all other party opposition. His virtual eradication of the Trotskyites during the 1930s was accompanied by a massive slaughter of the top strata of the party, the army, the state and all major institutions, as well as of vast sections of the population as a whole. Trotsky himself was assassinated in exile by Stalin's political police in 1940. From the time of Stalin's fiftieth birthday in 1929, he wielded well-nigh absolute power through his control of the political police, the Soviet Communist Party, the Soviet Union and the many Communist parties that belonged to the Third International founded by Lenin. In addition, he institutionalized the worship of his own person as a paramount—indeed, almost godlike—authority in all fields of activity.

Lenin's fateful decision affected not only Russia but the world. The chain of events it set in motion came to encompass vast numbers of people. Many countries on the western borders of the Soviet Union came under its power after Russia helped defeat Nazi Germany in World War II. China, in particular, was swept into the Communist orbit. In fact, Lenin's interpretation of Karl Marx molded the lives of more than a third of the human race and made Marxism one of the most potent forces in history.

JOEL CARMICHAEL

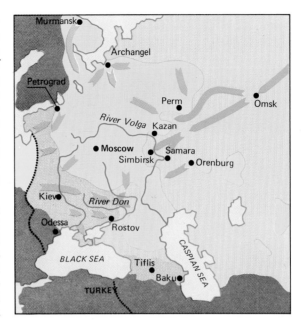

The Bolsheviks Fight for Survival

1918

○ Controlled by Bolsheviks

○ Occupied by Germany or her allies

⋯⋯ Russian front in 1918

⟫ Red Army advance

⟫ White Army advance

⟫ Allied intervention

⟫ German advance

○ Territory lost by Treaty of Brest-Litovsk Armies:

1919

○ Controlled by Bolsheviks

⟫ Red Army advance

⟫ White Army advance

⟫ Allied intervention

○ Controlled by Allies

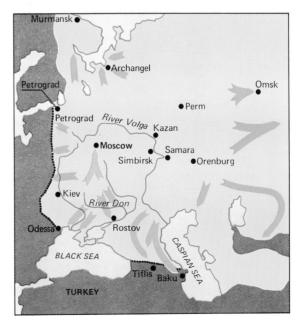

1920

○ Controlled by Bolsheviks

⋯⋯ Limits of Bolshevik power at the end of 1920

⟫ Red Army advance

⟫ White Army advance

Aviation

America's military role in World War I had been small. The first troops did not arrive on the Western Front until the spring of 1918, almost a year after the American declaration of war on Germany. Nonetheless, the American role as a supplier of equipment and food to the Allies had been an important one, and the Western Front would almost certainly have been lost if America had not joined the war when it did. But American intervention had a more important meaning for Europe and the world; traditional American attitudes of isolationism had been abandoned, and from 1917 America began to show an active interest in world affairs.

As far as the fighting itself was concerned, American intervention was less important than the use of the airplane. Until the outbreak of war—and even in its early years—aviation had been seen more as a sport—with large prizes for glamorous stunts or dangerously long voyages—than as a practical means of transport. Although airplanes had been used in the Balkan War of 1912, the advent of a larger struggle in 1914 had encouraged the substantial capital investment necessary to lead to more effective planes. The demand of military and naval authorities for aircraft that could fly higher, farther and faster, stimulated research, as did the need to carry bombs. At first, reconnaissance seemed the limit of airplane use; both planes and pilots were unarmed, and when French and German reconnaissance planes passed each other their pilots merely gave each other a friendly wave.

By 1918 all this had changed: German Zeppelins and Gotha bombers had attacked London and other British cities, dropping bombs as heavy as a thousand pounds. British Handley-Page bombers replied by attacking the industrial centers of the Ruhr Valley, and by 1918 a new model, capable of dropping up to two tons of bombs on Berlin, was under construction. But the thirteen-hundred-mile range of the Handley-Page was dwarfed by the achievement of a German airship, which traveled more than four thousand miles nonstop in a vain attempt to supply arms to troops in German East Africa. Fighter planes achieved

A British Handley-Page bomber.

records of a different kind: the German Baron Manfred von Richthofen (1892–1918), the "Red Baron," shot down eighty Allied planes. Although the Allies initially had no advantage in the air, during the last months of the war their air superiority played an increasingly important part in undermining German military confidence. By that time the rapid increase of British airpower had led to the formation of the Royal Air Force as a fighting force independent of the Army and the Navy; America's "billion dollar aircraft program" was under way—although it produced few planes until after the war ended; the Allies had taken more than a quarter of a million reconnaissance photographs—some from as high as eighteen thousand feet; over one hundred German submarines were sunk by Allied aircraft. By the end of the war American aviators—mostly flying in British and French planes—had shot down nearly one thousand German airplanes and airships. Ground warfare, however, remained far more important than air and the fighting on the ground was enormously influenced in the last months of the war by social disruption.

Russia's Revolution

During the five years immediately following the end of World War I, Europe was preoccupied with three issues that were to convulse the Continent until 1945. The rise of Communism belongs symbolically to one end of this period; the rise of Fascism to the other. The third issue derived from the Treaty of Versailles, which disguised the fact that Europe was no longer the focal

point of the globe. It was only because Russia and the United States withdrew into shells of isolationism that the illusion of Europe's preeminence was temporarily preserved.

The erosion of Russia's old order by revolution had begun during the war. In 1918, the new Bolshevik government published and denounced the secret treaties made by the Tsar's government with its allies. They then exhorted the workers of the West to begin their own revolutions—a move that alarmed Western European governments and in a short time effectively isolated the Bolsheviks.

The first hint of how extensive that isolation was to become came at Brest-Litovsk, where Germany and Russia met to make terms. Without troops in the trenches, the Bolsheviks were at a disadvantage at the treaty table. Realizing their weakness, they com-

pensated by using the negotiations as a forum for revolutionary propaganda. But, when the German forces ultimately advanced to within one hundred miles of Petrograd, the Bolsheviks were forced to sign away Poland, Finland, Lithuania, the Baltic Provinces, Transcaucasia and the Ukraine.

The Bolsheviks were busy looking for the outbreak of the proletarian revolution abroad, but they were in danger of losing power in Russia itself. By the end of 1918 they were only in control of a narrow strip of land running from Astrakhan on the Caspian Sea to Murmansk on the Arctic Sea. Elsewhere there were isolated pockets of Bolshevik control, but the situation had become increasingly complicated by the disunity and lack of cooperation between the leaders of the anti-Bolshevik forces, of whom Anton Denikin (1872–1947) and Nikolai Yudenich (1862–1933) were the most prominent. In addition, by the end of 1918 there were numerous foreign armies in control of parts of Russia: Germany and Rumania had armies in the west; Turkish, British and French troops were in the south; British and Americans in the north; and Japanese in Siberia. The Allied intervention in Russia was doomed to failure, partly because of disagreement about aims and methods and partly because of the efficiency and determination of the Bolsheviks. The Communist-controlled areas gradually grew, and by 1920 it was clear that the continued presence of the Allies in Russia could serve no useful function. The Allies had

The 1917 meeting at Brest-Litovsk, where Germany signed the armistice with Russia.

anarchy threaten established order

Grain deliveries by peasants to the Makugino railway station collection center in Kurgan Region, U.S.S.R.

problems enough of their own without involving themselves in those of Russia. The new Soviet State was left to the task of rebuilding the Russian economy in accordance with its revolutionary ideas.

The end of the war

The Germans' bold move at Brest-Litovsk seemed to prove the continued strength of imperial Germany, but that might was illusory. In January of 1918, over one million German workers went on strike against the harshness of the conditions imposed by their government at Brest-Litovsk.

In the same month, President Wilson published his Fourteen Points. The document proclaimed that the Allies were fighting for democracy and national self-determination. Wilson had already declared his intention of fighting for

... democracy, for the right of those who submit to authority to have a voice in their own government, for the rights and liberties of small nations, for a universal dominion of right by such a concert of free peoples as shall bring peace and safety to all nations and make the world itself at last free.

But before the future face of Europe could be drawn, Germany had finally to be defeated. Undeterred by the rising tide of civilian discontent and the danger of revolution, the German government decided to launch a vast all-or-nothing offensive in the West in March, 1918. Their armies got to within forty miles of Paris, but the

Allied lines held, and by August, thanks to Allied counteroffensives, the German offensive collapsed. The German fleet mutinied at Kiel and the long-awaited revolution began in Munich under the leadership of a former journalist, Kurt Eisner. Neatly evading responsibility, the German High Command resigned in October in favor of a democratic government led by Prince Max of Baden which then had to take the odium of defeat. On November 11, Germany signed an armistice with the Allies.

Revolution

By then, however, revolution had reached Berlin. Max of Baden had resigned and the Kaiser had abdicated. But, although the American insistence on democracy had brought revolution with it, it was not the proletarian revolution that the Communists had been waiting for. As the statesman and industrialist Walter Rathenau (1867–1922) remarked, "a general strike by a defeated army is called the German Revolution." The leaders of the left in Germany—unlike Lenin—believed that the revolution would result from a *spontaneous* workers' rising. As a result, these leaders, Karl Liebknecht (1871–1919) and Rosa Luxemburg (1870–1919), felt unable to take an active revolutionary role, and the situation that existed in Russia in 1918 never came into existence in Germany. The government, under Social Democrat Chancellor Friedrich Ebert (1871–1925), was able to maintain a semblance of order; both

Liebknecht and Luxemburg were arrested and killed by the police.

Elections in January, 1919, confirmed the Social Democratic hold over the National Assembly. The machinery of government, however, remained in the hands of a civil service that was dominated by Prussia's military traditions, and the government found itself almost powerless against the bureaucracy. Although several abortive risings took place during the next few years, the danger of revolution gradually receded. The army command saw Bolshevism as its enemy and expected the government's assistance in destroying it. As a result, little notice was taken of the foundation of the vigorously anti-

Revolution in Berlin: the German Republic is proclaimed in front of the Reichstag, November 9, 1918.

Communist National Socialist (originally German Workers') Party in 1919.

Germany narrowly escaped a real revolution but the danger remained present elsewhere in Europe. Wilson's personal adviser at the Paris Peace Conference noted in his diary, "Bolshevism is gaining ground everywhere ... we are sitting on an open powder magazine and some day a spark may ignite it." In a sense he was right, but Bolshevism was not the only spark that might ignite the powder barrel; the dangers of nationalism and of anarchy as causes of revolution were no less great. Whatever its social difficulties, Germany was at least united in language. The problems of Austria-Hungary went far deeper, and disaffection was serious even before it was exacerbated by the certainty of military defeat. Food supplies were low, and in some places strikes were followed by the establishment of soviets. In February, 1918, there was a mutiny in

the fleet. The trouble was suppressed, but there were other ominous signs. Matters were soon made worse by the arrival of prisoners of war released by the Russians. These ex-prisoners, who had been fed antiwar and revolutionary propaganda during their internment, had a corrosive effect on the rest of the Austro-Hungarian army, which resulted in a rash of mutinies. Alarmed by this trend, the Germans persuaded their Austrian allies to agree to joint military forces and to a customs union—a virtual abdication by the Hapsburgs, but in a sense the achievement of what they had always sought, a strong, unified German state. But even a solution

Rosa Luxemburg, German Socialist leader.

such as this could not make victory possible. The subject races of the Austro-Hungarian Empire were not slow to take advantage of the situation—Czechs and other Slavic groups soon demanded the setting up of a federation. It was against this background that the Treaty of Versailles was signed.

Treaty of Versailles 1919

At Versailles the victorious Allied powers gathered to agree on the peace treaty they would inflict on defeated Germany. Wilson's Fourteen Points—the core of the armistice agreement— were glossed over as Italy insisted on territorial gains, Britain and France on ruinous reparation payments, and France on the relegation of Germany to a powerless nonentity. The Germans finally signed the treaty, convinced they had no alternative. Its harshness and vindictiveness, however, caused widespread resentment and eased the way for nationalist extremists culminating in the rise of Adolf Hitler.

On the evening of April 29, 1919, the Germans who were to sign the peace treaty reached Versailles. Their reception at the station, their arrival at the Hôtel des Réservoirs, where they had to carry their own luggage to their rooms, the discovery that the hotel was surrounded by a barbed wire fence and was constantly patrolled by sentinels, all served to make them aware of how the Allies, and especially the French, regarded them: they were criminals, guilty of devastating France.

The conference room in the Trianon Palace to which the Germans were summoned on May 7 had been turned into a court of law. On three sides of the room sat over two hundred men, the representatives of nearly all the Allied and neutral nations. On the fourth side was what the French newspapers had described as "the dock"—the table of the German delegation. Once the Germans had been conducted to their seats Georges Clemenceau, the Prime Minister of France and the President of the Peace Conference, rose to his feet and addressed the German Foreign Minister, Count Ulrich von Brockdorff-Rantzau. He began formally enough, but was suddenly unable to contain his hatred. "You forced this war upon us," he exclaimed. "We shall take good care to prevent its ever happening again .... The hour has struck for the weighty settlement of our account." There were to be no negotiations. The Germans simply were to be given fifteen days in which to submit written "observations" on the terms. After that the final draft would be signed.

The German Foreign Minister requested permission to speak. Far from admitting that the Germans had "forced the war" upon the Allies, he suggested that the outbreak of hostilities was the consequence of "the imperialism of all the European states . . . the policy of retaliation, the policy of expansion and the disregard of the right of peoples to determine their own destiny." The Germans would make good to the best of their ability the damage they had caused, but the Allies should not forget the conditions on which the German government had accepted peace—the observance of President Woodrow Wilson's Fourteen Points. The object of the peace treaty should not be to ruin a nation; it should be to reconstruct Europe, and President Wilson's plan for a League of Nations was a noble attempt to do this.

Brockdorff-Rantzau's speech caused some irritation among the organizers of the conference. They found it too long; it was unsubmissive in tone; it reminded them of the principles that had been betrayed and the compromises they had had to reach; it implied, above all, that the Germans would not be ready to sign the treaty immediately. Besides, the draft of the peace treaty, a document of two hundred pages which Brockdorff-Rantzau took with him from the conference room to transmit to his government and to study at his leisure, was not to the satisfaction of any of the three men largely instrumental in drawing it up. Clemenceau found it too lenient, whereas the British Prime Minister, David Lloyd George, found it too harsh. President Wilson himself had said that if he were a German he would never sign it and most of the other delegates who saw it for the first time on the morning of May 7 concurred. The Germans, of course, were the most indignant of all. Brockdorff-Rantzau considered the "thick volume . . . quite unnecessary." The Allies, he said, "could have expressed the whole thing more simply in one clause— *'Germany gives up her existence.'*"

Six months before the German Foreign Minister had been presented with the draft of the treaty, another German delegation had received the Allied terms of armistice in a railway carriage in the Forest of Compiègne. This was on November 8, 1918. Three days later the armistice came into effect. The Germans evacuated their troops from France and the left bank of the Rhine and surrendered the

Georges Clemenceau, Prime Minister of France and chief proponent of Allied retribution. France had suffered the greatest damage during the war and was largely responsible for the reparation payments subsequently levied on Germany.

Opposite June 28, 1919. The signing of the Peace Treaty in the Hall of Mirrors, Versailles, by Sir William Orpen. Wilson, Clemenceau and Lloyd George are seated in the center. The two German delegates are on the near side of the table.

The Emperor Wilhelm II is vanquished ; a French poster on the theme of liberation. At the conclusion of the Franco-Prussian War in 1871, the victorious Wilhelm I had been crowned Emperor of Germany in Versailles' Hall of Mirrors.

Right The last German troops crossing back into Germany over a Rhine bridge, January 2, 1919. Although defeated, the German army retired in good order and was left structurally intact.

main part of their armaments, their aircraft and their navy. In the Allied capitals there was jubilation. After four years of fighting and destruction the war had ended, and with it an entire era. The time had now come to start anew, and there was no document so widely believed to provide the basis for this new era of history as President Wilson's Fourteen Points. The main principle on which the points rested was freedom and the right of self-determination of every nationality. There was to be absolute freedom of the seas and absolute freedom of trade. Secret diplomacy was to stop. "National armaments" were to be "reduced to the lowest point consistent with domestic safety." The Turkish and Austro-Hungarian Empires were to be broken up and each of the many nations included in them was to be entitled to independence. In the cases of the colonies an agreement was to be reached to the satisfaction of the indigenous inhabitants and the great power concerned. Finally, the fourteenth point provided for a "general association of nations" to guarantee world peace.

The main opposition to some of the Fourteen Points and to Wilson's German policy in general came from the other Allied leaders. Lloyd George was reluctant to accept the point concerning the freedom of the seas, which would have made a blockade by the Royal Navy illegal in any future war. Clemenceau was unwilling to agree to the abolition of secret diplomacy, an art in which he and his predecessors had specialized and to which France owed some of her most effective alliances. And though Lloyd George and Clemenceau approved of Germany's territorial losses they could hardly approve of Wilson's humane assurances that "no punitive damages" be imposed on Germany. American public opinion was indifferent to remuneration, perhaps because American losses in the war had been relatively small and none of them territorial. But the British and the French expected reparation payments for the damage they had suffered, and the political credibility of the two prime ministers depended on their obtaining them.

The first session of the Paris Peace Conference at which the terms of the peace treaty were decided upon took place on January 12, 1919. As time went by it became evident that each of the members of the "Council of Four" had different priorities. They were subject to a number of pressures—from their parties, their armies, their electorate and their governments. Vittorio Emanuele Orlando, the Italian Prime Minister, was primarily concerned with gaining the territorial concessions promised to Italy by the Treaty of London in 1915 in which she undertook to fight with the Allies. Many of these concessions were approved by Wilson but there was one city for which the Italians clamored on the grounds of self-determination, but which Wilson insisted be given to the new state of Yugoslavia—the port of Fiume. Orlando theatened to abandon the peace conference over the Fiume issue; the Italian public, which had been among his most enthusiastic admirers, turned against the American

Europe after the Treaty of Versailles

- Former territory of Imperial Russia
- Lost by Germany 1919 (Germany also lost Tanganyika and Southwest Africa)
- Saar: League of Nations control 1919-35
- Demilitarized Rhineland 1919-36
- Austria-Hungary until 1918
- Plebiscite Areas

President, but Wilson stood firm: Fiume was not to go to Italy.

The most adaptable member of the Council of Four was David Lloyd George, yet his adaptability verged on fickleness. He was the first to see his opponent's point of view; on a number of occasions during the peace conference he proved to be extraordinarily understanding of the Germans' predicament, and his own proposals for the terms of the treaty, the Fontainebleau Document, drawn up on March 26, 1919, were far-sighted and humane. But for all his awareness, for all the pliancy he displayed even after the treaty had been presented to the Germans, Lloyd George had his electorate to think about. "Fullest indemnities from Germany," he had promised the British in December, 1918, in addition to the trial of the Kaiser and the "punishment of those responsible for atrocities." Lloyd George was a man with commitments his intelligence prevented him believing. He could wriggle out of two of them.

Although he appeared to be the most vindictive of all the Allied representatives and although he alone of the Council of Four truly detested the Germans, Georges Clemenceau had also had to combat and satisfy men more extreme than himself. There was Raymond Poincaré, the President of the Republic. There was the French parliament which

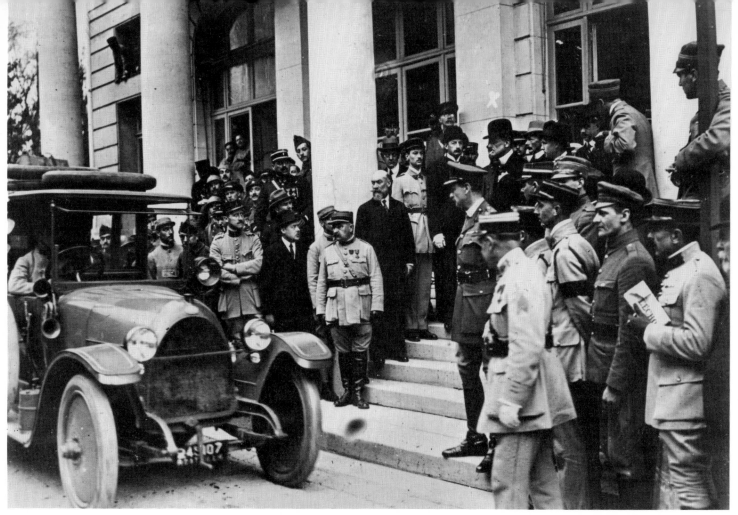

The German delegates at Versailles. Although Germany had signed the 1918 Armistice on the basis of President Wilson's Fourteen Points, the German delegation summoned to the conference at the Trianon Palace found itself arranged as for a trial.

believed that the only hope for France's future safety was to dismantle Germany, destroy her economy and surround her with well-armed and hostile states. There was the French army and its Commander-in-Chief, Marshal Ferdinand Foch, who wanted to advance as far as the Rhine and annex the ten thousand square miles of German territory to the west of the river. In addition there was the matter of the French budget. To every question concerning it Clemenceau's Minister of Finance, Louis Klotz, had replied "The Germans will pay."

In comparison with the volatile Lloyd George and the acrimonious Clemenceau, President Woodrow Wilson appeared as a paragon of disinterested justice. Yet even he was subjected to pressures and opposition. He had powerful enemies in the United States. The resentment he inspired in the Senate and the Republican Party was increased by his refusal to appoint a single senator among the five commissioners who accompanied him to the peace conference and by his acceptance of only one Republican, the elderly diplomat, Henry White, who had been politically inactive for more than ten years. Consequently Theodore Roosevelt had stated that the President had "no authority to speak for the American people" and the Senate, with its Republican majority, was ready to defeat any motion presented by Wilson. The Republican senators were ready, above all, to defeat Wilson's favorite project, the League of Nations. They argued that it was incompatible with the Monroe Doctrine and, although this had already been breached by Wilson when America entered the war, they were

determined that the United States would not again be involved in the defense of European countries.

An important section of the Treaty of Versailles was devoted to the League of Nations and what struck the Germans as particularly unfair was that they were to be excluded from it. Here, they felt, the most important of the Fourteen Points had been betrayed. But while the question of the League of Nations was more a matter of principle than anything else, the other clauses in the draft of the treaty were considered unacceptable on a practical level.

By these clauses Germany was to lose all her colonies and her concessions; she was to lose Alsace-Lorraine to France, the northern part of Schleswig to Denmark, Moresnet, Eupen and Malmédy to Belgium, and Upper Silesia, West Prussia and Posen to Poland. Danzig was to be a Free City, while East Prussia was to be separated from the rest of the country by the "Polish Corridor." The coal mines in the Saar were to be ceded to France "as compensation." After fifteen years a plebiscite would be held in the area and if the people voted to return to Germany, Germany would purchase the mines from France at a negotiable price in gold. The Rhineland was to be occupied for fifteen years by Allied forces to see that Germany met her obligations, and Germany was ordered to demilitarize the area permanently as well as to demilitarize the east bank of the Rhine to a depth of fifty kilometers (thirty-one miles). Any hope of Germany's uniting with Austria was to be renounced. The Germans had to give up the long-held dream of unification with Austria and were forced to "acknowledge and respect strictly the independence of Austria."

Considerable reductions were prescribed for the German army. It was to be reduced to a hundred thousand men with barely enough weapons to do more than serve as a police force. The German air force and navy were virtually to be abolished, the armament factories dismantled, conscription to cease, the General Staff to be dissolved and the cadet schools closed down. While the clauses regarding German armaments were precise, those concerning reparations, however, were vague. Germany was required to pay the Allies five billion dollars in gold before May 1, 1921, as well as to deliver consignments of chemicals, coal and other materials. In the meantime the Allied Reparations Commission would calculate the total amount owed and, in May, 1921, would inform the Germans of its conclusions and arrange for payment of the full sum over a period of thirty years.

Finally—and this was considered the most humiliating part of the treaty—not only was Germany to agree to hand over the Kaiser as well as any other German indicted by the Allies as a war criminal, she was also to "accept the responsibility . . . for all the loss to which the Allies and Associated Governments and their nationals have been subjected" in the war.

The two weeks accorded the German delegation to consider the treaty were extended to three, during which they complained about clause after

Civilians and soldiers dancing in the streets of Paris on the signing of the peace treaty. Despite the different priorities of the Allied leaders, there was a general feeling that the "war to end all wars" would produce a new international order, safeguarded by the League of Nations.

Destruction of German armor outside Berlin, 1919. By the terms of the treaty the German armed forces were to be drastically, and permanently, reduced.

clause. But the concessions granted by the Allies were so small that when the final draft of the treaty was presented to the Germans on June 16, almost three weeks after they had submitted their counter-proposals, the few amendments had merely been added in red ink to the text of the original draft. That night Brockdorff-Rantzau and his fellow delegates left France for Germany. They had been given barely a week in which to make up their minds about signing, and they had decided to put the matter in the hands of their government.

Brockdorff-Rantzau expected to find the German government as adamant in its refusal to sign the treaty as he was. This was not the case. The submissive attitude of the government was due to the realistic approach of one man, Matthias Erzberger, minister without portfolio in Chancellor Philipp Scheidemann's cabinet and leader of the Catholic Center Party, the second largest party in Germany. Erzberger had led the delegates to sign the armistice at Compiègne in November, 1918, and was considered one of the most courageous and level-headed politicians in the cabinet. His argument in favor of signing the peace treaty, however unfavorable the terms, rested on two assumptions. The first was that if the Germans refused to sign the Allied forces would invade the country and there was no possible chance of resisting them. The second was that when they were put into practice the harder clauses of the treaty would most probably be modified.

The German cabinet was divided. Scheidemann was forced to resign on June 20. Brockdorff-Rantzau also resigned, and it was only three days before the Allied deadline that the President, Friederich Ebert, succeeded in forming a new government with Gustav Bauer as Chancellor. Again the treaty was debated, again Erzberger advised submission, although he told the National Assembly that the Germans might succeed in having the "war-guilt" clauses removed. But the Allies accepted no modification. Either the Germans signed the treaty as it stood or the war would be resumed. Ninety minutes before the Allied troops were to invade Germany, the German government's unconditional agreement was announced to the Council of Four in President Wilson's study and, on June 28, the new German Foreign Minister, Hermann Müller, put his signature to the treaty.

Of all the prophets of the Treaty of Versailles Erzberger was one of the very few to prove to be right. The Allies did not after all apply the clauses stringently and the Germans frequently succeeded

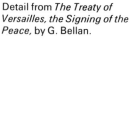

Detail from *The Treaty of Versailles, the Signing of the Peace,* by G. Bellan.

in evading them. In February, 1920, the Allies presented a list of war criminals whom they proposed to try, but the Germans were so indignant that the Allies let the matter rest and a small number of soldiers were tried and accorded minimal sentences in Germany itself. The Reparations Commission reached a far more moderate decision than the prophets of doom had expected. It was clear that Germany had been ravaged by the war and was in no position to pay an exorbitant sum. In 1920 the figure was put at 269 billion gold marks to be paid over a period of thirty-five years; the following year the Allies agreed to halve the amount; in 1924 the Dawes Plan was introduced and Germany started to borrow money from the United States and the other Allies with which to restore her economy and pay her indemnities. A further reparations settlement, the Young Plan of 1929, was abandoned on account of the Depression, and at the Conference of Lausanne in 1932 the Allies decided to absolve Germany of further payment after receiving from her a token three billion marks. The next year, however, Hitler came to power and the money was never paid.

German territorial losses were also modified. A plebiscite was held in Upper Silesia in 1921 and the northern half of the area was returned to Germany. The French troops began to withdraw from the Rhineland after the Treaty of Locarno in 1925, and in June, 1930, the Allies evacuated the area altogether. Despite the detailed instructions in the Treaty of Versailles as to the size of the army and the quantity of its armaments, the German army remained more than twice the prescribed size and managed to retain nearly all the weapons forbidden by the treaty.

The German economic crisis of the early 1920s was the consequence of the war and not of the Treaty of Versailles. Germany did, admittedly, lose much of her territory and her raw materials, but this did not prevent her from flourishing economically between 1924 and 1929. By the mid-1920s the Allies were prepared to treat her as an equal and in 1926 Germany was admitted to the League of Nations. Nevertheless a great many Germans continued to blame their misfortunes on the Treaty of Versailles. One nationalist leader after another promised his countrymen that he would revoke it. But when Hitler came to power in 1933 and proceeded to keep this promise there was surprisingly little left of the treaty to revoke.

ALASTAIR HAMILTON

We Are Making a New World, by Paul Nash. The World War scarred the consciousness of the generation that lived through it.

Vindictive peace terms

The uniform vindictiveness of the peace terms imposed at Versailles disguised Allied disunity, masking the falling out that had taken place between the British and the French. The fiercest critic of the terms, the English economist John Maynard Keynes (1883–1946), described them as "a web of sophistry." After the first surge of postwar belligerency, the British had shifted their stance, becoming more reasonable than the French. After all, British war aims were largely achieved. The German fleet had been scuttled and Germany's colonies forfeited. France, on the other hand, felt only slightly more secure than she had been before the war. Continued territorial disputes and a desire for revenge after the humiliating defeat of 1870 were not the only factors. Vanquished Germany seemed much stronger in men and resources than victorious France, and hence the French were anxious to humble Germany so completely that it might never rise again. Here again the treaty reflected neither viewpoint. Because the British would not agree to the total mutilation of Germany, the treaty was neither harsh enough to prevent German recovery nor lenient enough to encourage the Germans to accept it. It was not accepted as satisfactory even at the time. A British diplomat, summing up the failure of Versailles, declared: "We came confident that the new order was about to be established, we left convinced that the new order had merely befouled the old."

The whole of the Versailles settlement was based on the premise of American support. It was a sign of the shifting balance of world forces that when this American support failed to materialize, the settlement slowly began to disintegrate. The end of European domination of world affairs had been evident before 1914, but the war made the process irrevocable. With Wilson's declaration of the principle of self-determination and Lenin's denunciation of imperialism, permanent cracks appeared in the structure of European imperialism. No less important was the American determination to recover in full the large sums that it had lent the Allies, whom it had joined so late in the war. This led

Victorious British troops marching through the Strand in London, 1919.

to the beginning of widespread anti-American feeling in Europe. The British decision to demand only the repayment of enough of its loans to the other Allies to make it possible to repay the Americans heightened the anti-American feeling, but could not destroy America's new-found influence.

Colonial troops returned home from the battlefields of Europe with new notions of democracy, self-government and national independence. Together with a new self-confidence, these notions formed the basis of a resolve to obliterate the old concept of the inferior status of colonies. The revelation of the cynicism with which the Western powers bartered away colonial territories further discredited the imperialists and provoked violent reactions. Colonial attitudes were, however, too well established to be abandoned overnight, and, indeed, the Americans and the European Allies showed their desire to continue to extend their imperialist power. The main region left open for this was the Middle East, where there was a power vacuum caused by the collapse of Turkey.

Turkey, the Arab world and Africa

Just as the Austro-Hungarian Empire had been fragmented as a result of defeat in war, the growth of nationalism and the Versailles Treaty, so the other great monarchy of southeastern Europe, the Ottoman Empire, was dismembered. It was reduced to 300,000 square miles by the removal of the Arab regions. Seeing the impossibility of continuing to fight the Allies, the new Sultan, Mohammed VI, sought to cooperate with them. This proved to be a foolish policy as the Allies, who were themselves preparing to partition the country, did nothing to prevent an invasion from Greece; the failure of the Sultan to stand up to the Allies led to the rapid decline of his authority. A number of associations for national protection were set up both in the east and in the west of Anatolia, and these showed little respect for the Sultan, who was regarded as the Allies' servant.

Disturbed by this development, Mohammed sent Mustafa Kemal Pasha (1881–1938), an officer who had distinguished himself in the defense of the Dardanelles, to keep the situation under control. The choice proved a bad one; Kemal encouraged the nationalists to rise and became their leader. After resigning from the army Kemal presided over a hastily summoned and unrepresentative National Assembly, which declared the Sultan deposed. In 1920, after a brief rapprochement with the nationalists, the Allies and the Sultan struck back by imprisoning nationalist supporters in Istanbul. This led to the outbreak of civil war, and the nationalists were for a short time in danger of losing power altogether, even in their capital, Ankara. The army, however, showed itself more loyal to the rebel Pasha than to the Sultan, and Kemal was soon the master of most of eastern Anatolia. The Allies did not want to become too closely involved themselves, so they encouraged the Greeks to extend their invasion. The Greek army, however, was soon beaten back and destroyed, and by 1922 Kemal was the master of Turkey. In the following year, by the Treaty

Kemal Atatürk, leader of the nationalist cause against the discredited Sultan and creator of modern Turkey.

nationalism take root in the colonial world

of Lausanne, the Allies recognized the nationalist government.

Kemal had proved himself a capable general; he now proceeded to drag his backward country of thirteen million inhabitants into the twentieth century. Privileges—religious, military and civil—were swept away; the sultanate and caliphate were abolished; a civil code, based on that of Switzerland, was introduced; Roman orthography replaced Arabic; women—who were now forbidden to veil their faces—were given the vote; and imperialist ambitions were abandoned. Although Kemal was only able to carry through his programs by banning opposition, he was able to turn the most backward state in Europe into a socially advanced nation, and in 1935 when family names were introduced, he took the name Atatürk (Father of the Turks) in recognition of his services. Although Turkey began to stagnate once again after Atatürk's death, he had shown how rapidly a backward state could advance, and was one of the most important figures in twentieth-century history.

In the Arab world, which had hoped that the assistance given to the Allies in World War I would lead to independence, the disclosure of the Sykes-Picot agreement gave a sharp boost to Arab nationalism. There were few objections to the idea of Jewish immigration to Palestine, but the thought of French hegemony in

Syria and Lebanon and of British in Iraq and Jordan created enormous ill will. In Egypt, nationalist ideas had already become widespread by the end of World War I, and the independence-minded Wafd Party was founded in 1919; three years later the British granted independence to Egypt. The Kingdom of the Hejaz, which had been part of the Ottoman Empire, remained independent, and in 1926 the ruler annexed the huge neighboring desert territory of Nejd to form Saudi Arabia. Elsewhere the colonial powers showed less willingness to abandon their gains, and the formation of the nationalist Destour Party in Tunisia in 1922 was not looked upon with favor by the French.

Elsewhere in Africa, too, the current of anti-imperialist feeling was rising. The year 1919 saw the convention of a pan-African congress in Paris. Those who sought independence soon found that the Bolsheviks had been quick to realize the revolutionary potential of oppressed or discontented colonial peoples, and the Russians kept a stream of anti-imperialist propaganda flowing into Africa.

Colonial self-awareness

Throughout Asia these same factors contributed to an increased sense of self-awareness among colonial nations. This was particularly so in India. In accordance with the

The young Mohandas Karamchand Gandhi.

promises made in 1917, the British began implementing self-government for the Indians. The resulting Government of India Act of 1919 was something of a sham, however, for it retained complete British control of the central government. The legislature was to contain democratically elected Indians, but it had no control over ministers. Indian nationalists were bitterly disappointed. In view both of the 1917 promise and the great efforts made by Indians on Britain's behalf during the war, much more had been expected. Throughout 1918 there were riots and disturbances, and they grew worse as demobilization of European troops took place.

At this point, Mohandas K. Gandhi emerged as the leader of the Indian nationalists. Throughout 1919, he inspired outbreaks of civil disobedience. Initially, those outbreaks were confined to the educated classes, but with the help of Jawaharlal Nehru, Gandhi managed to extend the Congress movement to other social classes as well. The process of welding a political machine that would embrace every village and province was barely in its infancy, but it did mark a great step forward for Indian nationalism. Disorders reached a climax in 1919 at Amritsar in the Punjab, when troops under British control fired on a mob of rioting Indians, killing

379 and wounding about 1,000. Amritsar became a symbol of British cruelty and did much to increase the trend toward militancy.

The revolt against the West continued in China, where revolution was progressing with Mandarin slowness. During the war, the European powers had more or less abandoned China. Japan had been allowed to seize German territory and had taken the opportunity to overrun large areas. Chinese President Yüan Shih-k'ai hesitated to resist, and a series of army mutinies destroyed his power. Army generals began to rule in their own interests, and during this period the Chinese countryside was pillaged and robbed. Robber bands and private armies roamed the land. In the long run this devastation turned the peasantry into a revolutionary force that longed for a strong, stable, reforming government of the sort that the Communists were ultimately to offer. In the short run, the main result was a revulsion against the Western powers, who were held responsible for the chaos.

Discontent in Europe

Bleak as prospects seemed for the West in Asia, things hardly appeared much better in Europe. In the aftermath of war, rising prices and inflation created discontent among the lower middle classes, especially in Germany and Italy. In Germany that discontent combined with resentment against the harshness of Versailles; in Italy, with disappointed war aims. Patriotic disappointment was swelled by the existence of large numbers of ex-servicemen. All over Europe, demagogues emerged who were ready to exploit discontent, ready to throw the blame on socialism and democracy, and ready to launch aggressive programs of nationalist expansion. Before the war, violence had been advocated in many quarters as a mode of political action; after the war, those who had advocated violence as a political tool saw their advice put into practice in Italy. In 1919 the poet Gabriele d'Annunzio (1863–1938) led an unofficial Italian army to seize the Croatian port of Fiume (Rieka), which had been assigned to Yugoslavia at Versailles. This proved to be a dress rehearsal for a coup d'état in Italy four years later.

King Fuad opening the first Egyptian Parliament. On the right the Premier Zaghoul Pasha reads the King's speech.

The Blackshirts March on Rome

"Either the government of Italy is given to us, or we shall seize it by marching on Rome!"
Benito Mussolini's bold declaration electrified the thousands of Fascists who had gathered in the
Piazza del Plebiscito in Naples on October 24, 1922, to hear their fiery young leader.
Responding to Mussolini's oratory, the crowd chanted "Roma! Roma! Roma!" Il Duce's words
had convinced the Blackshirts that a march on Rome would topple Luigi Facta's already troubled
government; those words had not convinced Mussolini himself. Indeed, his indecisiveness was so
acute that the leaders of the march gave serious thought to proceeding without him. By the time
Mussolini did reach Rome, Facta had resigned and King Victor Emmanuel had called upon the
Fascist leader to form a new government. The task of restoring order fell to Mussolini, who two
years later became the youngest Prime Minister in Italy's history.

During the afternoon of October 24, 1922, thousands upon thousands of black-shirted Fascists marched into the Piazza del Plebiscito in Naples. They stood at rigid attention in the square and listened to the words of their leader, Benito Mussolini. "I assure you in all solemnity that the hour has struck," Mussolini called out to them in his deep, emotive voice. "Either the government of Italy is given to us, or we shall seize it by marching on Rome. It is a matter of days, of hours. ... I guarantee, I swear to you, that the orders will reach you." Responding to the power of Mussolini's oratory, the assembled Fascists took up his cry, shouting in unison, *"Roma! Roma! Roma!"*

Later that day Mussolini and other leading officers of the Fascist Party held a secret meeting in the Hotel Vesuvio. They discussed the arrangements for the march on Rome that Mussolini had proposed. It was decided that the Fascist militia should be mobilized as soon as the Blackshirts returned to their homes from the party congress in Naples. Four days later—following Fascist-provoked riots in which police and radio stations, post offices, prefectures, trade union premises and the offices of anti-Fascist newspapers would be occupied in all the principal towns—the Fascist militia would concentrate at various selected points and then converge upon the capital. The march was to be directed by four leading Fascists into whose hands all power was given.

Those *Quadrumviri*, as they were later to be known, were Michele Bianchi, a thirty-nine-year-old journalist who was Secretary-General of the Party and a dedicated, not to say fanatical, Fascist whose proud claim it was that he had been a member of the Party "from the first hour"; Italo Balbo, twenty-six years old, brave, good-looking, intelligent, the hero of the *squadristi* (the violent Fascist action groups); Cesare Maria de Vecchi, a landowner and lawyer, conservative and monarchist, who had distinguished

himself as an army officer during World War I; and General Emilio de Bono, a small, frail, white-bearded officer of fifty-eight who had taken over the leadership of the Fascist militia while remaining in the regular army.

Mussolini himself remained outside the quadrumvirate. Indeed, in Balbo's opinion, his hesitant, capricious character entirely unsuited him for the organization and leadership of a determined coup d'état. Balbo noted afterward that Mussolini was so vacillating that he had to be firmly told: "We are going to Rome, either with you or without you. It's up to you. Make up your mind."

Mussolini prudently returned to Milan as soon as the decision to march on Rome had been taken at Naples, and he determined to remain there until the crisis was resolved either by force or by compromise. He had not yet finally decided, despite his forthright address to the Blackshirts in the Piazza del Plebiscito, that a peaceful solution might not be reached even then.

There is little question that the Prime Minister, the good-natured and easygoing Luigi Facta, was prepared to make a deal with the Fascists if, by doing so, he could prolong his own government's life. So were the three other principal contenders for Facta's office, Antonio Salandra, Saverio Nitti and Giovanni Giolitti, all of whom had held the office in the past and with each one of whom Mussolini was in touch either directly or through an intermediary.

All over Italy the Fascists were preparing for action. Mobilization had started: public buildings had been occupied; prominent anti-Fascists had been detained; telephone wires had been cut, trains requisitioned, rifles and cars commandeered. And the militia had begun to concentrate for the coming march. Perugia, where the *Quadrumviri* had

A Fascist poster from the 1930s.

Opposite Benito Mussolini, Italy's "man of destiny," dominating the ancient city of Rome.

Fascist leaders arrive in the capital after the march on Rome, October, 1922.

Mussolini taking the salute at a shipping review at Portofino, 1926.

established their headquarters in the Hotel Brufani, was one of several towns already firmly under Fascist control. In Rome, at eleven o'clock on the night of October 27, 1922, Luigi Facta handed his government's resignation to the King.

Remaining in office until a successor could be found, Facta called an emergency cabinet meeting for five o'clock the next morning. The cabinet members decided to proclaim a state of siege at noon. The proclamation, drafted on the spot, was to be fixed to the walls of Rome at 8:30 A.M.; the Italian army was to be commanded to prevent the threatened march on the capital; all Fascist troublemakers were to be arrested to prevent outbreaks of violence.

Facta departed immediately for the Villa Savoia, Victor Emmanuel's official residence, where he planned to obtain the King's signature on the proclamation. But in the night Victor Emmanuel had been warned that the army might well refuse to oppose the Fascists; he had also been advised that opposition might lead to civil war. Therefore, to Facta's consternation, he refused to sign.

When Mussolini heard that the King's refusal to sign the proclamation had forced the government to revoke the state of siege, he knew that he had won. Urged on all sides to leave immediately for the capital, he confidently replied that he would do so only when he received a written request from the King to form a government. When that request at last arrived, he left immediately for the railway station.

The march on Rome—so feared by the government, so revered in the party's later propaganda—was less than orderly. The headquarters of the *Quadrumviri*, isolated in Perugia, was able to exercise little control over the converging columns in a situation that changed confusingly from hour to hour. The various groups marched independently, without a coordinated plan. Four thousand men came down to Civitavecchia, two thousand to Monterotondo, and about eight thousand to Tivoli. (Some three thousand more remained in reserve at Foligno, near Perugia.) The men in each of the three marching columns were unaware of the progress of their comrades. No arrangements had been made for sleeping quarters on the way; most groups were short of food; some were unarmed. By the time they reached their concentration points north of Rome, a heavy rain had begun to fall, and some of them,

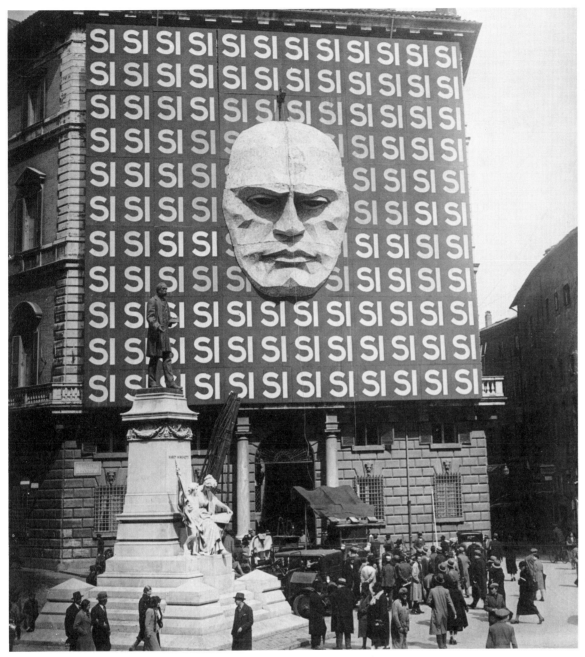

Gabriele D'Annunzio, poet, and war hero.

wet and hungry, decided that they had had enough and went home.

Yet under the threat of less-organized opponents than these, stronger governments have fallen. And when, on the day after Mussolini's arrival in Rome, the thousands of *squadristi* still encamped outside the city were brought in by special trains to march in triumph past the Quirinal, the world could no longer doubt that a new age in the history of Italy was dawning.

To most Italians that dawn was both overdue and welcome. Italy had been on the victorious side during World War I, but she had failed to gain most of the territories that her allies had promised her. She obtained some islands in the Aegean and the Adriatic, parts of the Dalmatian coast, the Tyrol and Trieste. Yet she was denied the former German colonies, and she was also denied the Yugoslavian port of Fiume. Fiume had been seized by the nationalist poet and aviator Gabriele D'Annunzio in a characteristically theatrical gesture in 1919; however, D'Annunzio's eagle-plumed followers had been thrown out of Fiume with their cloaks and daggers after three months of rodomontade.

Reviled by disappointed nationalists, Italy's successive parliamentary governments, weak and irresolute, were equally reviled by the country's workers. Strikes and industrial revolts were as widespread in the north as was brigandage in the south. Workers' soviets were set up in the factories; Socialists and Communists marched through the streets shouting revolutionary slogans; rioters, protesting against the ever-rising cost of living, attacked public buildings, barracks, banks and trains. Inflation was aggravated by subsidies which did not relieve the distress of a painfully impoverished

Above A rally in Rome's Piazza Venezia in 1939.

Below Victor Emmanuel III, King of Italy, meets Mussolini after the Fascist takeover.

Porto a Vostra Maestà l'Italia di Vittorio Veneto riconsacrata dalla Vittoria

country that had been left billions of lire in debt by the sudden end of economic help from her allies. At the same time, the problems of unemployment were increased by the demobilization of thousands of soldiers, and the problems of crime were magnified by the army of no less than 150,000 deserters who had grown accustomed to living by their wits.

It was in those conditions of violence, distress and industrial unrest that Fascism had been born. In March, 1919, a group of men had met in a room at the Milan Association of Merchants and Shop-keepers in the Piazza San Sepolcro. The group in-cluded a disparate ragbag of discontented Socialists and syndicalists, republicans, anarchists, unclassifi-able revolutionaries and restless soldiers. Many of the latter had been *Arditi* (commandos in the Italian army), and some of them were wanted by the police. Their self-appointed leader was Benito Mussolini, the son of a blacksmith from the Romagna. Musso-lini was an ex-soldier himself, formerly a school-teacher and now a journalist. As early as February, 1918, this dynamic young man with the pale face and staring dark eyes had been advocating the emergence of a dictator "ruthless and energetic enough to make a clean sweep." Three months later, in a widely reported speech at Bologna, he had hinted that he himself might prove such a man.

At the meeting in Milan, he advocated the for-mation of a *Fascio di Combattimento*, a group of fighters. Their insignia was to be the fasces, symbol of author-ity in ancient Rome—an axe surrounded by rods tightly bound together for strength and unity. The "Fascist" movement spread rapidly, gaining wider and wider support from the discontented young, from the frightened middle class, from industrialists and merchants who deeply resented the growing power and pretensions of the workers, from land-owners who feared for the loss of their rents, and from patriots who believed that the Fascists were members of the one movement that could bring Italy to a position of respect and power in Europe.

By the time of the elections of 1921, the movement had gained sufficient support for thirty-five of its candidates, including Mussolini himself, to be elected to Parliament. The following November the Fascist Party was founded—and thereafter Fascism grew more and more arrogant, meeting violence with greater violence. Squads of Fascists armed with knives and cudgels (or with revolvers brought back from the war) attacked their enemies with a ferocity and regularity that soon resulted in a situation almost comparable to civil war.

Yet although Mussolini had achieved power by force, he exercised it initially with restraint. He seemed anxious to demonstrate that he was not only the leader of Fascism but the head of the government of a united Italy. Less than a third of his cabinet were members of his party. He made it clear, however, that he intended to govern authoritatively and per-sonally. He appointed himself President of the Council, Minister of the Interior and Minister of Foreign Affairs. He demanded—and obtained by an overwhelming majority—full dictatorial powers for a year to carry out what he considered to be essential reforms. And that year proved long enough for him to push through a law guaranteeing the party that secured the largest number of votes in the elections the right to claim two-thirds of the seats in the Chamber. In the elections of 1924 the Fascists received over 65 percent of the votes, and Mussolini, the youngest Prime Minister the Italians had ever had, was confirmed in an office that he was to retain for twenty years.

The first few years of those two decades were the halcyon days of Mussolini's party. The people were tired of strikes and riots; they were responsive to the flamboyant, choreographic techniques and the medieval trappings of Fascism; they were ready to accept a dictatorial regime—and the so-called corporative state—if the dignity of the country were to be restored and its national economy stabilized. And Fascism in those halcyon days—although never achieving the miracles claimed for it by its tireless propagandists—*did* seem a worthwhile adventure. Something *was* done to improve the conditions of the workers, to stabilize the economy, to inaugurate an ambitious program of public works (including the draining of the Pontine Marshes), to induce greater administrative efficiency, to promote national interests.

Thus it was that Mussolini's popularity was able to survive the violence and fraud of the 1924 elections and the murder of the brave and gifted Socialist leader Giacomo Matteotti by Fascist thugs. Skillfully presenting himself to the people as Italy's man of destiny, Mussolini was accepted as such—and it was not only Italians who fell under the sway of that proudly jutting jaw, those black wide-open eyes, those wonderfully expressive gestures. He was compared—without a hint of irony—to Napoleon and to Cromwell, and hailed as a genius and as a superman by public figures all over Europe and in America. Had he not reinvigorated his divided and demoralized country? Had he not succeeded—where even Cavour had failed—in reconciling the state with the papacy? Had he not carried out his social reforms and public works without jeopardizing the interests or losing the support of the industrialists and landowners? Who else could have achieved all this? No one but Mussolini, *Il Duce*, who—as slogans painted on walls all over Italy proclaimed—*ha sempre ragione* (is always right).

Yet all the while an anti-Fascist resistance was at work, increasing in numbers as the dictatorship grew more oppressive and as it became increasingly evident that Mussolini was, behind the bluster of his brilliant propaganda, childish and coarse, unstable and irresolute, constitutionally deceitful and pathologically egotistic. As the years progressed, *Il Duce* revealed that he really had little conception of how to run a government, no patience with difficult work, a horror of decisions. He was capable of writing "approved" on two conflicting memoranda emanating from two different ministries—and then of going into another room where one of his mistresses lay waiting to satisfy the urgent demands of a sexual

Su loro ricade la colpa!

An Italian war poster: an attack on Churchill and Roosevelt as murderous gangsters.

appetite that approached satyriasis. In his callous xenophobia, his wild arrogance, and his willful misapprehension of Italy's fundamental necessities (and with his health rapidly deteriorating and his gifts declining) he led Italy first into the invasion of Abyssinia and then into an alliance with Hitler and a world war that destroyed the power of Italian Fascism forever.

In April, 1945, as the World War II Allies drove the Germans into headlong retreat, Mussolini was shot by Communist partisans while attempting to flee into the mountains. His body was later strung up by the heels in front of a screaming mob in Milan, the city where Fascism had been born—the city where Mussolini first learned he had come to power through the Fascist march on Rome.

CHRISTOPHER HIBBERT

Confusion in Eastern Europe

Mussolini's march on Rome was not the only disturbance in the years after Versailles. In the newly created states of Eastern Europe, political disorder was the rule rather than the exception, and attempted risings were frequent. Hungary, for example, was a battle-ground of warring factions. Governments rose and fell rapidly as different classes and interests seized or attempted to seize power. Nor was the situation helped by the efforts of the Hapsburgs to regain power—by force if necessary—or by the continual erosion of the country's borders by its neighbors. It was only gradually under Count Stephen Bethlen, who was Prime Minister from 1921 to 1931, that a semblance of normal government was reintroduced. Although deeply conservative, Bethlen got rid of the most obviously reactionary aspects of the counterrevolutionary government that he replaced.

The fundamental problem in Eastern Europe remained that of the nationalities: should an area peopled by a single nationality be regarded as an independent state? The failure of the Versailles Settlement to produce a satisfactory answer to this problem made further disorder in Eastern Europe inevitable.

Ireland: the threat of nationalism

Western Europe could afford to ignore this problem, but in Ireland, "John Bull's other island," Britain was forced to take more decisive action. The British government had found itself faced from 1914 onward with two extremist factions—Roman Catholic Nationalists and Protestant "Unionists," who wanted the closest ties with Britain. Although the majority of the population was Roman Catholic and favored separation from Britain, the Unionist minority was more militant and far better organized, with a volunteer army of 100,000 men. Two and a half centuries of religious and national intolerance and bigotry made civil war likely.

A minority of Nationalists, however, decided on rebellion against the British and asked Germany for help. On April 20, 1916, Sir Roger Casement, the Irish leader, landed on the Irish coast from a German submarine to start the rebellion; and four days later, on Easter Monday, the Nationalists seized the Dublin post office and declared Ireland a republic. The rising was quickly suppressed by the British army, but it had helped to focus Nationalist aspirations on the Sinn Fein (Ourselves Alone) Party, which had supported the rising. In the general election of 1918, seventy-three Sinn Fein candidates were elected to Parliament (against thirty-two elected from other parties in Irish constituencies). The Sinn Feiners refused to attend the Westminster Parliament and set up a separate assembly (Dail) as the "government" of Ireland. Anxious not to offend the Americans—much influenced by Irish opinion—the British could do nothing. Gradually Unionist and Republican violence mounted; the government banned the Sinn Fein and its illegal army,

The Easter Week Rising in Dublin, 1916. Violence continued in Ireland in spite of World War I.

the I.R.A. (Irish Republican Army), in 1919, and set up a new para-military force, the "Black and Tans" whose brutal methods and partisan support for the Unionists helped the Republicans to gain widespread popular support.

The British government sought a political compromise solution by dividing the country into two—largely Protestant Ulster with six counties, and the twenty-six counties of the South—giving each a parliament with limited powers. Sinn Fein refused to accept this as any sort of solution, although its candidates stood for election in the South. In all the county and borough constituencies of the South, Sinn Feiners were elected unopposed—and when Parliament met only the four members for Trinity College, Dublin, attended. It was clear to all that the attempted compromise had failed.

In 1921 the British government at last accepted reality while the Nationalists showed increasing willingness to accept a compromise that would give them most of Ireland. A treaty was signed between the British government and the still illegal Sinn Fein. The twenty-six counties of the South became "the Irish Free State," while Ulster, politically dominated by the Unionists, retained its links with Britain and its Parliament at Stormont Castle, Belfast.

On October 25, 1922, a new republican constitution was approved for the South. A minority of the Nationalists refused to accept the compromise, and as a result the new Irish government, which was dominated by Eamon de Valera (1882–   ), banned Sinn Fein and the I.R.A. Neither in the North nor in the South was the settlement of 1922 seen as a final solution; it was only regarded as a temporary compromise. It was not until 1968 that the compromise collapsed, although it had soon shown signs of wearing thin. The fundamental causes of disorder in Ireland—religious intolerance and biased government—died down in the South after 1922, but they had not been eradicated in Ulster.

Locarno: a truce of exhaustion

Meanwhile, on the mainland of Europe, France's attitude toward Germany poisoned international relations by strengthening both Germany's distrust of the Western

The Treaty of Locarno, with the signatures and seals of Britain, Belgium, Germany, Italy, Czechoslovakia and Poland.

powers and her determination to break the 1919 settlement. Britain was no less determined to smooth things over and moved to cancel all war debts, a major cause of bitterness between France and Germany. The British move was blocked by Washington, but this new spirit of appeasement did achieve a major success in France, where there was a dawning realization that the nation's vindictive postwar policy was merely playing into the hands of nationalist extremists in Germany. The efforts of British Prime Minister Ramsey MacDonald created an atmosphere of mutual sympathy that was crowned in 1925 by the Treaty of Locarno. At that gathering MacDonald convinced Edouard Herriot of France and Gustav Stresemann of Germany to agree to a treaty in which Britain guaranteed the frontiers of France and Germany against aggression by either side.

Locarno was perhaps as much a truce of exhaustion as a triumph of appeasement. There had been too much violence and hatred in the preceding decade for it all to be resolved overnight. Germany was still resentful of its defeat and anxious for a chance to recover. And France was still conscious of the German capacity for recovery. Moreover, the Germans never seriously believed that the British would support them in a crisis. Therefore France went on seeking a net of encircling alliances and Germany went on stealthily rearming. In time Locarno might have worked, but before it had a chance to inspire the necessary confidence, the world economic crisis broke. Thereafter, extremists were able to distract attention from

Communism to the needs of the Soviet Union

Leon Trotsky with newly graduated Red Commanders of the Military Academy, Moscow.

domestic, social and unemployment problems by attacks on the Treaty of Versailles.

While Western Europe was blindly heading for catastrophe, events of enormous significance were taking place in Russia. During these years, Russia's bureaucracy began to develop into the monolith that it remained. The growth of an antiterrorist police force started at an early stage, for, in a world of civil war, foreign intervention, economic chaos and counterrevolutionary enemies, the Bolsheviks soon became obsessed with the need to crush opposition before it crushed them. Absolute power was taken by the Communist Party on the theory that vast tracts of land stretching across two continents could only be ruled by a strong bureaucratic structure.

The Bolsheviks, who had taken up revolution in the first place in order to eradicate oppression, injustice and terror, and all the things associated with absolute power, were soon faced by a dilemma. They were forced to sacrifice their ideals in order to protect the essential framework of the Revolution. During the hard period of the civil war and the Allied intervention, grain had to be forcibly requisitioned, and opposition was wiped out, often by the most brutal methods.

Conditions became so bad in 1921 that the sailors of the Kronstadt naval base—the most revolutionary force in the country—mutinied against the government. A heartbroken Trotsky put down the revolt. It had become clear as a result of the war against the White Russians that if Communist government was to function effectively it would have to be able to speak with one voice. At the Tenth Party Congress, Lenin placed a ban on opposition within the party, thereby changing it from a free association of independent, critical-minded ideologists to a tightly disciplined bureaucratic and

monolithic machine. At the same time Lenin instituted the New Economic Policy, whereby direct economy was to be revised by the temporary introduction of free enterprise. But all of these measures were seen as being only temporary. By the end of 1923, Trotsky was advocating the waiving of the ban on opposition, and the economy was visibly stronger.

The death of Lenin

At this point the greatest tragedy of the Bolshevik Revolution occurred. In January, 1924, Lenin died. His death resulted in a struggle for power, the outcome of which molded contemporary Russia. The ultimate victor of this struggle was Joseph Stalin (1879–1953), a cold, brutal bureaucrat from the Cauca-

Joseph Stalin, Lenin's heir.

sus. Unlike most of the Bolshevik leaders, who were cultured and cosmopolitan, Stalin was narrow and crude, and bitterly jealous of Trotsky's many-faceted genius. He had risen in the party through his ability and his willingness to take over the administrative tedium that the other Bolsheviks shunned. Through his posts on various committees, Stalin had accumulated vast power and had filled the ranks of the party with his nominees.

Just before he died, Lenin began

to sense that the bureaucratic machine was moving independently of him, and in his political testament he wrote: "I propose to the comrades to remove Stalin from that position (General Secretary of the Central Committee of the Party)." Lenin's proposal was buried with him a short time later, and Stalin used his accrued powers to gain the leadership of the party.

The effects of Stalin's victory in the Soviet struggle for power are incalculable. The main tenet of Stalinism was "socialism in one country." Originally used to counter the Trotskyite notion of "permanent revolution," Stalin's phrase struck a chord in the hearts of thousands of party workers who were tired after eight years of war and revolution. The concept involved the abandonment of the universality of Marxist thought and a concentration on Russia's well-being. As Trotsky put it, the Comintern was transformed from the vanguard of the world revolution into the frontier guard of Russia.

Communism outside Russia

This had momentous results for Russia's foreign policy; it meant that the interests of world Communism might have to be sacrificed to the immediate needs of the Soviet Union. During Stalin's long rule, foreign Communist parties allowed themselves to be almost totally subjected to orders from Moscow. The dangers inherent in this acceptance of Russian leadership soon became apparent. In Germany, for example, the Communist Party embarked on a series of blunders that facilitated the rise of Hitler. Meanwhile, the Spanish Communist Party concentrated on persecuting anarchists and Trotskyites rather than on fighting the far more dangerous threat of nationalism. In the other Western states, too, Communists found themselves forced to defend the harsh measures of the Russian government, although they were often measures of which they disapproved strongly.

The first country to suffer from Stalin's jaundiced interpretation of the prospects of world revolution was China. At the time, the Chinese Communist Party was extremely small, and the Russians tended to back Sun Yat-sen's nationalist Kuomintang. In 1925, Sun Yat-sen died, and the leadership of

Chiang Kai-shek, Kuomintang leader.

the Kuomintang was taken over by Chiang Kai-shek. In 1927, Chiang began to take advantage of a national feeling of revulsion against the power of the warlords. As his campaign progressed, the Communist Party made large numbers of conversions. The merchant and landlord classes that formed the basis of Chiang's backing grew fearful of social revolution, and to quiet their fears Chiang began to move against the Communists. Stalin, who believed that the first stage of the Chinese Revolution could only be won through an alliance with the Kuomintang, ordered the Communists to surrender to Chiang. He, however, made plain his attitude toward the Chinese Communists by ordering

Mao Tse-tung, head of the Chinese Communists.

their massacre at Shanghai in 1927. Led by Mao Tse-tung the shattered remnants of the Communist Party began a guerrilla war against a program of encirclement by the Kuomintang.

Stalin's abandonment of Communism as an international movement did, however, allow him to concentrate on internal matters. He began to organize the collectivization of agriculture and introduce the first of his five-year plans.

The New Socialist Offensive 1928

On taking power, Lenin and his associates adopted "War Communism" to convert Russia from an agrarian to an industrial economy, but the results were ineffective and they soon resorted to semicapitalism. On Lenin's death, Stalin took over, slowly centralizing power in his own hands. His one-man rule enabled him to move firmly and ruthlessly, and the First Five Year Plan required both. By it, Stalin collectivized agriculture, built up heavy industry, created a command economy and instituted political totalitarianism in Russia—at the cost of millions of lives. In so doing he created the modern U.S.S.R.

By 1928 Joseph Stalin's mastery over the Communist Party of the Soviet Union was complete, enabling him to control the fate of 150 million people. The launching of the First Five Year Plan that October has been called, with justification, a Third Revolution. It was, in fact, a more fundamental revolution than either of the two revolutions of 1917.

The four elements the plan involved were the collectivization of agriculture, the building of basic heavy industries (on which subsequent Russian industrialization has depended), the imposition of totalitarian party control over the whole of Russian society in a way previously unknown, and the creation of the command economy. This economic system replaced the market and price mechanism of a capitalist economy—in which the needs of consumers determine production through supply and demand—with a gigantic system of administrative controls. It allowed the rulers to decide what was produced, and then to allocate this as they saw fit—to further investment, for state military requirements or to consumers.

For the first time in history, the socialist alternative to the market economy was put into effective operation. The previous attempt to do so, immediately after the Revolution in the period known as "War Communism," had not been effective. The four elements of the Third Revolution were all linked together; none could have been realized without the three others, and together they made up a coherent system, which has since governed the development of the Russian economy, society and politics.

Stalin was able to exercise such power because in 1923 Lenin's illness had made him unable to rule. The Russia he had created was in many ways an odd, even a paradoxical, society. It was a peasant, agrarian society, ruled by a tiny elite of socialist ideologists, mainly middle-class intellectuals in origin, who claimed to represent the industrial proletariat, itself only a small minority of the total population. The constitutional framework of soviets, or elected councils, was a sham. Real political power was concentrated in the Communist, formerly known as the Bolshevik, Party, which had suppressed all its rivals. In 1921 even the other socialist parties, the Mensheviks and Social Revolutionaries, had been banned. Lenin believed that it would still be possible to preserve democracy and freedom within the party, but his methods had already created the situation in which the party itself was controlled from the top. The decision of 1921, to allow the Central Committee to expel dissident members, marked the end of genuine freedom of discussion within the party. By 1923 the secret police (G.P.U., later O.G.P.U.) was being used against party members. Soon the whole process of electing party officials and delegates to party congresses was controlled by the Secretariat, that is, by Stalin, who was made General Secretary in 1922 by Lenin.

Stalin moved cautiously at first, as he had much less prestige than his rivals at the top, notably Trotsky, who controlled the army from his position at the War Commissariat and who seemed the obvious successor to Lenin. But Trotsky allowed himself to be outmaneuvered. Stalin first allied himself with two other party leaders, Zinoviev and Kamenev, against Trotsky. When Trotsky had been rendered powerless within the party, Zinoviev and Kamenev belatedly realized that the real victor was Stalin. Trotsky, Zinoviev and Kamenev then tried to form an "anti-Stalin bloc" within the party. But it was too late to challenge his control of the party machinery, and in October, 1926, all three were expelled from the Politburo. They made a pathetic attempt to use methods that had worked in the days of tsarism, setting up an illegal printing press and organizing street demonstrations. This last flicker of organized political opposition in Russia was easily suppressed by the G.P.U. The

Lev Borisovich Kamenev, leading leftist opponent of the compromise N.E.P. and a member of the triumvirate ruling Russia after Lenin's death.

Opposite A billboard calling for increased production in Karelia, 1926. Due to Lenin's partial return to a market economy, production in industry and agriculture had returned to prewar levels.

Working the fields of Soviet
Central Asia, c. 1934. Stalin
forcibly wrenched the
U.S.S.R. into the twentieth
century.

attempt only gave credence to charges of treachery
and allowed Stalin to expel his rivals and their
supporters from the party. The leaders went into
exile in Siberia, and on January 22, 1929, Trotsky
was expelled from the Soviet Union, to begin the
eleven-year journey that was to end with his murder
in Mexico by Stalin's agents.

The essence of this conflict was the personal rivalry
among Lenin's political heirs. However, it took the
form of resolutions debated and voted at the party
congresses in ideological terms regarding the speed
at which the transition to socialism could be
achieved. The left, Trotsky and his supporters,
with Preobrazenski as their economic expert,
demanded a more revolutionary policy in all fields.
On the international scene they opposed Stalin's
policy of cooperation with the bourgeois Kuomintang Party in China and the relatively moderate
policy imposed on the European Communist parties.
Within Russia the left envisaged rapid economic
development based on industrial growth, and the
ending of the existing policy of cooperation with the
peasants. The right, with Bukharin as their main
theoretical spokesman, had the support of Stalin
from 1924 to 1928. Zinoviev and Kamenev had
originally supported Stalin's right-wing position,
but then had swung left in order to join Trotsky
against him.

Once Stalin had defeated his rivals he adopted
an even more extreme left-wing line than they had
advocated. There is no comparison between the
revolutionary ruthlessness imposed by Stalin in the
First Five Year Plan, and the much more modest
proposals advocated by the left in the inner-party
debate of the previous years, then rejected by Stalin
as unrealistic.

To understand the problems debated by the
party in these years a recapitulation of Russia's
economic history since 1917 is necessary. Marxist
theory before 1917 had been based on the assumption that socialism could only develop when capitalist society had reached its apogee, using the most
advanced technology and methods of mass production, and when vast amounts of capital had been
accumulated by the "exploiters." Russia did have
a small industrial sector that had been developing
rapidly in the last years of tsarism, but it was still
far behind Western European countries. Lenin had
turned Marxism on its head by seizing power in the
name of the industrial proletariat in a predominantly
rural and peasant society. Thus, the Communist
Party, instead of taking over a developed capitalist
economy, was faced with the task of stimulating and
controlling the industrial revolution that had been
produced in the West by capitalism in the nineteenth
century.

The Communists at first thought this industrial
revolution could be achieved almost at once,
showing almost total ignorance of both economics
and technology. "Communism," declared Lenin
in 1920, "is Soviet power plus electrification." He
expected miracles from the introduction of electricity, when oil for the peasants' lamps would have
been more appropriate. The first three years after

Lenin's seizure of power saw the virtual breakdown of the economy, resulting from these attempts to introduce a completely socialist system when the necessary administrative machinery was lacking, and the physical possibilities of production were severely limited due to the World War and the civil war.

In March, 1921, however, Lenin's realistic side reasserted itself, and he announced the New Economic Policy, a strategic retreat at least halfway back to the market economy. The essence of the N.E.P. was the abandonment of the attempt to force the peasants to deliver a certain portion of their crop to the state, in return for an allocation of industrial goods which usually did not arrive. Peasants were allowed to sell their produce, after paying a fixed tax to the government, either to state buying agencies or to private traders. This was only part of a general return to a market economy. Most large-scale industry remained nationalized, but small firms were allowed to be run for private profit. It was no longer illegal for an individual to hire labor, and private employers reappeared both in agriculture and industry. Even the nationalized industries bought and sold between themselves, and to the general public, at prices fixed by supply and demand. Russia's partial return to a capitalist economy produced an economic miracle. Production in both agriculture and industry recovered from the abysmal levels of 1920–21, and by 1926 was back to prewar levels. But the N.E.P. was always seen as merely a strategic retreat after which would follow a further advance to socialism. The argument between right and left in the party concerned the rate and methods of this progress.

The main problem was the acquisition of resources from the private sector, consisting essentially of peasants, for investment in the public sector of large-scale nationalized industry. An agricultural surplus was required to feed an expanding industrial work force, and to export in order to pay for new machinery from the West. The right argued that this surplus could be gained by offering the peasants better industrial goods, thus encouraging them to market more grain, and could lead to the balanced growth of the whole economy. The trouble from a socialist point of view was that this meant the strengthening of the capitalist elements in the economy—this being the richer peasants who hired laborers and alone were able to offer much surplus for sale. To be effective this policy would have necessitated a reversion to a more capitalist economy, causing a weakening of the party's political control, and a general relaxation of ideological fervor and dynamism. In the end it probably would have meant the return to a more liberal system of government. On these grounds the policy was opposed by Trotsky and the left, but they did not offer an effective alternative. Coercion of the peasants had been tried in 1920 and had failed. The peasants, finding that surplus crops were confiscated, had sown only enough for their own immediate needs.

Beginning in 1929, Stalin's ruthless genius pro-

The first electric bulb is lit in a village of the Bryansk Gubernia, 1928.

vided a way out of this dilemma in the form of collectivization, a solution not tried in 1919–20. By forcing the peasants into huge collective farms, cultivation of crops was controlled by party members sent out into the countryside. It did not matter that production fell disastrously. Under the new system the state's requirements came first: vast quantities of grain were collected to feed the towns, and for export to the West at rock-bottom prices. Millions of peasants starved to death, while grain was dumped onto the world market at the bottom of the Depression, driving the world price even lower. Primary produce such as grain and timber was all Russia could offer to pay for the imports of Western machinery. Between five and six million people perished, half of them in the Ukraine, in the worst peacetime famine of modern times. A further three million peasants, were dragged away to slave labor camps, from which few were freed.

Not only grain production suffered; cattle and horses were either killed by the peasants or died in the chaos collectivization produced. Not until long after the end of World War II did the livestock of Russia return to the 1929 level. Agricultural production revived to some extent when the peasants were allowed to cultivate small private plots and to keep a few animals of their own in a modern version of serfdom, but agriculture remains today, as in 1929, the Achilles' heel of the Russian economy.

The second part of the Third Revolution of 1928–32 involved the creation of vast new heavy industrial complexes. The years of the First Five Year Plan

French cartoon of the *Soviet Paradise*, 1935.

Left Advertising the progress of the Five Year Plan. A barrage of propaganda accompanied the systematic terror and economic chaos.

Opposite Poster showing the development of the economy. Child-care amenities enable women to participate in the socialist reconstruction.

saw so much disorganization and chaos, and their statistics have been so falsified for propaganda purposes, that it is impossible to say with any certainty what happened to production. But it is clear that the goals of the plan, in any of its versions, were not attained. The overambitious aims of the First Plan were several times increased, in the spirit of Stalin's dictum, "There are no fortresses Bolsheviks cannot storm," and the first draft of the Second Five Year Plan called for even greater production. The result was the disastrous year of 1933, in which disequilibrium among the different parts of the economy was so great that production no longer increased. A more realistic analysis eventually prevailed and in the Second Five Year Plan, as redrafted and submitted to the Seventeenth Party Congress in 1934, the production figures were revised downward. This period saw the beginning of a more realistic approach to the actual management of a bureaucratic command economy. It is best, therefore, in estimating the industrial growth of Russia to look at the entire period 1928–40.

Favorable weather and a good harvest in the year 1937 represented the high point of this period. After 1937 the economy was again disorganized, first by the purges and then by the war. During the period 1926–39 the number of industrial workers in Russia increased from 15 million to 45 million and the production of the main items of industrial raw materials and energy increased as follows:

				1928	1940
Coal	(million metric tons)			35·8	166
Pig iron	,,	,,	,,	3·4	15
Steel	,,	,,	,,	4·3	18·3
Oil	,,	,,	,,	11·5	31
Electricity	(billion Kwh.)			5·1	48·3

This was an industrial revolution in the real sense of the term. The capitalist countries had never seen such a rapid transition from a traditional and largely agricultural economy to a modern, large-scale factory system. In these years were laid the bases for the subsequent development of the Russian economy after World War II. It was also important that much industrial development was on sites east of the Urals, where it remained safe during the war.

This massive increase in industrial production was achieved by the switch of the economy from consumption to investment. More than twenty percent of the total national income was devoted to investment, such as the building of factories that produced steel in order to build more factories. The industrial base was not allowed to turn toward consumer goods until after Stalin's death more than twenty years later. There was an enormous fall in the standard of living, shown in most dramatic form by the deaths of millions of peasants, and the

Smiling peasants handing in their applications to enter collective farms in Byelorussia, 1931. Collectivization, in fact, was rigorously enforced and three million peasants were deported to labor camps.

enrollment of millions more in slave labor camps. This fall in living standards was also seen in the effect inflation had on wages for the industrial workers of the towns. Wages actually increased, but prices went much higher, and real wages were cut by half. Only a minimal amount of investment was devoted to new housing, and the rapid increase in the urban population resulted in a great decline in housing standards, one room per family becoming the norm. Only long after World War II did the housing available in large cities return to the standards of tsarist times.

The other important factor in the increased production was that the Russian economy in 1929 was so far behind the advanced capitalist countries in technological advances. Thus huge gains in productivity resulted from adopting modern methods, despite the inefficient bureaucratic planning methods of the command economy.

The third element of Stalin's revolution was the creation of an administrative system to run the economy. Under the control of the State Planning Commission (G.O.S.P.L.A.N.), which decided production goals, an enormous bureaucratic system developed to run the different industries, to set goals for individual factories, to reward managers who attained them, and to punish those who failed.

Theorists of the socialist economy have worked out ingenious systems of equations by which such a system could optimize its performance by dovetailing the millions of interconnections involved. Such academic exercises were far removed from the "heroic" planning of the First Five Year Plan, which involved little more than continued exhortation to produce more basic industrial materials. The gross distortions—a country littered with half-built factories and machines, inoperable because of the lack of raw materials—and the overloading of the railway system led to more attention to the problem of dovetailing different economic sectors in the Second Five Year Plan. By a process of trial and error a working system of economic allocation by the administrative hierarchy developed. It worked, albeit not efficiently. Adherents of *laissez-faire* economics, who had argued that bureaucratic allocation of resources could not work, were proved wrong. It could work, but only at enormous cost; the doubters were only wrong because they had no inkling of the degree of political control possible for a ruthless dictatorial party, and of the deprivation such a party could impose on the population in the name of Socialism.

The fourth component of Stalin's revolution was political. The party had used violence against

opponents since 1917, but it reached a new level of tyranny in these years. The countryside, home of the great majority of the population, was brought under party control for the first time. The tendency toward relaxation, after the fervor of the first revolutionary years, was now reversed. A new atmosphere of desperate struggle against a hostile world of foreign capitalists, reactionary peasants and apathetic non-party workers, was created. There could be no room, it seemed, for inner party debate; party unity and obedience to the leader were necessary. Thus party control over all aspects of life and over all Russia was strengthened, and Stalin's control over the party reinforced. Non-party specialists, who had played an important role in the 1920s, were arrested and found guilty in trials staged to show them as "saboteurs," or disappeared without a trace. The whole atmosphere of desperate struggle, the battle for the creation of socialism, was an essential element in the evolution of Russia into a completely totalitarian society. The arbitrary arrests and concentration camps, initially used for non-party members, were eventually to be used on party members themselves in the great purges of 1936–39, when Stalin fully developed the potentialities of the instruments he had forged for personal control of an entire society.

Thus Stalin launched the Russian economy and society onto the path it has followed ever since. He produced something unknown since the Pharaohs devoted so much of the manpower of ancient Egypt to the building of the pyramids. He created an economic system whose main aim was not the satisfaction of individual human wants, but the fulfillment of production goals which to the rulers were ends in themselves. The Russian economy became one of conspicuous production; the aim was to produce ever more spectacular figures of economic growth. Until Stalin's death, the only other aim of the economic system was the production of military hardware.

Stalin's economic system served both these purposes with remarkable success. His successors, however, have found it difficult to produce the goods consumers actually want, at the right time and place, and in the appropriate quantities. It is now clear that the spectacular annual figures for economic growth, which used to be flaunted at the "flagging" capitalist economic system, bore very little relation to the growth of real welfare. Perhaps the most ironic victory for Stalin is that an ever larger gross national product is now accepted even in capitalist countries as a sensible aim of economic policy.

D. R. WATSON

Harvesting in Russia, October, 1923. Stalin's Five Year Plan caused a disastrous drop in agricultural output—millions of peasants died of starvation —and production did not return to the levels of Lenin's N.E.P. until after World War II.

Above left A young woman member of Komsomol repairing a machine. Stalin's program of massive indust-rialization effected a true industrial revolution, laying the basis for Russia's subsequent economic development.

121

Russian collectives

Having won the struggle for power within the Communist Party, Stalin ruthlessly began thrusting barbaric, semi-Asian Russia into the twentieth century. By the end of the 1920s, the Communists realized that drastic action was necessary to solve Russia's economic problems. The New Economic Policy had brought production back to prewar levels, but they knew that capital was necessary if the economy were to expand further. The world's credit was closed to Russia, and so capital would have to be accumulated within Russia itself. Such a goal could only be achieved by drastic reductions in domestic consumption, and this in itself involved an enormous problem. The Bolshevik Revolution had originally been a proletarian revolution of urban industrial workers bent on the socialization of property, but because the industrial proletariat was

agriculture was fragmented into millions of small holdings, the rate of production necessary for economic expansion could never be reached.

In 1929, Stalin embarked upon a program of forced collectivization of agriculture to solve the dual problems of increasing production and socializing the peasantry. Trotsky and Grigori Zinoviev had long advocated the need for a collectivized system of agriculture, one which they suggested could be built gradually by first setting up model collectives that would convince the peasants of the benefits of collectivization. Stalin brutally implemented this scheme. He ordered villages surrounded by companies of machine gunners who herded the villagers into collectives that often had no tractors or fertilizers. At the same time, the First Five Year Plan in industry was begun. Peasants were uprooted to work under harsh factory conditions and were forced to live in hovels in shantytowns. Ruthless

run Russian industry was to reap the benefits of the regimen imposed by Stalin. Other aspects of Stalinism had more tragic results. In his passion to protect Russia from a hostile capitalist world, the Soviet leader subjugated foreign Communist parties to the needs of Russia's domestic policy.

In a world hit by the Great Depression, the opportunities offered the Communist movement were many. But Stalin, who feared that a global upheaval might damage Russia's plans for reconstruction, refused to sanction all-out revolutionism by the parties of the Comintern. He shattered working-class solidarity by authorizing attacks on non-Communist workers' parties, and in all corners of Europe that directive fostered the growth of Fascism. In Germany, for example, the Communist Party might have rallied the German working class by cooperation with Social Democrats. Instead, they helped the Nazis destroy the government's followers.

The "Black Bottom," a dance of the 1920s.

and insecurity. Before it was over the decade was to witness the beginnings of political terror in Soviet Russia, the emergence of Nazi gangsterism in German politics, a great general strike in Britain and revolutionary rumblings in China and India. The war left in its wake the economic uncertainties of dwindling credit and rising unemployment. And the aftermath of the Versailles Treaty saw the beginnings of a new quest for security by Western diplomats. Portents of a second war loomed.

Economic insecurity affected an enormous number of people. The war left a much-impoverished Europe, and Europe's poverty affected most of the rest of the world. The demographic cost, in terms of those killed and those not born because of the war has been estimated at twenty million. Death on such a large scale—an entire generation of young men had died for their countries in a war that had brought little benefit and great suffering—had a catastrophic effect.

Before the Depression

According to popular myth, the decade of the 1920s was a rowdy, rollicking era between World War I and the Great Depression. The decade has consequently acquired a sort of happy-go-lucky glamor, symbolized by the flapper, the "good-time girl" of the speakeasy, whose search for pleasure was probably an expression of postwar anxiety. But the almost legendarily vice-ridden Berlin in the Weimar Republic is a better symbol of the period.

Behind the sequined façade of the Jazz Age lay a world of violence

Board members of a new collective farm.

small and weak, the Bolsheviks had increasingly identified themselves with the peasants. In fact, it was the sheer weight of peasant discontent that overthrew the Tsar. But the peasant was only an inadvertent revolutionary, one whose main aim was the personal ownership of land. Thus the Bolshevik Revolution was based upon a contradiction between the socialist revolution of the towns and the bourgeois revolution of the countryside. Socialism could not be built until the peasantry ceased to be a conservative property-owning force. And as long as Russian

drill and discipline forced them into the routine of modern industry. In the country, peasant groups responded by slaughtering livestock and burning crops; in the towns, by smashing machinery. Stalin replied with a comprehensive system of terror that prevented rebellion by destroying all sense of security. Midnight arrests, torture and imprisonment became common.

The price paid by the Russian people for industrialization was large in terms of cultural sterility, loss of personal freedom and drab living conditions. But in the long

During the Jazz Age some women were able to shake off the restrictions of convention.

Gold bullion bars. The collapse of the New York stock market and the subsequent depression forced many nations to abandon the Gold Standard.

Trading on the floor of the Stock Exchange.

1929 is that so many thousands of Americans had been seized during the previous years by the fever of speculation (which pushed them into investments well beyond their resources) that a disastrous finale was inevitable. Bernard Baruch referred to the "frenzy of stock market gambling that preceded the 1929 crash [as] a reflection of the curious psychology of crowds which has been demonstrated again and again in human history." Those who were in New York in 1929 recall how obsessed the whole city seemed, bankers and brokers, taxi drivers and shop assistants, with the possibility of growing rich overnight by dealing in shares. Speculation ran wild, indulged by the bland optimism of most of America's political and financial leaders.

The prices of shares had begun to climb in 1927, and in 1928 the boom moved into top gear and finally lost touch with industrial reality. More and more people began not only to invest in shares in the confident hope of rapid gain but to invest on borrowed money. The practice of margin trading—that is, buying additional stock with money borrowed against previously purchased shares—became commonplace. The interest paid by margin trading was so high that it in turn attracted a rising volume of finance into New York.

Meanwhile, the small investor's position was made more dangerous by the fact that the industrial boom

in America—soundly based a few years before on increasing productivity and the rising sales of such products as cars, houses and electrical equipment—was tailing off. A disastrous paradox was emerging: anyone with a rudimentary knowledge of economics knew that the value of shares ultimately depended upon the prosperity and earnings of the companies in which they were held—but as shares rose to new speculative heights in the United States in 1928 and 1929, industrial prosperity was faltering.

There seem to have been two main reasons for the Depression in the United States: the saturation of the market for industrial goods and the policy of the financial authorities (which aimed at keeping prices and wages steady and, as a result, directed the benefits of rising productivity into profits without stimulating fresh consumer demand). By mid-1929, there were fairly clear signs of overproduction. Moreover, there were serious weaknesses in the country's financial and economic structure, weaknesses that the Great Crash was sharply to expose. According to Professor Galbraith, those flaws were: the inequitable distribution of income, which gave too much economic influence to investment and luxury spending; a corrupt company structure, with too many grafters and swindlers; an archaic banking structure, overstretched and overfragmented; the persistent surplus in American trade, leading to an

influx of gold into the United States and an outflow of dubiously secured loans; and the poor economic thinking on the part of those in authority. These factors served to worsen and to prolong the Depression once it was truly launched by the Great Crash.

Like the toppling of great financial empires in the United States in the autumn of 1929, the exposure in England, a short while before, of the swindles of Clarence Hatry (who built up a great business empire that foundered on forgery) made industry more vulnerable to the onset of depression. But Europe's economic weaknesses, so glaringly revealed by the financial collapse of 1929, could be traced back to the end of World War I, eleven years earlier.

Economic historians point to a tangle of events and errors that made a slump of some kind almost inevitable. World War I had left a sorry legacy of dislocated world trade, along with vast problems of war debts and reparations. It also brought about a substantial increase in production of raw materials and foodstuffs, which led to surpluses and sagging commodity prices when the war was over, and in turn to less demand for industrial products. Agricultural gluts were further increased by improvements in farming techniques and science.

The financial systems of the major industrial countries grew more and more unstable. In particular, Germany was forced to borrow from the United States to pay for reparations; France suffered from the flight of capital abroad; and the United Kingdom struggled unsuccessfully to rebuild its position as the world's great source of capital. For a time, the system was held together largely by American willingness to send money abroad. But when the Stock Exchange boom tempted investors to keep their dollars at home, where they earned more, the pressure on debtor nations to cut back on their imports and increase their earnings at each other's expense became immense. The Great Crash was like a match applied to high explosives.

In 1934, a few years after the Crash, Professor Robbins of the London School of Economics reflected the shocked reaction to the Great Depression that is still discernible in the attitudes of millions of people today. The world depression that followed the stock market crash, he wrote:

… has dwarfed all preceding movements of a similar nature both in magnitude and in intensity. … Production in the chief manufacturing countries of the world shrank by anything from 30 to 50 percent, and the volume of world trade in 1932 was only a third of what it was three years before. It has been calculated by the International Labor Office that in 1933, in the world at large, something like 30 million persons were out of work. There have been many depressions in modern economic history, but it is safe to say there has never been anything to compare with this.

In Europe, the financial crisis was triggered by the collapse of Austria's largest bank—the Credit-Anstalt—early in 1931. Banking assets held in Austria were immediately affected, notably those of the German banks that felt the first shock. Despite British and American efforts to help the Germans

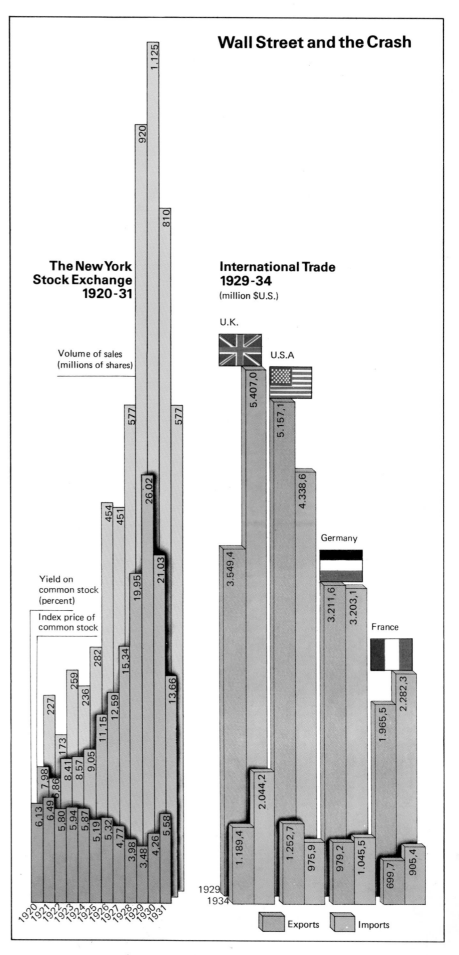

Wall Street and the Crash

The New York Stock Exchange 1920-31

Volume of sales (millions of shares)

Yield on common stock (percent)

Index price of common stock

International Trade 1929-34
(million $U.S.)

U.K.

U.S.A

Germany

France

1929
1934

Exports   Imports

Right Crowds waiting to hear the latest news outside the Stock Exchange at the height of the crisis.

financially, the Reichsbank was forced to impose controls on foreign exchange, and this in turn prompted panic withdrawals of funds from London and other financial centers in Europe. As confidence in Britain's abilities to sustain its industry and maintain the Gold Standard was eroded, and as the country's financial reserves ebbed away, the only solution seemed to be the formation of a National Government. This was followed by the abandonment of the Gold Standard in September, 1931.

For Germany, the Depression meant the final loss of American finance and a swift rise in unemployment, the latter being one of the factors that helped the Nazi Party climb to power and led to Adolf Hitler's assumption of the chancellorship in 1933. For the United States, the Crash brought about the New Deal policies of President Roosevelt. In Japan, the Depression caused a rise in unemployment, possibly to as high as 3 million. The Japanese economy was still heavily agricultural, while industry relied

for its basic labor on thousands of small workshops. The shock of the Depression stimulated Japanese industry to achieve a vigorous expansion in the 1930s, chiefly through the development of heavy industry and exports, which were stimulated by government subsidies, protection and low wages.

In these ways, the Great Crash on Wall Street helped to shape the world economic and political structure in the 1930s. The years 1929–34 were a true watershed of history. The 1920s, for all the problems that existed—and despite a shaky world economy and the lingering shock caused by the slaughter of World War 1—were years tinged with optimism. Universal peace seemed within grasp. The problems of industry were grave but also, most people seemed to believe, soluble by free societies. The Soviet Union, the great dissenter, stood aside, revealing only its progressive aspects to the few admirers from the West.

In the economic field, the belief that the clock should and could be put back was nicely exemplified by Britain's return to the Gold Standard in 1925, a decision announced by its Chancellor of the Exchequer, Winston Churchill. But the return to the Gold Standard heralded increasing financial turbulence, not a return to the calm and prosperity of the days before World War 1. For the Gold Standard had been effect as much as cause: it had worked before 1914 because of comparative political stability, economic confidence, and the steady flow of gold discoveries. And it had worked because of the industrial lead established by Great Britain as center of the Empire and creator of the Industrial Revolution, a lead that enabled the City of London

Selling a car to raise money. Many hard-pressed investors were forced to take even more drastic steps.

$100 WILL BUY THIS CAR MUST HAVE CASH LOST ALL ON THE STOCK MARKET

President Roosevelt, who faced the task of reconstruction after the Depression.

to finance world trade with supreme confidence, based on fairly small gold reserves.

The 1930s were the years of slump, mass unemployment, protection, increasingly bitter class warfare, and a desperate nationalism that fostered the totalitarianisms of Germany, Italy and Japan. Those movements won sympathizers for reasons that included the disillusionment of millions with the capacity of liberal capitalism to withstand the challenge of Communism. In the 1920s, men still tended to look back to the partly imaginary halcyon days of pre-World War I and to believe that these could be restored. The Great Depression shattered those imaginings: there was clearly no going back. The choice in the 1930s seemed to be to go forward to the controlled societies of either Fascism or Communism. Only after World War II did the strength of modern capitalism, reformed by welfare and by Keynesian economic ideas that had been rejected in the late 1920s, emerge as a challenging and highly successful contender for men's allegiances.

The kind of abuses that led to Black Thursday and its aftermath would be impossible in the established stock exchanges of the world today, since regulations are stricter and perhaps economies more balanced, even if people are no less greedy and gullible. But for millions, those abuses are a symbol of the black side of financial capitalism. For many others, by no means hostile to free enterprise, they are a reminder that the price of prosperity, like the price of freedom, is constant vigilance.

GEORGE BULL

Above The front page of the *Boston Daily Globe* on Friday, October 25, 1929. The Crash did not immediately affect the attitudes of investment analysts, as the stockbroker's advertisement at the foot of the page shows.

Below Brokers relaxing on the floor of the Exchange in mid-October, 1929. The Crash wiped the smiles from many faces.

Economic instability gives an added luster

Recession

The administration of Herbert Hoover was stunned by the great stock-market collapse and failed to see the impact that it would have on the American economy. In any case, Hoover found his ability to maneuver severely circumscribed by sharply declining revenues from taxation in 1930 and 1931, and this in turn caused a deterioration in government services, which added to the problems of the Depression. By 1930 there were more than three million unemployed, and the number continued to rise rapidly, reaching a peak of about thirteen million in the winter of 1932–33.

It was only in 1932 that the administration began to take any action to relieve the situation, and it was only pressure from a new Democratic-controlled Congress that forced the reluctant President to take action. Unemployment benefit, which Hoover had recently denounced as a "gigantic pork-barrel" was begun, a Reconstruction Finance Corporation was set up and the Federal reserve system was reformed. But Hoover had acted too late and done too little. The close links between the Hoover administration and the corruption of big business added to public discontent. In the fall of 1932 a series of revelations of business scandals helped the Democrats; Hoover received no more than 59 electoral votes out of a total of 517 and Franklin Delano Roosevelt was swept into office in an electoral landslide unequaled until the 1960s.

In the wake of the Great Depression

Before the Great Depression, Europe was already experiencing major economic and political upheavals. Social and economic troubles had brought Mussolini to power in Italy, had fed Nazi propaganda in the Weimar Republic and had produced a general strike in Britain. But it was the crash of the American stock market that really crippled the world's economies, for as a market and supplier of capital the United States was foremost in the world. The Crash hit America worst—national income fell thirty-eight percent between 1929 and 1932—but other nations suffered almost

Addressing the masses in Munich.

as badly as a result of the collapse of world trade. As America withdrew capital from abroad, debtor nations cut their imports, causing prices to plummet. There was less demand for raw material in developed countries and less demand for manufactured goods in underdeveloped countries. International trade ground slowly toward a halt.

It is in the light of this economic disaster that most of the significant events of the 1930s—from the rise of Hitler to the coming of World War II—must be viewed. Until late in the 1930s the world suffered from America's economic collapse. In the big-money years of the Jazz Age, successive u.s. governments had declined to intervene to limit overspeculation. Under President Calvin Coolidge inflation had free range, and industrial production rose so sharply that high-pressure advertising had to be developed to market the surplus goods. But affluence hid poverty. While industry and commerce boomed, farming languished. Agriculture rapidly became a semidepressed sector of the economy, and even before the Crash took its toll, the conditions later described in John Steinbeck's novel *The Grapes of Wrath* (1939) were destroying the small farmers of the Midwest. It

was the same story after the Depression, only in more extreme terms. For the majority, the Crash brought hunger and poverty; for the lucky few, it brought enormous wealth.

After America, Germany was hardest hit by the Depression. Massive unemployment and other miseries following the Crash created a recruiting paradise for extremist groups, and savage street fighting erupted between the Communists and the Nazis. German industrialists began subsidizing Hitler in the hopes that they could use him to destroy socialism.

The instability of the post-Depression years was spread far and wide. Germany owed America more than a billion dollars; Australia owed 181 million; Canada, 164 million. These were all short-term loans and they were called in with catastrophic speed. Australia and Canada were forced to devalue their currencies and to reduce wages, and both suffered a drop in living standards. France did not owe nearly as much, but in the collapse of world trade its economy was badly hit. Economic instability bred political unrest there as elsewhere. France had thirteen changes of government between 1929 and 1933.

The British also suffered badly in terms of unemployment, although many of their problems were caused by the obsolescence of basic industries. Asian competitors were ruining Britain's textile industry, and the coal and steel industries were hit when postwar reconstruction drew to a close and the European railroad network was completed. Political instability of the sort that affected the rest of Europe never hit Britain, but economic problems did produce the British Union of Fascists, called Blackshirts, a fascist group led by Sir Oswald Mosley.

Economic nationalism in South America

Elsewhere, perhaps the most significantly affected area was South America. The Crash underscored Latin America's highly precarious dependence on foreign capital and markets. Aware that their natural resources, properly developed, could provide decent living standards, many governments embarked on policies of economic

Lázaro Cárdenas being greeted by a worker.

nationalism, often based on the corporatism of Mussolini's Fascism. Authoritarian regimes proliferated: in Brazil, the "disciplined democracy" of Getulio Vargas; in the Dominican Republic, the dictatorship of Rafael Trujillo; in Argentina, Augustín Justo's state planning of a New Deal. In Mexico, by way of exception, Lázaro Cárdenas founded his socialist regime on labor support. The Depression brought massive unemployment to South America and shattered working-class living standards by reducing the prices of raw materials, especially coffee. The consequent discontent was often savagely repressed: in El Salvador, by the fascist dictatorship of Hernández Martinez; in Honduras by the military dictator, Tiburcio Carías; and in Guatemala, by the regime of Jorge Ubico.

The Japanese in Asia

Western influence in Asia was largely economic, and the Depression naturally cut back investment there as well. British economic influence declined sharply and the Japanese were able to advance into former British spheres of influence, largely at the expense of the Americans (for whom dominance of the Far East seemed a vital strategic interest). Japan, which had been a major power in Far Eastern affairs from the time of the Sino-Japanese War of 1894–95, suffered a great population

Sir Oswald Mosley, founder of the British Union of Fascists, at a rally.

to fascist and nationalist groups

A demonstration in London against Japanese goods in 1933.

explosion in this period. That increase, coupled with an urgent need for resources, forced Japan to adopt an expansionist foreign policy to provide outlets for both emigration and raw materials.

The overpopulated island empire soon moved against both Manchuria and China—traditional targets of Japanese expansion—and by 1931, Japan had outstripped its Western rivals in China. (This was a relatively easy task because Chiang Kai-shek's weak Kuomintang government was preoccupied with subduing Mao Tse-tung's growing peasant army.) Ruthless Japanese competition had long kept Chinese industry in a subservient position, and while the financial crash reduced the influence of other powers, Japan had avoided most of the worst results of the Depression by a program of large-scale rearmament. Thus, by the time Japan was ready to move into Manchuria in September, 1931, its forces were strong and China's economy, weak. Japan's aggression was the first serious blow to the system of international relations established at Versailles; the League of Nations was unable to effect Japanese withdrawal, and that demonstration of its weakness would encourage similar moves by Hitler and Mussolini.

India

Another area of Asian opposition to Western encroachment was India, where the increasingly militant Congress movement was gaining strength. British government readiness to meet the movement's demands proceeded less from Britain's economic weakness than from the recognition of a growing chorus of discontent. The work of Gandhi —by now called Mahatma, "great souled," by the people—and Nehru in organizing the Congress Party into a mass body with support from the educated middle classes and the peasants was beginning to bear fruit. This highly integrated party, which was rapidly mobilizing the masses, could not be ignored, and in 1926 the British set up the Simon

Indians in Madras protesting against the Simon Commission.

Commission to look into the question of India's readiness for self-government. Indians boycotted the Commission both because it contained no Indians and because it seemed insulting to have an inquiry into their fitness to govern themselves. Motilal Nehru, father of Jawaharlal, said the British were treating the Indians like schoolboys who could go up a class if they were good. The Commission ultimately recommended a measure of pro-

vincial self-government and a federal state structure, and in 1930 a round table conference met in London to discuss these points.

At the conference, Congress leaders demanded immediate self-government and dominion status. Gandhi began his second civil-disobedience campaign by distilling salt from sea water, which symbolically challenged Britain's salt monopoly. Violent riots swept India, and Gandhi and other leaders were arrested. The Mahatma was released in 1931 after he had called off the campaign, and he was invited to London for the second round table conference. While there, he disconcerted George v by appearing at Buckingham Palace "with no proper clothes on and bare knees." The King's parting remark to this saintly leader of millions was: "Remember, Mr. Gandhi, I won't have any attacks on my empire." The conference ground to a halt over the issue of minority representation, but by that time nationalist enthusiasm had dwindled to the point where Gandhi was forced to abandon his policy of civil disobedience.

Dictatorship in Europe

Authoritarian government had become necessary in India, and South America had become a continent of dictatorship, but Europe too had its troubles. The determined belief of police and politicians in most European states that there was a serious threat of socialist revolution had given right-wing groups a valuable boost. Economic instability provided the opportunity for fascist and nationalist groups to attempt coup after coup. In the kingdom composed of Serbia, Croatia, Slovenia, Montenegro and Dalmatia, King Alexander overthrew the constitution, introduced

a monarchical dictatorship and renamed his kingdom Yugoslavia in 1929. There were attempted fascist coups in Finland in 1930 and 1932 and Lithuania adopted a fascist outlook in 1932. The republican government of Spain faced a military rising in 1932, when General José Sanjurjo rebelled briefly in Seville. In Portugal, also in 1932, the junta that had controlled the country since 1926 made Oliveira Salazar Prime Minister.

But it was in Central Europe that fascism and nationalism had dug their roots in deepest. In part this was as a reaction against the unfairness of the Treaty of Versailles. Economic difficulties also played a large part. When relatively prosperous Britain was forced to

Funeral of President Gömbös.

abandon the Gold Standard, which it did in 1931, the problems of Hungary, Germany and Austria were bound to be far greater. In 1932 Julius Gömbös, an anti-Semitic nationalist who admired both Mussolini and Hitler, became premier of Hungary. The threat of a fascist rising in Austria materialized in the wake of the collapse of Credit-Anstalt, the largest bank in the country; although the rising was suppressed, it showed that there was widespread support for fascism.

It was in Germany that fascism was most organized and had its widest electoral appeal. The weakness of the Weimar Republic was in sharp contrast to the clearly formulated views and the activity of the National Socialist Party. By the end of 1932 there were more than thirteen million unemployed in Germany. On January 30, 1933, Hitler became Chancellor of Germany. A month later the Nazis were able to consolidate their power by suspending civil liberties. The excuse for this was the Reichstag fire.

The Burning of the Reichstag

The flames that consumed Germany's parliament building on the night of February 27, 1933, also destroyed the tattered remains of the Weimar Republic—and with it Germany's post-World War I democracy. A young Dutch Communist was arrested and charged with the crime, but by that time the opportune burning of the Reichstag had given Adolf Hitler and his Nazi Party an excuse to seize control of Paul von Hindenburg's tottering regime. On the day after the fire, Hitler—who had been Germany's Chancellor for less than a month—persuaded Hindenburg to sign a decree suspending those sections of the constitution dealing with civil liberties. Hitler moved swiftly in the resulting vacuum, purging Communists and Social Democrats from the government and then moving against trade unions, Jews, intellectuals, pacifists, liberals and dissidents of all kinds. The process of Nazification had begun; before it was ended, it would affect the entire world.

On the night of February 27, 1933, the German parliament building in Berlin, the Reichstag, was set on fire. The culprit apparently was a young Dutch Communist, Marianus van der Lubbe, who was found in the empty building even as the flames were consuming it. Symbolically and in harsh reality, the fire marked the death of German democracy. Called a Communist prelude to revolution, the fire was used as an excuse to destroy the left-wing and democratic forces that still stood in the way of the total Nazification of Germany.

On January 30, 1933, Adolf Hitler had been made German Chancellor as a result of a deal with anti-Republican conservatives who had hoped to use him to destroy the Weimar Republic. Hitler had accepted because his farcical attempt to seize power in 1923 had convinced him that his revolution could best be made with, rather than against, the power of the state. But although he had the Chancellorship, the Nazis were still in a minority. Even at the crest of their popular success in the elections of July, 1932, they had polled only 37 percent of the vote. Hitler's immediate task was to overcome the opposition of the other 63 percent of the German people. New elections were arranged for March 5, 1933. For the first time, the Nazis would have at their disposal state resources of press and radio, together with police rights to smash the meetings of their opponents.

The election campaign built up throughout February, with posters, bonfires, marches and film shows (backed by the naked terror of the brown-shirted thugs of the *Sturmabteilung*, the Nazi militia). Then, at a most opportune moment, came the Reichstag fire. So opportune was it, in fact, that it might almost have been planned by the Nazis themselves. Years of speculation on this point has made it clear that the whole truth will never be known.

Despite the great doubt there may be as to who was responsible, there is none regarding who reaped the benefit. The Nazis had been anxious for something sensational to terrify the public before the election and for an excuse to smash their left-wing rivals. On the day after the fire, Hitler got President Paul von Hindenburg to sign a decree "for the Protection of the People and State" that suspended those sections of the constitution dealing with individual and civil liberties. It was the beginning of the process of *Gleichschaltung*, or "coordination," whereby the whole of German life and culture was to be totally Nazified.

The Reichstag fire was merely an occasion and not a cause, however. Indeed, many historians have seen the events of 1933 as the inevitable outcome of German history. It can hardly be denied that Hitler found his greatest support among educated, respectable people, nor that most of the Nazis' ideas were widely current and eminently respectable before World War I. From the middle of the nineteenth century on, many of these ideas had become intellectual commonplaces in Germany. They sprang both from the hopes placed in German unification and from disappointment when these hopes were not fulfilled. Because Germany remained split into many small states for so long, many thinkers began to search for a cultural German unity. To find it, they were willing to return to a romanticized medieval age.

When Otto von Bismarck achieved political unification in 1871, there was nonetheless bitter disappointment: the new empire failed to provide spiritual unity. The backward-looking search for a cultural unity became more intense. A reaction against the reality of modern Germany began, and a scapegoat was found in the Jews, who symbolized modernity.

Propaganda for the Hitler Youth.

Opposite The burning of the Reichstag on February 27, 1933. Symbolically, and in harsh reality, the fire marked the death of German democracy.

Hermann Göring addressing the Reichstag in September, 1932.

Georgi Dimitrov, an associate of van der Lubbe. After World War II Dimitrov became President of Bulgaria.

Here was a crisis in Germanic culture, and it was not just confined to a few intellectuals. Widespread spiritual despair produced its own prophets, and their books were read by millions. In the 1890s Julius Langbehn published *Rembrandt Als Erzeiher*, a confused essay on Germanism. It asserted the physical superiority of the Germans, argued the need to exterminate lesser races—especially the Jews—and called for a great Führer to lead Germany to greatness. Such ideas were very popular, and by the end of the century the conflict between everyday materialism and the potential spiritual vitality of the German race was a cliché of right-wing thought.

These ideas provided a sympathetic context for the Nazis later on, but the really influential set of ideas was the mixture of racism and social Darwinism propagated by Houston Stewart Chamberlain, an English friend of the Kaiser. In a series of books, notably his *Die Grundlagen des Neunzehnten Jahrhunderts* (*The Foundations of the Nineteenth Century*), he interpreted world history as a ruthless struggle for the survival of the fittest nation and depicted the German race as locked in a mortal struggle with the Jews.

Most of the men behind such ideas were eccentrics, yet they became completely respectable. *Volkish* ("folk," or "nationalist") ideologists, rabidly nationalistic Pan-Germans, and anti-Semites were prominent in the teaching profession. History textbooks under the Empire and the Weimar Republic were soaked in such notions. The *Wandervogel* movement, which gave rise to the world youth hostels, was permeated with anti-Semitism and the leadership cult. The Pan-German League, nationalistic, anti-Jewish and imperialistic, had a considerable influence among generals, admirals, industrialists, civil servants, agriculturalists and university pro-

fessors, who enthusiastically embraced Pan-German schemes for the Germanization of Eastern Europe and for the clearing away of the Slavs. It is not surprising, then, that Hitler was so readily accepted by upper and middle classes.

Between 1909 and 1913, in the doss houses and gutter politics of Vienna, Hitler formed the ruthless ideas that were to bring him to power in the 1930s. There he developed the notion that brutality is the essential life-force; acquired the ability to cheat, lie, deceive and flatter; and gained considerable skill in manipulating others' weaknesses. In Vienna, too, he learned his political stock in trade: his obscene anti-Semitism, his crude social Darwinism, his Pan-German clichés. Added to the unprecedented ruthlessness of his ideas was the manic power of his personality. Many witnesses say that when talking to Hitler, it was impossible to resist falling under the spell of his eyes.

The main factor in Hitler's favor in the twenties and thirties was the sheer weakness of the Weimar Republic. The currency of *Volkish* and anti-Semitic ideas was itself inimical to democracy. But more particularly, in the years of insecurity after 1918, Weimar was physically threatened by both the right and the left wings. The right associated the Republic with surrender and treachery. The aristocracy, the Junker landowners, industrialists, bankers and the officer corps opposed it from the first. Former servicemen, fueled by right-wing propaganda, identified their personal grievances with Germany's humiliation, a resentment that was channeled into violence against the regime. The Social Democrats, the presumed guardians of the Republic, had lost much support by their deal with the German army at the beginning of the regime. Their failure to proceed to social reform left them open to attack by the Communists, who concentrated on creating disorder and confusion in the belief that a revolutionary situation would carry them automatically to power. All they achieved was to increase the unscrupulousness of German political life and to make the way easier for the real cutthroats.

Perhaps the greatest burden carried by the Weimar Republic was its reliance on the German army, which placed it at the mercy of the hostile right and deprived it of support from the left. Throughout the twenties, the army, by its enthusiastic opposition to the left and its ambiguous sympathy toward the right, dangerously hampered the Republic in its freedom of action.

An equally dangerous thorn in the side of the Republic was the judiciary. Political opposition by the left was ruthlessly crushed, thereby discrediting the Republic with its supporters. Attacks by the right, vicious slander and numerous political murders were condoned because the judiciary, permeated with *Völkish* and Pan-German ideas, felt that these attacks were more patriotic than was support for the democratic Republic.

In this environment, Hitler began building his movement. The support of veteran Ernst Röhm brought him former servicemen for his paramilitary s.a., as well as the patronage of the Bavarian authorities. At the same time, Hitler was attaining a mastery of propaganda, of simple repetitions, of black-and-white statements. Believing that passion and aggression attract the masses, he developed a technique of verbal violence. Virulent posters, salutes, uniforms and a hierarchy of command gave his movement a veneer of power. Mass meetings created a sense of belonging. Gang fights and the smashing of opponents' meetings gave an impression of irresistible strength.

Hitler's debut on the national stage came in 1923. The French had occupied the Ruhr to speed up reparations payments, and the German government had replied by encouraging passive resistance. More paper money was printed to make good the wages of Ruhr workers, and an already inflationary situation spiraled absurdly. When Chancellor Gustav Stresemann made the sensible and courageous decision to recommence reparations, the right howled about betrayal.

In Bavaria several groups toyed with the idea of overthrowing the Republic. Hitler in particular worked his supporters into such a state that even when the Berlin government began to master its difficulties, he could not draw back. After trying to take over the government of Bavaria, Hitler marched his troops into Munich. But the police and the German army for once held firm, and the Nazis lost their nerve. It was a total fiasco—yet Hitler managed to profit from it. Above all, he learned that power could not be taken without the support of the establishment and the army. At the same time, he turned his trial into a political triumph before the press of Germany and the rest of the world. With the compliance of the judges, he put the prosecution witnesses in the dock, indicted the Republic, and gained much praise from the right wing for his forthright declaration of war on democracy.

Hitler received a five-year sentence, of which he served only nine months. During his imprisonment, he began the dictation of *Mein Kampf*. The royalties from that book were to be his main income for the next few years, for after the 1923 crisis, things improved for the Republic and simultaneously went badly for the Nazis. Membership in the party increased slowly, but Hitler kept it together until his big break came in 1929.

Stresemann was then negotiating to fix reparations for fifty-nine years in return for evacuation of the Rhineland. The parties of the right—Alfred Hugenberg's Nationalists, Class' Pan-Germans, Franz Seldte's *Stahlhelm* veterans party—were joining in a huge protest. Hitler was enlisted to drum up mass support. The campaign failed to stop implementation of the Young Plan—by which Germany was to pay reparations over a period of fifty-nine years on a graded scale—but the resources of Alfred Hugenberg's vast newspaper empire made Hitler a national figure and attracted for him the attention of industry and big business.

This attention put Hitler in a strong position when the Depression broke out at the end of 1929. Unem-

ployment rocketed to 3 million in September, 1930, and to 6 million the following year. Again the middle classes were hit. The loss of their respectability enabled Hitler to exploit their fears and resentments. For the elections in September, 1930, the Nazis launched a violent campaign. Slogans, posters, demonstrations, rallies, mob oratory gave the impression that the Nazis were the party of energy, determination and success—a party that could get Germany out of its economic chaos. Hitler offered the middle classes the nationalistic, virile solution that they had previously found only in their *Völkish*

Left Policemen looking at the gutted Reichstag.

Marianus van der Lubbe, the young Dutchman who was supposedly responsible for the Reichstag fire. Göring later said "The only one who knows about the Reichstag is I, because I set it on fire."

A room in the Reichstag. Within minutes of the start of the fire, the whole building was ablaze.

Adolf Hitler, Reichsführer. "We may go under but we will take the whole world with us."

reading. He gave them objects for their resentments: the French, the corrupt politicians of the Weimar Republic, Jewish speculators. Nazi propaganda appealed to everyone, in particular the youth of Germany. In the elections, the Nazis received 107 seats, making them the second largest party in the Reichstag.

The increasing precariousness of the government encouraged the Nazis to attack it. At the same time, Hitler was consolidating support with the conservative right, whose members found his extremism distasteful but who were basically sympathetic to his ideas. In September, 1930, he made an open overture to the army during a trial of officers accused of spreading Nazi propaganda. He spoke flatteringly of the great German army and promised that a Nazi regime would build a huge one. Nazi strength was attractive to General Kurt von Schleicher, the power behind the German army, who was trying to organize a government satisfactory to the armed forces. Schleicher had hopes of using the Nazis to build a strong government. Hitler, for his part, began to realize that for all his increased strength

he was no nearer power, and so he grew more sympathetic to a partnership with those who could get power for him.

As 1932 approached, the economic crisis worsened—and in state elections the Nazis polled 35 percent of the votes. Hitler resisted overtures from Schleicher because he hoped to gain an absolute majority in the national elections in March. The campaign was fought with unprecedented bitterness. The Communists weakened the left by attacking the Social Democrats on orders from Moscow. A huge push with posters, films, records, marches and rallies brought the Nazi vote to 11.5 million, and in the April reelection the vote increased to 13.5 million. Yet Hitler was still faced with the problem of how to turn an electoral success that fell short of a majority to political advantage.

At this stage Schleicher adopted the tragic role of *deus ex machina*. He informed the Chancellor, Heinrich Brüning, that Brüning no longer enjoyed the support of the army. Schleicher, who felt it his duty to the Reich to find a strong chancellor, drafted Franz von Papen, a conservative dandy. But von Papen and his cabinet of barons were so unpopular that they had to rule by presidential decree. Meanwhile, the Nazis unleashed a wave of violence. On July 17, at Altona, 19 people were killed and 285 wounded. Schleicher and von Papen used the incident as an excuse to remove the Social Democratic government of Prussia, one of the last bastions of the Republic. In the July elections, the Nazis received 230 seats, making them the strongest single party. Yet they were as far away from power as ever. The S.A. was getting restless, but Hitler was determined to gain power legally. The Nazis demonstrated their indispensability to the government in September when they voted with a Communist motion of censure against von Papen. However, in the elections that followed von Papen's defeat, the Nazis, while they remained the largest party, lost 2 million votes. Their myth of inevitable success was broken, and von Papen was confident that another election would see their downfall. Unfortunately for von Papen, Schleicher decided to intervene at this stage. He was jealous of von Papen's growing independence and of his influence over President Hindenburg, and he was annoyed at the hostility between von Papen and the Nazis, since his object in giving von Papen power had been to get Nazi support for strong government. Schleicher therefore told Hindenburg that von Papen's policy of doing without the Nazis could not work. On December 2, 1932, Schleicher became Chancellor himself, confident that he could both get the support of the Nazis and keep them under control.

Schleicher was to be defeated by the same sort of intrigue as that which had brought him to power. Hitler was making a deal with von Papen, and between them they could muster the support for a government, which Schleicher could not. Hindenburg was impressed by the extent of the Nazis' electoral backing. By January 20, it was obvious that Schleicher's attempt to build a national front had

Hitler with Paul von Hindenburg, Germany's President, on January 29, 1933. On the following day Hindenburg asked Hitler to form a government.

A military parade in the 1930s. Hitler bought the support of the army by promising to modernize and enlarge it.

failed. When he asked for emergency powers, Hindenburg refused. Hitler by this time had also secured the support of Hugenberg's Nationalists. On January 28, Schleicher resigned; on the thirtieth Hindenburg offered Hitler the chancellorship.

Hitler had made it. Von Papen was as confident of controlling him as Schleicher had been. But with the power of the state behind Hitler, there would be no moving him. The aftermath of the Reichstag fire showed his determination to destroy his enemies and entrench his own power. Hitler had gained power by the skill and unscrupulousness with which he had exploited the selfishness of the right, the complaisance of the army, the weakness of the left, and the general confusion of the period. Yet there was more to his victory than trickery. The fact remains that the Nazis received more votes than any other party. There was widespread sympathy for them throughout the right, and enthusiastic support among the middle classes.

Hitler might have been unique in his sheer unscrupulousness, but there were other parties of the right near enough to him to suggest that the Nazis were far from being a lone aberration of German politics. If they were unique, it was in the intensity of their urge for naked power. Indeed, the real significance of the Reichstag fire may be seen to be its illustration of this. In 1932, Hitler said to Hermann Rauschning: "We shall never capitulate. We may go under but we will take a whole world with us." On the day that he was made Chancellor, he said: "No power in the world will ever get me out of here alive." The Reichstag fire was the prelude to a series of events, from the liquidation of the Jews to World War II, which showed that Hitler meant exactly what he said.   PAUL PRESTON

M. Hitler déclare la paix au monde.

Above Hitler declares peace on the world, a French cartoon published in 1936.

Hitler ascending the steps at the beginning of the Nürnberg rally, 1933.

The Nazification of Germany

The emergency decree signed by President Hindenburg on the day after the Reichstag fire gave Hitler free rein to begin the Nazification of Germany. A series of political purges followed. The most significant of these was the Night of the Long Knives, June 30, 1934. On that night, Ernst Röhm and a number of other leaders of the leftist group known as the *Sturmabteilung* ("stormtroopers"), or simply the S.A., were hauled from their beds and shot. At the time the S.A. was locked in an intense rivalry with the German army, and Röhm had aroused the jealousy of both Hermann Göring and Heinrich Himmler. The army, overjoyed at the removal of the S.A., swore its undying loyalty to Hitler. (That loyalty would not be shaken until after Hitler had overrun most of Europe and his army faced defeat at Stalingrad.) The German army was not the only group that supported Hitler with equanimity. When Hindenburg died in August,

Persecution of the Jews in Germany in the 1930s: a Jewish woman, sitting on a bench marked "Only for Jews," hides her face.

1934, a ninety percent majority of the German people approved Hitler's assumption of the presidency.

Most Germans regarded the Nazi regime with hope and confidence. The violence that had helped bring it to power was ignored and few took any notice of the danger signals. Indeed the destruction of the S.A. seemed a portent, suggesting that Hitler would now firmly eschew extra-legal violence. Only a minority of liberals, pacifists and

Jews lived in terror of the Gestapo and concentration camps; the majority rejoiced over Hitler's intention to make Germany a great military power once again and to free it from the shackles of the Treaty of Versailles. The promise of economic change and improvement led the German public to accept the Nazis.

The last page has yet to be written explaining the history of Nazi Germany and the psychology behind such excesses as anti-Semitic legislation that deprived Jews of basic human rights, forbade their marrying gentiles, and barred them from making a career in all but the most menial occupations.

The cultural cost of Nazism was gigantic. In the process of creating a specifically Nazi culture, the liberal humanitarianism of Goethe and Beethoven, and the sophisticated art of Heine, Mahler and Kafka were abandoned; in their place a mindless and barbaric cult was erected.

Rearmament was the key to Hitler's economic success. And while this was secretly taking place, Hitler pursued a foreign policy designed to throw other world powers into confusion about his ultimate aim. Still not absolutely sure of his position, Hitler played the respectable diplomat during this period. For the moment, the dreams of his revealing book, *Mein Kampf* (1924), of sweeping aside the Slavs in search of *Lebensraum* ("living space") for a greater Germany, were shelved. In 1934, Germany was still militarily weak, and its neighbors to the east and west — Poland and France, respectively — were hostile and suspicious. The long-term aim of Hitler's policy — world domination — was temporarily dropped in favor of the short-term aims of destroying

the Treaty of Versailles and of rearming without provoking war.

The Nazi leader inaugurated his ambitious scheme on May 17, 1933, with a "peace" speech that completely disconcerted the Western powers. In that speech he renounced all offensive weapons — provided everyone else did the same. Hitler's declaration was only a means to an end, however, for as the Führer himself observed: "My party comrades will not fail to understand me when they hear me speak of universal peace, disarmament and mutual security pacts." Less than six months later, Germany withdrew from the disarmament conference in Geneva on the grounds that the other participants had not renounced offensive weapons. Neither Britain nor France protested Hitler's move; he had successfully cashed in on the superficial reasonableness of his case and on the eagerness of Britain and France to appease him. The Nazi leader followed this first diplomatic triumph with an even greater one; in January, 1934, he signed a nonaggression pact with Poland and thereby created a huge breach in France's security network of Eastern alliances.

Hitler's policy was always double-edged. While he spoke publicly of peace, he secretly encouraged the subversive activities of Austrian Nazis. In July of 1934, this group organized a putsch in which the Chancellor, Engelbert Dollfuss, was shot and killed. Nothing came of the attempted coup, but it did demonstrate Hitler's determination to effect a union with Austria. In March, 1935, Hitler announced Germany's rearmament, but the other major powers did nothing until April, when representatives of Britain, France and Italy issued a joint condemnatory declaration after conferring in the Italian resort of Stresa. No effective action was taken, however, largely because Hitler softened the blow with verbiage about war never coming again. Each time he circumvented another provision of the Treaty of Versailles, his position at home strengthened. The German leader's most brilliant diplomatic stroke was yet to come, however. In the spring of 1935, Hitler offered Britain a limitation of German naval strength to thirty-five percent of that of the Royal Navy, and Britain promptly took the bait. The Anglo-German Naval Agreement, signed in June of that year,

Bowing obsequiously, Hitler, newly appointed Chancellor of the German Republic, greets the ageing President Paul von Hindenburg.

success by means of large-scale rearmament

Thousands of books smolder in a huge bonfire as Germans give the Nazi salute during the wave of book burnings that spread through Germany. Only those works that followed Nazi racial and political theories were approved reading for the people.

there that the Germans had been harshly treated at Versailles because of French vindictiveness. In both Britain and France, there was a strong determination to avoid a repetition of the holocaust of World War I.

Appeasement was no answer to an Adolf Hitler bent on war, but few saw this at the time. An informed minority, Winston Churchill and Robert Vansittart among them, saw the danger, but their warnings fell on deaf ears. The British Ambassador in Berlin, Sir Horace Rumbold, wrote home that "the German is an inexorable Oliver Twist. Give him something and it is a jumping-off ground for asking for something else."

Both the French and British governments were preoccupied with unemployment, however, and the enormous social problems left in the wake of depression. There was no enthusiasm in either country for a resolute foreign policy. The people were war weary, and the governments hoped to spend what little money they had on something more socially useful than armaments. France in particular was faced by violence from the extreme

The New Deal

In the United States, Roosevelt's New Deal was consolidating American capitalism and democracy. The horrors of Nazism were largely ignored in the United States as they were in England and France, for America had troubles of her own. Franklin D. Roosevelt became President in March, 1933, at a time when national income and productivity were only half what they had been in 1929. Bread lines, vagrancy and shantytowns bore witness to the crippling poverty that had left thirteen million workers unemployed. America also faced a political problem, a threat to democracy that was perhaps best illustrated by Senator Huey Long's attempts to set up a somewhat ruthless populist regime in Louisiana.

To avoid social, economic and political catastrophe, Roosevelt pledged himself to "a new deal for the American people." He began by restoring confidence in the banking system. After temporarily closing all banks, Roosevelt re-

convinced the British of Hitler's sincerity and, in the process, destroyed the four-month-old Stresa Agreement (which had established a common British, French and Italian front against Germany). This made it possible for Germany to continue rearming without

Dr. Engelbert Dollfuss, the Austrian Chancellor murdered by the Nazis.

danger of outside interference.

Hitler's bold foreign policy led to fresh triumphs in 1936. Complaining that the Franco-Russian alliance invalidated the Treaty of

Locarno, he shattered that treaty by marching his troops into the Rhineland. On the same day, he proposed a nonaggression pact with France and Belgium. Behind a smokescreen of rationality, he had destroyed the Versailles system, and the meek reaction of the Western powers convinced Hitler that he could do with them as he wished.

The era of appeasement

The Western policy of appeasement was shown at its most flaccid later in 1936, when Hitler joined Mussolini in openly aiding the uprising headed by General Francisco Franco in Spain. Appeasement, which culminated in the betrayal of the Czechs at Munich, proceeded from understandable, if not entirely creditable motives. In the twenties the policy in Britain sprang from a widely held belief that prolonged and strenuous efforts to secure peace were of greater value than the politically easy resort to war. It also derived from the belief

Sir Robert Vansittart, one of the few people in the mid-thirties to realize the danger of Hitler.

right and left. Accordingly, both of the Western democracies listened eagerly to Hitler's talk of peace, hoping against hope that war could be avoided. Even those who suspected that war could not be avoided hoped it might be put off for a time. The determination not to antagonize Hitler was an indication of the enduring exhaustion of World War I. In America, too, the dishonesty of Hitler's policies aroused few fears. In general Americans were impressed by Hitler's promise of firm government and economic improvement. Besides, the United States had problems and preoccupations of its own that had led it to have little interest in Europe.

opened first the Federal Reserve Bank and then those private banks that were solvent. A huge program of public works raised wages, created more purchasing power and rejuvenated the entire economy. Agricultural production was limited in order to raise prices. The popularity of the New Deal was such that in the 1936 elections, Roosevelt was reelected with a plurality of ten million votes.

The New Deal was to bear its greatest fruit during the war. Measures first adopted to counter the Depression were later to be the basis of America's huge wartime program. But the immediate impact was felt most strongly as a result of the 1933 Social Security Act.

Insurance for the Elderly   1935

With FDR's *election as President on a promise of "a new deal for the American people,"
hundreds of bright and eager people flocked to Washington to help pull the nation out of the
Great Depression. Led by an inner circle known as the Brain Trust, they drafted and saw
through Congress legislation dealing with everything from banking to work projects. Among
the significant measures of Roosevelt's first term was the Social Security Act. For the first time
in the nation's history, the American government was underwriting social benefits for its elderly.*

On March 4, 1933, a cold wind and dark sky greeted the crowds gathering in front of the Capitol and along Pennsylvania Avenue for the inauguration of Franklin D. Roosevelt as the nation's thirty-second President. The weather mirrored the country's mood; three years of depression in America had left nearly thirteen million people without jobs and forced thousands of farms and businesses to close. On inauguration day banks in thirty-eight of the forty-eight states were shut and commodity markets in two large cities suspended trading.

In his inaugural address Roosevelt promised to "act and act quickly" on the nation's problems. The following day executive orders were issued calling for a special session of Congress and declaring a bank holiday. Saving the banking system took first priority and Roosevelt directed the Secretary of the Treasury, William Woodin, to produce a program for presentation to Congress when its special session began—only five days later.

Immediately after the opening ceremonies were completed a copy of the Emergency Banking Bill was handed to House Speaker Rainey, who read its provisions aloud while some Congressmen were still finding their seats. Forty minutes of debate followed and then, with most representatives never having read the bill themselves, it was passed unanimously. The Senate took only a slightly longer time considering the measure and that same evening the President was able to sign the Emergency Banking Act. Just a week after his inauguration Roosevelt spoke to some sixty million Americans in the first of his popular radio broadcasts known as "fireside chats." He announced that the banks would reopen the following day on a firm financial base and he urged the public to resume normal use of the banks. Contrary to fears that there would be further panic withdrawals after the week-long bank holiday, Americans deposited more money than they withdrew during the first days of full bank operations.

Roosevelt's immediate action on the banking crisis and the public's positive response presaged a halt in the downward slide of the Depression that would be borne out in the events of Roosevelt's first hundred days in office. In contrast to the aloof and controlled style of his predecessor, Roosevelt's personal dynamism and natural warmth infused the presidency with a new vigor and promise of accomplishment that seemed to restore the country's self-confidence.

The personal differences between himself and Herbert C. Hoover had been a principal issue in the 1932 presidential campaign—much to Roosevelt's favor. In a striking break with tradition Roosevelt flew to Chicago to accept the Democratic Party's nomination for the presidency personally. During his acceptance speech Roosevelt declared that the Democrats would provide "a new deal for the American people," a phrase picked up by editorial writers and political cartoonists that quickly became the catchwords of his campaign and later his presidency.

At speeches and rallies across the country Roosevelt attacked Hoover's handling of the economic crisis. Although he did not spell out his own program for recovery, Roosevelt had been busy throughout 1932 assembling a group of experts in economics and government to formulate a new strategy. Known popularly as the Brain Trust, the study group included such men as Raymond P. Moley, Adolf Berle, Basil O'Connor, Rexford Tugwell, Felix Frankfurter, Hugh S. Johnson, Henry Morgenthau Jr., later Treasury Secretary, and Roosevelt's political mentor, Louis Howe. In groups of two or three they would travel to Roosevelt's home in Hyde Park or to the New York governor's mansion in Albany and stay late into the night presenting ideas and answering FDR's questions.

Franklin Delano Roosevelt, thirty-second President of the U.S.A. His introduction of social and economic legislation led the country to economic recovery and stability.

Opposite Businessmen pay homage to the golden calf while the factories stand idle. Roosevelt's election reflected a change in the country's mood. The "old guard" leadership, the business community, lionized in the twenties, was discredited and blamed for the Depression.

The two-million-strong National Recovery Administration publicity parade passing New York Public Library on Fifth Avenue, 1933. Roosevelt's instrument of industrial recovery, the NRA drew up a code regulating working conditions and competitive practices.

Frankfurter and Jerome Frank. They floated airily into offices, took desks, asked for papers and found no end of things to be busy about."

During the period between his election and inauguration Roosevelt assembled his cabinet, and on his second day in office administered the oath of office to the nine men and one woman he had selected. Among the most prominent individuals were Henry Wallace, appointed Secretary of Agriculture; Frances Perkins, the first woman to hold a cabinet post, as Secretary of Labor; the distinguished Tennessee lawyer and former Senator Cordell Hull became Secretary of State; William Woodin took over as Director of the Treasury Department; and the one-time "Bull Moose" Republican and progressive Harold C. Ickes became Secretary of the Interior. Raymond P. Moley was designated Assistant Secretary of State, a post which allowed him to take on a wide range of tasks for the President, many outside the area of foreign policy. Other members of the Brain Trust were not immediately given government posts, but continued to advise FDR as private citizens.

Although Roosevelt originally planned to allow Congress to end its special session immediately after the banking bill was passed, the legislative branch's quick action on that bill and subsequent measures concerning government spending and repeal of the eighteenth amendment to the Constitution—prohibiting sale of alcoholic beverages—caused him to change course. Congress remained in session until June 9 and approved fifteen major pieces of legislation, a record that Roosevelt noted made it the most productive legislative meeting in the nation's history. But the session—often called "the Hundred Days"—was noteworthy not only for the sheer number of bills acted upon, but also for the governmental philosophy they represented.

Members of Roosevelt's Brain Trust concluded that economic recovery and stability could be obtained through government and business cooperation to regulate economic growth. Technological innovations gave unfair advantage to large corporations and permanently reduced the effectiveness of competition. They suggested that regulations could restore the necessary balance. The Agricultural Adjustment Act (AAA) and the National Industrial Recovery Act, which set up the National Recovery Administration (NRA), were the cornerstones of this New Deal philosophy—two great experiments in national planning within a capitalist economic system.

Although people from every economic group suffered during the Depression, American farmers bore an unusually heavy burden. Real farm income dropped by one-third between 1929 and 1933; prices were down fifty percent in the same period. Violence flared in farm states throughout the winter of 1932 and spring of 1933 as mobs of farmers gathered to prevent produce from reaching markets or sheriffs from carrying out foreclosure orders. The situation threatened to worsen when the Farmers' Holiday Association called a national farm strike

From these discussions and other work, separately or in groups, the conduct of the early New Deal was charted.

As the 1932 campaign drew to a close it became apparent that Hoover and the Republicans were going to be rejected decisively. Hoover's campaign oratory took on an increasingly shrill and desperate tone as he promised to reverse the Depression in another term. But when the final election returns were tallied Roosevelt won the electoral votes of all but six states and amassed a total of 22.8 million votes against Hoover's 15.7 million.

Roosevelt's election not only meant a shift of power to the Democrats after twelve years of Republican administration; it also signaled a new mood on the part of the electorate. The sudden change from prosperity to depression had forced many stereotypes to be challenged. Businessmen who had been lionized during the boom years of the 1920s now were discredited and blamed for the collapse. The world's most productive nation was unable to feed and clothe its citizens adequately. In the opinion of many Americans the "old guard" had failed and so a new and largely unknown leader was voted in.

A feeling of change began to permeate Washington as soon as FDR took office. Hundreds of new people arrived in the capital to staff the New Deal. One observer noted "a plague of young lawyers settled on Washington. They all claimed to be friends of somebody or other and mostly of Felix

for May. Roosevelt realized the need for initiating his farm policy quickly and pressed Congress to pass the program devised by Agriculture Secretary Henry Wallace and Assistant Secretary Rexford Tugwell. The House responded by passing AAA, but in the Senate the separate and highly partisan issue of hard *vs.* soft money held up action. With the strike threat growing nearer a compromise was reached on the question of currency that swung the necessary support to pass AAA.

Secretary Wallace's first actions under AAA were as distasteful as they were necessary. Hundreds of acres of corn, wheat, and cotton crops had to be destroyed in order not to glut already full markets. During the winter, herds of young pigs were slaughtered and winter wheat plowed under. The following year, 1934, severe drought and dust storms achieved much the same results, while price subsidies and a system of voluntary production limits were instituted. These harsh measures yielded remarkable success as farm income rose by fifty percent during Roosevelt's first term. Moreover, AAA succeeded in convincing fiercely individual farmers that collective action was necessary to save their livelihood.

In the area of industrial recovery an even more ambitious program of regulation and planning was instituted. Authorized by Congress in May, 1933, and in operation only a few weeks later, the National Recovery Administration (NRA), led by the energetic and outspoken General Hugh S. Johnson, succeeded in enlisting the ten largest American industries in its code system during the first three months of its existence. The codes were charters that regulated such matters as working hours and conditions and competitive practices. Through an adroit use of public relations, Johnson made the NRA, its symbol the Blue Eagle, and its slogan "We Do Our Part" a familiar part of the American landscape. The culmination of this effort resulted in an NRA march down New York City's Fifth Avenue in which an estimated two million people participated.

Despite the public's enthusiasm for NRA, problems developed in two areas: prices and labor-management relations. Johnson could do no more than urge businessmen to hold the line on prices and as a consequence they rose steadily throughout NRA's existence—a disastrous condition for housewives trying to stretch weekly budgets. In the area of labor relations, Johnson was often caught in the middle as unions tried to press for enforcement of Section 7a of the NIRA—the right of employees to bargain collectively. Management made an effort to circumvent this provision by organizing company-sponsored unions that mitigated against outside unions covering their employees. Inevitably jurisdictional fights ensued that were ultimately settled —often to the satisfaction of neither side—by the National Labor Board. By most economic yardsticks the success of NRA was marginal, but in the area of social change the record is clearer. Such things as an end to child labor and sweatshops, a national minimum wage, the right to collective bargaining and limits on unfair business practices can all be credited to NRA.

Other important initiatives against the Depression were passed by the seventy-third Congress: $500 million was appropriated under the Federal Emergency Relief Act for distribution to relief projects organized by the states, and the Public Works Administration (PWA) received $3.3 billion. As administered by Interior Secretary Ickes many worthwhile projects received PWA grants, including funds for completion of the Triborough bridge in New York City and the Thirtieth-Street railroad station in Philadelphia. The establishment of the Tennessee Valley Authority—a government operated, non-profit corporation empowered to develop the Tennessee River Valley—represented a bold new approach in regional conservation and economic planning. Action was also taken to protect stock investors in the "Truth in Securities" Act.

While Congress worked on his legislative program Roosevelt maintained a high public profile. In addition to his radio programs, the President made ten major speeches during the Hundred Days. News conferences were held twice weekly under a new format—questions no longer had to be submitted in advance, but Roosevelt reserved the right to keep some answers "off the record." Cabinet meetings also became more frequent.

When Congress returned to Washington in 1934 a slowdown in activity was inevitable. Although several important pieces of legislation were passed—

FDR signs the Social Security Act in Washington, August 14, 1935. The act provided a nationwide pension for the elderly and insurance for the temporarily unemployed.

ROOSEVELT AND GARNER ©

An auto tag from the 1932 election campaign illustrating the Prohibition issue. Part of the comprehensive New Deal legislation, the Beer-Wine Revenue Act of March, 1933, legalized and taxed alcoholic beverages.

including establishment of the Securities and Exchange Commission—it was a time of consolidation and evaluation of bills already enacted.

The Congressional election of 1934 naturally became a referendum on the first two years of the New Deal and FDR's leadership. Contrary to the normal political wisdom, which dictates that the party in the White House loses strength in midterm elections, Democratic majorities in both the House and Senate increased. Yet even in the midst of this triumph strong challenges to Roosevelt's reelection in 1936 were beginning to form.

After Roosevelt was elected in 1932 the business community, although traditionally Republican, united behind the President and his programs. But in late 1934, and even more strongly in 1935, opposition to FDR began to surface. Some business leaders rallied around chapters of the newly formed American Liberty League, a nationwide organization dominated by northern industrialists like the Du Ponts and dissident, conservative Democrats led by Al Smith. At its 1935 national convention held in Washington, the U.S. Chamber of Commerce voted to oppose a two-year extension of NRA.

Criticism from business was echoed among upper-class Americans who characterized Roosevelt—a man of considerable personal wealth—as a traitor to his class. Roosevelt became particularly incensed by these rebukes and likened his critics to a man in top hat and tails who upon being rescued from drowning first thanks his savior, but then chastizes him for failing to retrieve the top hat as well.

A more serious political threat appeared in the burgeoning nationwide popularity of the Democratic Senator from Louisiana, Huey P. Long, and the Chicago radio priest, Reverend Charles Coughlin. Long was a highly intelligent and ambitious politician whose folksy, down-to-earth style had an undeniable mass appeal. After building an efficient political machine in Louisiana, Long turned to national politics and promoted a scheme for redistributing wealth through locally organized "Share the Wealth" clubs. Of incalculable aid to Long was the support shown him by Father Coughlin. A consummate radio performer, Coughlin's sermons against big business, Communism, and the New Deal reached an estimated 35 million people a week, primarily in the urban centers of the East and Midwest. Coughlin spoke favorably of Long and his constituency dovetailed nicely with the Louisiana Senator's strength in the South and Southwest. The true extent of Long's challenge to Roosevelt can never be judged because Long was assassinated in the fall of 1935 while on a visit to his home state. But the popularity of Long and Coughlin and other radical reformers such as Upton Sinclair and Dr. Francis Townsend indicated the restlessness and disorder under the surface of American political life.

The program Roosevelt presented to Congress in 1935 represented a departure from the direction set by the Hundred Days. At heart Roosevelt was a pragmatist who wanted to give the public what he termed "concrete achievements that people could touch and see and use" and so he turned to a more aggressive reform program. In addition, the President's inner circle had changed and under the prodding of Harry Hopkins, Thomas Corcoran, Benjamin Cohen and Felix Frankfurter the Works Progress Administration, the Rural Electrification Administration, the Eccles Banking Bill, the Public Utilities Holding Act and a new tax reform act were formulated. But perhaps Roosevelt's new approach was best typified in the Social Security Act passed in August, 1935.

As drafted by the administration in January, 1935, the Social Security Act had two separate goals—to provide a nationwide pension for the elderly, financed entirely by a payroll tax, and to extend a small cash benefit to temporarily unemployed workers, also financed through taxes but administered by the states. Interest in a benefit for the elderly had been increasing as a result of Dr. Townsend's campaign for a weekly cash payment to all Americans over sixty and the realization that individuals living on a fixed retirement income could be wiped out entirely in an economic emergency such as the Depression. A proposal for unemployment insurance had been presented to Congress in the Wagner-Lewis Bill of 1934, but effective lobbying on the part of business had prevented the legislation from coming to a vote.

Hoping to gain time to rally supporters for both issues, Roosevelt sent a message to Congress in June, 1934, reaffirming his support for legislation in this area, but suggesting that discussion be postponed until the next session of Congress. In the meantime, he appointed Labor Secretary Perkins to chair a cabinet Committee on Economic Security that was charged with presenting a feasible proposal to the President by winter.

Roosevelt received the Committee's report in January and immediately submitted it to Congress. Although business opposition to the Social Security Act remained strong, popular sentiment in favor of the bill proved even more forceful and the Act was passed. In the early years of its history Social Security did not pay high benefits, but it was a crucial step in the development of an acceptance by the federal government of responsibility for the future security of Americans.

The final important achievement of the seventy-fourth Congress was passage of the Wagner Labor Relations Act. In spite of the fact that Senator Wagner's bill is usually counted among the major measures of the New Deal's labor program, it did not receive any administration support until shortly before passage. The Wagner Act attempted to rectify many of the inadequacies that appeared in enforcement of Section 7a of NIRA and was a key factor in labor's growth during the 1930s and 1940s.

Debate over the efficacy of the programs passed during the first Hundred Days as opposed to those approved in the 1935 session of Congress was rendered academic when the Supreme Court, whose justices had been appointed in earlier administrations, declared NIRA unconstitutional. That was only the first of several Court decisions dismantling many of the New Deal's achievements.

The shock of the Supreme Court decision sent Roosevelt to the offensive. Looking toward the 1936 presidential election he built solid alliances with labor, ethnic groups and progressives that were to be the Democratic Party's greatest strength in the decades to come. Indeed Roosevelt created a new Democratic Party based in the large urban centers, cutting American politics sharply along class lines.

The campaign of 1936 proved to be a tremendous vindication of Roosevelt and his policies. The President pointed with pride to reports showing a

With its vast organization under one management, economies are effected which Certain-teed passes on to you in the form of better quality.

definite upturn in business activity. More than six million new jobs had been created in four years and while unemployment figures remained formidable the outlook for more employment opportunities in the future seemed favorable. Roosevelt's Republican opposition, Kansas Governor Alfred M. Landon, was a moderate who could not outflank the President's liberalism nor convincingly portray himself as a conservative. Any apprehensions FDR may have harbored about the outcome of the election were dispelled shortly after the polls closed and first returns were received at the Roosevelt home in Hyde Park. The President swept every state except Maine and Vermont, carrying in even larger Democratic majorities in Congress.

In the remaining years before the outbreak of World War II it became apparent that the reforming spirit of the early New Deal was spent. Roosevelt's plan to circumvent the ageing Supreme Court justices who had vetoed his program by increasing the size of the Court sparked an extremely bitter split within the Democratic Party and marked the end of Roosevelt's mastery of Congress. Economic recovery continued at a slow pace, marred by a slight recession in 1937. But the inevitable setbacks of the years after 1936 do not detract from the magnificent accomplishments of the New Deal. In a very real sense Roosevelt saved the spirit of the country and demonstrated that a democratic system was flexible enough to reform itself without giving up any of the freedoms that make it valuable.

ELLEN KAVIER

Advertisement for a giant business corporation. Business interests united behind Roosevelt in 1933, but the workings of NRA to break monopolies and in the fields of prices and labor-management relations soon caused defections. The administration's social reforms were passed in the teeth of business opposition.

145

The burial of the Weimar constitution

Reconstruction

The New Deal was part of a wider economic reconstruction after the difficulties of the years that followed the Great Crash of 1929. Across the world a new—and more soundly based—prosperity was beginning to emerge. During the later years of the 1930s real incomes rose steadily. Social legislation was introduced in many countries. By the outbreak of World War II universal literacy had become the rule rather than the exception in all advanced countries; mass-circulation newspapers and radio broadcasting brought a wide range of information to a vast public. The dangers inherent in this did not become apparent until World War II, when the German propaganda machine of Doctor Joseph Goebbels disseminated misinformation and distorted facts. Popular entertainment, too, was making great changes in social life. The rise of the movie brought a vision of faraway places to many who could not afford to travel, and internationalism in sport flourished also. The Berlin Olympic Games of 1936 provided Hitler's Germany with a propaganda opportunity that was not neglected. All this was made possible only by continued industrial growth.

Industrialization in Russia

In Stalin's Russia, industrialization and collectivization were proceeding at an enormous human cost. Thousands were shot or deported as full collectivization began; while in industry, gigantic strides forward were accompanied by huge sacrifices of human life. An American engineer who worked for five years on the Magnitogorsk project, reported: "I would wager that Russia's battle of ferrous metallurgy alone involved more casualties than the Battle of the Marne." The priority of heavy industry over consumer production, of reasons of state over popular interest, resulted in the terrible conditions described by the novelist Arthur Koestler who espoused Communism only to break with it at the time of Stalin's purge trials: "I could not help noticing the Asiatic backwardness of life; the apathy of the crowds in the street, tramways and railway stations; the

incredible housing conditions which make all industrial towns appear one vast slum (two or three couples sharing one room divided by sheets hanging from washing lines)."

The catastrophic reduction in living standards necessitated by Stalin's rapid industrialization resulted in a tremendous conflict between the people and the Communist Party. An increase in coercion and an intensification of police methods became essential, since the party was forced to carry out enormous social and economic transformations in a hostile environment. Toughness in carrying out unpopular orders became the highest qualification for Communist Party office, and men like Vyacheslav Molotov (1890–) and Lazar Kaganovich (1893–) came to the fore. Old Bolsheviks recoiled at the excesses of Stalinism—compulsory direction of labor, imprisonment in work camps, mass terror, the growth of crude Russian nationalism. Occasionally, when the old guard seemed to forget its responsibilities to the ideals of Bolshevism, Trotsky, a lone voice in exile, reminded them through the pages of his *Bulletin Oppozitsii* that the Revolution was being betrayed. And when members of Stalin's own clique began expressing their fears that the Revolution's ideals were being buried in a mound of tyranny, suffering and oppression, the Russian leader decided that the old guard had to be eliminated.

At the time, Politburo member Sergei Kirov was advocating a liberalizing of the regime, and when Kirov was mysteriously assassinated in Leningrad in December, 1934, it was a signal for the purges to begin. Absurd charges—of attempting mass poisoning of the workers, of being Nazi agents, of attempting to restore capitalism—were used to justify the liquidation of the great figures of the Revolution. Lev Borisovich Kamenev, Grigori Zinoviev, Aleksei Rykov, Nikolai Bukharin, Mikhail Tukhachevski and a host of lesser figures were shot after humiliating confessions had been wrung out of them.

Stalin thus created the Russia of cold-war legend, the police state, where free thought is ruthlessly stifled and insufferable living conditions prevail. The positive achievement of Stalinism was that it tore primitive, rural Russia out of its feudal backwardness, hurling

Nazis force elderly Jews to scrub the sidewalks in Vienna.

it, almost fully industrialized, into the twentieth century. When Hitler attacked Russia, it would be his undoing. This was so because Stalin had prepared Russia for modern warfare.

Realizing "Mein Kampf"

Economic improvements in the United States, Russia and Western Europe did not, however, basically alter the major issues of European foreign policy. By 1937, Hitler was ready to switch from the restricted policy of removing the limitations of the Treaty of Versailles to the bolder course of implementing the aims outlined in his book *Mein Kampf*. The British and French made a massive diplomatic effort to turn the tide of Hitler's ambition, but from 1936 to 1939 German aggression proceeded unchecked. During that period, Hitler kept to his shrewd policy of conquering his

victims one at a time. In Austria and Czechoslovakia, for example, Nazi-inspired disruption of public life created fruitful problems for Hitler to "solve." *Anschluss* (Union) with Austria was achieved under the pretext of preventing the maltreatment of Austrian nationalists. (Hitler was able to point out that he was merely applying Wilsonian principles of national self-determination.) *Anschluss* completely changed the Central European balance of power and opened the way to further expansion, for Vienna was the traditional gateway to southeastern Europe. The German army was at the edge of the Hungarian plain and at the threshold of the Balkans. In the north, Czechoslovakia's defenses were outflanked.

The ease with which *Anschluss* was effected in Austria and the absence of protest by the democracies tempted Hitler to look next to Czechoslovakia. Created in 1919

Lighting the Olympic flame at the Berlin Olympiad, 1936.

marks the birth of European dictatorships

as a democracy and an ally of France, Czechoslovakia was a hateful symbol of Versailles. Moreover, the crack Czech army had to be eliminated before any move to the East could be made. The takeover of Czechoslovakia resembled that of Austria; the Sudetenlanders, residents of a heavily German section of eastern Czechoslovakia, began making unacceptable demands and creating unrest. Hitler was then able to intervene to "prevent civil war and the oppression of a minority."

The British Prime Minister, Neville Chamberlain, believed that conceding the Sudetenland might tempt Hitler into a negotiated settlement of other pressing issues. But Hitler played on Western fears by parading his own readiness for war, and was therefore able, in the ill-famed Munich Agreement, to persuade Chamberlain to concede German occupation of Sudetenland.

Italy in Africa

While Germany's claims to hegemony in Central and Eastern Europe were growing rapidly, the Italian dictator Benito Mussolini was watching with admiration. Although his longer period in power had changed Italy far less than Germany had been changed by Hitler, Mussolini had some reason for pride in his domestic record; as his apologists in France and Britain pointed out, he had achieved the almost impossible by getting the railroad trains to run on time; the papacy had been persuaded to recognize the existence of Italy and had concluded the Lateran Treaty with Mussolini in 1929; the worst effects of the Depression had been avoided by an increase in the public works program; Fiume had been reoccupied.

But Mussolini's ambitions went much further; he saw himself as the heir of the Roman emperors and set about building himself an empire. There was no possibility of expansion in Europe and despite Italy's possession of Libya there was no possibility of controlling the Mediterranean, but further south in Africa there was one country, Ethiopia (Abyssinia) which seemed to beckon enticingly. Not only was it the only substantial country in Africa not already under European domination, but most of its coast-

Italian troops during the invasion of Ethiopia in 1935.

line already formed the Italian colonies of Somaliland and Eritrea, and Ethiopia had itself been an Italian protectorate for a brief period in the 1890s.

Ethiopia was socially and culturally backward and Mussolini foresaw little difficulty in annexing it. A large number of Italian "consuls" were appointed, each of them with an armed guard of about a hundred men. The son-in-law of Emperor Haile Selassie was persuaded to rebel at the beginning of 1935. Mussolini's plan to foment a more general civil war failed completely, but he had at least found an excuse for invasion. Against the Ethiopian army of forty thousand men, many of them equipped only with swords, Mussolini flung nearly a quarter of a million well-armed troops, backed up by tanks and four hundred bombers. The outcome was obvious; Haile Selassie could do no more than fight a delaying action and hope that the League of Nations would come to his support. Yet, despite the massive use of poison gas and the bombing of Red Cross hospitals, it took Mussolini's men eighteen months to conquer even the capital, Addis Ababa.

Although the creation of Mussolini's Roman Empire in Ethiopia had little strategic importance on a world scale, it showed that the League of Nations was totally ineffective in dealing with any serious problem. It underlined the failure of Britain, the United States and France to stand up to the dictators and encouraged the dictators to push forward their plans.

The abdication crisis

While Germany and Italy expanded their influence in Europe and Africa, Britain was busy showing the world what its priorities were. The country that had watched the rise of Hitler with complete equanimity was deeply shaken constitutionally and socially because its King wanted to marry an American

divorcee. King George V died in 1936 and was succeeded by his fun-loving son, the forty-two-year-old Edward VIII. The new King wanted to marry Mrs. Wallis Simpson. The establishment—represented by the Archbishop of Canterbury, Cosmo Gordon Lang, the Prime Minister, Stanley Baldwin, and the editor of *The Times*, Geoffrey Dawson—was determined that he should not do so and remain King. The outcome was that Edward was forced to abdicate. The crisis had little intrinsic importance, but it showed clearly how difficult Britain was finding it to discover a new role in a world that seemed to have passed her by.

In India, for example, the balance of power was shifting further away from the British. Increasing numbers of influential people were acknowledging that Britain must either recognize the power of the Congress movement and transform India into a self-governing dominion and a loyal member of the Commonwealth or else embark on a savage policy of repression that would benefit no one and would shatter India's economy.

Middle Eastern troubles

In the Middle East, British hegemony was further threatened by the Palestine problem, which was making enemies for the British on both sides. There had been sporadic violence between the local Arabs and Jewish settlers for many years, but Hitler's rise to power brought a new urgency to the problem. Many previously assimilated Jews were forced to turn to Zionism in their search for decent human rights, and as the Zionist movement grew, Arabs became alarmed at the prospect of increased Jewish immigration. To the consternation of the British, riots and assassinations increased. It was thus an unusually troubled world that received the news of the outbreak of the Spanish Civil War in July, 1936.

King Edward VIII of England with the Prime Minister Stanley Baldwin.

The Spanish Civil War

The strongly worded pronunciamiento *broadcast by a Canary Islands radio station on July 18, 1936, was aimed—both literally and figuratively—at Madrid. The bold rhetoric of the manifesto was attributed to "the Commanding General of the Canaries"; its actual author was General Francisco Franco, who was soon to emerge as the leader of the military cabal that was bent on overthrowing the Second Spanish Republic. Assisted by the Axis Powers, which provided air transport for his troops, Franco landed some 15,000 members of his personally trained Army of Africa on Spanish soil in August of 1936. Romantics have tended to view the three-year civil war that followed as a contest between democracy and fascism; the truth is a little less clear-cut. The country that Franco invaded was rapidly sinking into anarchy. The authoritarian regime that Franco established at least gave Spain its first stable government in more than a century.*

The badge worn by members of the International Brigade, which fought against Franco in the Spanish Civil War.

Opposite A poster issued by the Republicans attacking Franco's supporters for their vested interests.

The military conspiracy against the Second Spanish Republic began in earnest in February, 1936, but General Francisco Franco did not commit himself to it until the end of June. On June 23, from his "exile" in the Canary Islands (where the newly elected Popular Front government had sent him as military governor), he made what he considered a final attempt to bring the government to its senses. In a long letter to the new Prime Minister, Casares Quiroga, he dwelt at length upon army grievances and gave warning of "grave dangers" facing Spain. In Franco's mind, this curious letter hinted that he was available to restore order in an increasingly chaotic situation—if called upon to do so.

Casares Quiroga, who suffered from advanced consumption and had no desire to acknowledge that the Republic was in danger, ignored Franco's warning. His silence was the nonevent that ended Franco's prolonged season of doubt. Just in time—for the conspirators were about to act without him—he decided to join the military rebellion.

General Emilio Mola, known to the plotters as *El Director*, had planned to act on July 14, but he postponed his move until the seventeenth because of some last-minute quarrels on a common program acceptable to the disparate groups on the Nationalist side. The extra three days gave the Nationalists time to complete arrangements for conveying Franco from the Canaries to Morocco, where he was to take command of the insurgent forces in Africa. A British civil plane, chartered by the Nationalists, picked the General up at Las Palmas. News that the uprising had begun reached Franco before he left. He immediately telegraphed all divisional generals in Spanish Morocco and throughout Spain, appealing to them to rally to the Nationalist cause.

Franco also drafted an old-style *pronunciamiento*, known today as the Manifesto of Las Palmas, which was remarkable on several counts. For one thing the manifesto, as broadcast by Radio Tenerife on July 18, 1936, was not attributed to Franco by name but to "the Commanding General of the Canaries." This reticence on Franco's part is explained by the fact that the General, a latecomer to the conspiracy, was not at that time the leader of the Nationalist movement. With Mola as the organizer, the conspirators had, in fact, designated General José Sanjurjo—a prestigious officer then in exile in Portugal—as Commander in Chief. Nevertheless, the tone and wording of the manifesto made it quite clear that Franco considered himself the natural leader of the rebels now that he had decided to join them. That was the second remarkable aspect of the manifesto.

A third point was that, in the face of the fact that the Republic's persecution of the Church was a major issue on the Nationalist side (and for all Franco's later reputation for piety), the manifesto made no mention of religion. Instead, it promised "liberty and fraternity without libertinage and tyranny; work for all; social justice, accomplished without rancor or violence, and an equitable and progressive distribution of wealth without destroying or jeopardizing the Spanish economy."

Franco's immediate problem was how to convey the Army of Africa across the Straits of Gibraltar. This small but formidable force, whose professionalism owed much to Franco's efficient discipline, was potentially the key to a Nationalist victory. But it was almost useless where it was. The bulk of the Spanish fleet was in Republican hands, the crews having turned on their Nationalist officers and murdered them. The vessels, led by the battleship *Jaime* I, were steaming toward the international port of Tangier, where their presence would threaten any attempted crossing by sea.

In this situation, Franco made the fateful decision to seek the assistance of the Axis Powers. He first turned to Mussolini, who rebuffed his emissary. A second emissary, sent by Mola on July 25, persuaded *Il Duce* to change his mind. Five days later, twelve three-engined Italian Savoia-Marchetti 81s took off for Morocco; only nine actually arrived. Meanwhile,

Los Nacionales

MINISTERIO DE PROPAGANDA

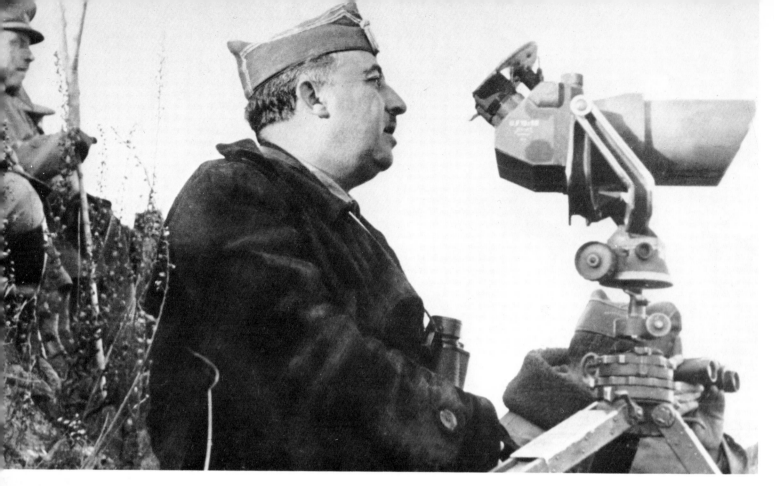

General Franco directing operations on the Catalonian front in January, 1939.

Franco put his case to two local Nazis, who took off for Berlin on July 22. Hitler received them on July 26 at Bayreuth, where he was attending a Wagner festival, and on the advice of Admiral Canaris, the head of German military intelligence—who thought highly of the Spanish general—he decided to back Franco. Shortly after the two Nazi emissaries returned to Morocco, Hitler's first planes started arriving. The first group consisted of twenty Ju 52 maximum-capacity transports and six Heinkel 51 fighters. They immediately started ferrying Nationalist troops across to the mainland. Together, the German and Italian aircraft transported up to five hundred men and fifteen tons of material a day across the Straits. Within a few weeks, some 15,000 men were ready for action against the Republic.

Franco, meanwhile, was neutralizing the Republican fleet and preparing a naval convoy of his own. Five warning telegrams were issued to the control committee of the international zone at Tangier, and on August 7, they were followed by an ultimatum that gave the committee forty-eight hours to get rid of the Republican fleet. In a crucial vote, the British member of the control committee sided with the Italian member in supporting a motion that Madrid should be requested to remove its warships. On the ninth, the last of them steamed out of Tangier.

Although this removed an immediate danger, the Republican naval blockade was still in force. Overruling objections from his naval staff, Franco had already decided—before sending his ultimatum to Tangier—to go ahead with his convoy plan. At 5 P.M. on August 5, three thousand troops set off from Ceuta, in the gunship *Dato*, the coastal patrol ship *Uad Kert*, a tugboat and three merchantmen. Chal-

Franco addressing the crowds in Burgos after being proclaimed Supreme Head of the Nationalist Government in 1936.

lenged by the *Alcala Galiano*, a Republican destroyer, the *Dato* engaged her in an unequal artillery duel, which ended in the *Dato's* favor when the Nationalist Air Force put the *Alcala Galiano* to flight.

Franco had won the Battle of the Straits and had gotten his troops to the mainland. Within two months, his tough and professional Army of Africa had a string of military successes to its credit, and Franco had been proclaimed Chief of State and Generalissimo of the armed forces of Nationalist Spain. His one serious political rival, General Mola, met his death in an air crash on June 3, 1937. Less than two years later, the Republic was crushed.

And thirty years after the Republic's defeat, Generalissimo Francisco Franco y Bahamonde was still Chief of State in the Nationalist Spain that was his by military victory.

The Spanish Second Republic was the direct outcome of the municipal elections of 1931, elections in which nearly all the cities and large towns voted overwhelmingly in favor of the Republican parties. King Alfonso XIII, fearing civil conflict, went into voluntary exile, though he did not abdicate—a fact that made it possible for the Monarchists to deny the legitimacy of the Republic. The Monarchists, and the King himself, had largely discredited themselves in public opinion by Alfonso's tolerance of the dictatorship of General Primo de Rivera (1923–30), which began well with modernizing achievements but ended in financial decline and general discontent. The first years of the Republic were dominated by Manuel Azaña, who began as War Minister and later became in turn Prime Minister and President. A gifted writer, Azaña was determined to curb the power of two of the three pillars of traditional Spain —the Church and the army. (The third pillar, the monarchy, had already been broken.)

However defensible these objections may have been, Azaña aroused much antagonism by the arrogance and tactlessness with which he pushed through his anticlerical and antimilitary reforms. Conservative opinion had already been alarmed by Azaña's declared indifference in the face of a wave of church and convent burnings in the early days of the Republic. An ill-timed and ill-organized attempt to overthrow the Republic was made in August, 1932, by General Sanjurjo, who was first sentenced to death but was later reprieved and exiled. A fellow plotter, Colonel Varela, was won over to the ultra-conservative Carlist cause during his imprisonment and later trained the "God, King and country" *Requetés*, or militias, of the Traditionalist Communion, as the Carlists should properly be called. (The Carlists were supporters of Don Carlos, pretender to the Spanish throne.) Although he had been approached by the plotters, Franco stayed aloof.

The Azaña phase of the Republic ended (as it had begun) in a wave of strikes and violence, in which the hand of the Anarchists and their trade union organization, the C.N.T., was visible. The next phase was dominated by the young right-wing Catholic leader Gil Robles, whose party, the C.E.D.A., topped the polls in the general elections of November, 1933, though it did not gain an absolute majority and was not included in the first post-election government. The two years of center-right government that followed are known to the Spanish left as the "two black years" (*bienio negro*). The trend toward extremism gathered speed and strength. Primo de Rivera's son, José Antonio, founded a Spanish fascist party, the Falange Española, with a radical social program and—in distinction to Nazism and Italian Fascism—support for religion. On the left, the Anarchists declared war on the new government, called strikes, burned churches and proclaimed "libertarian communism" in the villages. The small

Hitler and Franco inspecting a guard of honor before their meeting at Hendaye, France, in 1940.

Communist Party gained new members and fresh influence in alliance with the revolutionary left-wing Socialists, led by Largo Caballero. Political murders became commonplace.

The entry of Gil Robles' party into the government in October, 1934, sparked a left-wing revolution that took the form of a Socialist-led general strike, the proclamation of Catalonia's independence, and a miners' insurrection in Asturias jointly led by the Socialists, Communists and Anarchists. Called in by the War Ministry, General Franco restored order with brutal efficiency and considerable loss of life. The crushing of the Asturian revolt left the army (except the officers promoted by Azaña) determined to combat revolutionary anarchy —which they called "communism"—and the left bent on revenge against the "fascists."

The general elections of February, 1936, confirmed the race to extremism. The Popular Front of Azaña's left-center, together with the Socialists and Communists—and supported by Anarchist and Trotskyite votes at polling time—dominated the Cortes, or Parliament. The Front won 258 seats, as opposed to 152 for the right and only 62 for the center. Street clashes became more and more frequent, not merely between the Falangists and Communists, but also between the relatively moderate Socialist followers of Indalecio Prieto and the Largo Caballero Socialists, who preached violent revolution. The climax was the abduction of the Monarchist politician Calvo Sotelo, who was murdered on July 13 by uniformed Republican police in retaliation for the murder of a policeman by Falangists the previous day.

By this time, the military plot against the Republic was far advanced. The Carlist *Requetés* were well

Don Manuel Azaña, who succeeded Zamora as President of the Republic.

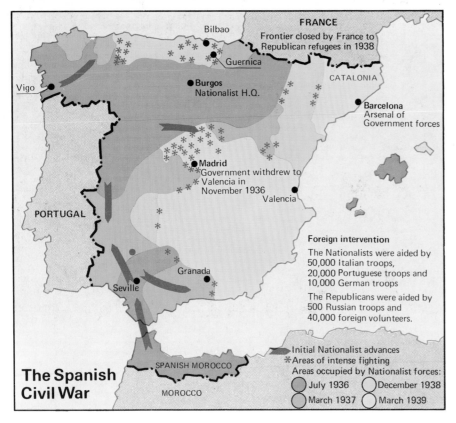

The Spanish Civil War

Bilbao

FRANCE

Frontier closed by France to
Republican refugees in 1938

Guernica

CATALONIA

Burgos
Nationalist H.Q.

Vigo

Barcelona
Arsenal of
Government forces

Madrid
Government withdrew to
Valencia in
November 1936

Valencia

PORTUGAL

Foreign intervention

The Nationalists were aided by
50,000 Italian troops,
20,000 Portuguese troops and
10,000 German troops

The Republicans were aided by
500 Russian troops and
40,000 foreign volunteers.

Granada

Seville

▬ Initial Nationalist advances
✳ Areas of intense fighting
Areas occupied by Nationalist forces:

⬤ July 1936   ⬤ December 1938
⬤ March 1937   ⬤ March 1939

SPANISH MOROCCO

MOROCCO

A painting showing soldiers
being executed by a firing
squad.

In terms of serious organization, Mola's conspiracy began at the time of the Popular Front's electoral victory. It was his achievement to unite the rival Monarchist groups (called Carlist and Alfonsist from their support of rival Bourbon contenders for the vacant throne) with the anti-Monarchist and anticapitalist Falange, and to win financial support from bankers and industrialists.

The polarization of Spanish politics coincided with the rise of the totalitarian dictatorships in Europe: those of Stalin in the Soviet Union, Hitler in Germany, and Mussolini in Italy. In the age of appeasement, the dominant concern of the Western democracies, especially Britain, was to keep out of the Spanish Civil War when it began. Hence their support for a nonintervention policy. Despite the Nonintervention Committee, however, the Spanish Civil War became an international free-for-all, with Russia, Mexico and France aiding the Republic, and Germany and Italy intervening with decisive effect on Franco's side. The popular concept of the war as a struggle between democracy and fascism is rooted in these circumstances. But this was essentially a true civil conflict, with indigenous Spanish origins.

Franco's decision to join the military rebellion against the Spanish Republic was one of the turning points of contemporary history. Under any of the General's contemporaries, Nationalist chances would have been considerably slimmer. If Franco had stayed out, the mantle of leadership would have presumably fallen upon the swashbuckling Queipo de Llano, the "radio general" who had bluffed his way into Seville at the outset of the Civil War. It is

trained and organized, and the Falangist militias were training too. Within the army, opposition to the Republic had crystallized around the semisecret *Union Militar Española* (U.M.E.) formed in 1934.

difficult to imagine the more conservative National-ists taking orders from this flamboyant character with vaguely leftist views (who was the initiator of an abortive coup against Alfonso XIII).

Nor is it at all certain that Hitler would have provided transport for the Army of Africa had it not been under Franco's orders. And Mussolini, though he had promised planes, did not actually send them until he was sure that the Nazis were doing likewise. In all senses, then, Franco's belated decision to intervene was decisive.

The historical consequences of that decision, and of the victory guaranteed by his inflexible will as much as by Axis aid, were, however, ironical. Public opinion, identifying Franco with his Axis allies, wrongly saw the Nationalist conquest as the murder of Spanish democracy by international fascism. It would have been truer to see it as the victory of traditional Spain over the revolutionary left and international communism.

To present the outcome of the Civil War in this way is not to accept the Nationalist myth in preference to the Republican. What the Nationalists called "communism" embraced Azaña's anticlerical radicalism as well as revolutionary anarchism and the Spanish Communist Party, with its international allies. But Spanish democracy was already menaced when the Civil War began, and it died shortly after that. Law and order began to collapse in the political violence that occurred from February to July, 1936. Thereafter two developments marked Republican Spain: first, a sweeping Anarchist revolution, with destruction of records, the emptying of prisons, the seizure of properties, the burning of Church property, and the torture and killing of clergy; and second, a carefully planned takeover of the Republican state by the Communists, carried out under the supervision of Comintern officers who, for Stalin's purposes, "used" such public figures as Largo Caballero and Dr. Negrin (who shipped the Republic's gold to Russia). The takeover would doubtless have been

more complete had it not been for Stalin's reluctance —probably for general foreign-policy reasons—to let the Spanish Communist Party be shown to be in control of the Republican government. If the Republican forces had won, Spain would probably not have been a parliamentary democracy, but a Communist-controlled "people's democracy"—an outpost of the Soviet Union.

Paradoxically, the fact that Franco was in power in Madrid, helped to victory by Nazi aid, did not much help Hitler in World War II—for Franco, proclaiming Spain's neutrality or nonbelligerency (the formula varied to meet the fluctuations of fortune in World War II), resisted all Hitler's threats or blandishments. Losing patience, Hitler planned to invade the peninsula, but abandoned his plans when the bulk of his forces got bogged down on the Russian front. Gibraltar stayed British; the Allied campaign in North Africa was safeguarded; and Rommel was defeated. In the House of Commons on May 25, 1944, Winston Churchill praised Franco's Spain's contribution to the Allied successes in the Mediterranean. On the Axis side, General Jodl singled out "General Franco's repeated refusal to allow German armed forces to pass through Spain to take Gibraltar" as one of the major causes of Germany's defeat.

Franco's decision to seek Nazi and Italian Fascist help, however, was fateful in other ways. The "fascist" label stuck, and Spain was ostracized for many years after the defeat of the Axis Powers, deprived of Marshall Aid for postwar reconstruction and kept out of NATO. Some would see in this international odium a fitting punishment for Franco's original sin in seeking Axis aid. But his importance in European history cannot be denied. He gave Spain the longest period of peace it had known for a century and a half; his resistance to Hitler's demands contributed to the Allied victory; and he prevented the spread of Soviet Communism to southwestern Europe.

BRIAN CROZIER

Picasso's painting commemorating the bombing of Guernica.

General Francisco Franco, photographed in 1968.

Georges Clemenceau 1841–1929
French statesman

Paul von Hindenburg 1847–1934
German general, statesman

Paul Gauguin 1848–1903
French painter

Ivan Pavlov 1849–1936
Russian physiologist

Horatio Herbert Kitchener 1850–1916
British soldier

Henry Cabot Lodge 1850–1924
U.S. statesman

Ferdinand Foch 1851–1929
French general

Joseph Joffre 1852–1931
French general

Vincent van Gogh 1853–90
Dutch painter

James Keir Hardie 1856–1915
British socialist statesman

Theobald von Bethmann-Hollweg 1856–1921
German statesman

Woodrow Wilson 1856–1924
U.S. President

Hussein ibn Ali 1856–1931
Grand Sharif of Mecca

Sigmund Freud 1856–1939
Austrian psychoanalyst

George Bernard Shaw 1856–1950
British writer

Theodore Roosevelt 1858–1919
U.S. President

Max Planck 1858–1947
German physicist

Wilhelm II 1859–1941
German Kaiser

Raymond Poincaré 1860–1934
French statesman

Vittorio Emanuele Orlando 1860–1952
Italian statesman

Douglas Haig 1861–1928
British soldier

Franz Ferdinand 1863–1914
Archduke of Austria

Gabriele d'Annunzio 1863–1938
Italian writer and soldier

Edvard Munch 1863–1944
Norwegian painter

David Lloyd George 1863–1945
British statesman

Henry Ford 1863–1947
U.S. industrialist

Erich Ludendorff 1865–1937
German general

Jean Sibelius 1865–1957
Finnish composer

Sun Yat-sen 1866–1925
Chinese statesman

J. Ramsay MacDonald 1866–1937
British statesman

Wilbur Wright 1867–1912
U.S. aircraft inventor

Marie Curie 1867–1934
French physical chemist

Stanley Baldwin 1867–1947
British statesman

Robert Falcon Scott 1868–1912
British Antarctic explorer

Nicholas II 1868–1918
Tsar of Russia

Maxim Gorky 1868–1936
Russian writer

Neville Chamberlain 1869–1940
British statesman

Victor Emmanuel III 1869–1947
King of Italy

Mohandas Gandhi 1869–1948
Indian leader

Henri Matisse 1869–1954
French painter

Frank Lloyd Wright 1869–1959
U.S. architect

Rosa Luxemburg 1870–1919
German socialist

Nikolai Lenin (V.I. Ulyanov) 1870–1924
Russian revolutionary leader

Marcel Proust 1871–1922
French writer

Ernest Rutherford 1871–1937
British physicist

Orville Wright 1871–1948
U.S. aircraft inventor

Grigori Rasputin 1872–1916
Russian monk

Roald Amundsen 1872–1928
Norwegian polar explorer

Bertrand Russell 1872–1970
English philosopher, mathematician

Guglielmo Marconi 1874–1937
Italian inventor

Arnold Schoenberg 1874–1951
Austrian composer

Chaim Weizmann 1874–1952
Russian-British Zionist leader

Herbert Clark Hoover 1874–1964
U.S. president

Winston Churchill 1874–1965
British statesman

Carl Gustav Jung 1875–1961
Swiss psychiatrist

Albert Schweitzer 1875–1965
Alsatian philosopher, missionary

Mohammed Ali Jinnah
Pakistani statesman

Konrad Adenauer 1876–
German statesman

Leon Trotsky (L. D. Bronstein)
Russian revolutionary leader

Joseph Stalin (I. V. Dzhugashvili)
Russian statesman

Albert
German-

Franz
German

Wings Over Kitty Hawk   1903
Orville Wright's brief flight over North
Carolina sand dunes realizes one of man's
oldest dreams and revolutionizes
transportation

1907   **Picasso Revolutionizes Art**
Picasso renounces traditional painting,
emphasizing conceptual rather than
perceptual methods of vision

1904
The Russo-Japanese War
Abandoning isolation, Japan collides
with Russia and emerges as the first non-
European nation to win great power
status

An Automobile for the Masses   **1908**
An innovative mechanic from Detroit
perfects an unlovely, inexpensive motor
car — the Model T — and puts America
on wheels

Einstein 1879–1955
American physicist

Isoroku Yamamoto 1884–1943
Japanese admiral

von Papen 1879-1969
statesman

Harry S. Truman 1884–1972
U.S. President

Douglas MacArthur 1880–1964
U.S. army officer

David Ben-Gurion 1886–1973
Israeli statesman

Kemal Atatürk 1881–1938
Turkish leader

Chiang Kai-shek 1887–
Chinese general, statesman

Béla Bartók 1881–1945
Hungarian composer

Bernard Law Montgomery 1887–
British soldier

Alexander Fleming 1881–1955
British bacteriologist

John Foster Dulles 1888–1959
U.S. statesman

John XXIII 1881–1963
Pope

Adolf Hitler 1889–1945
German dictator

Kliment Voroshilov 1881–1969
Russian field-marshal

Jawaharlal Nehru 1889–1964
Indian statesman

Alexander Kerensky 1881–1970
Russian statesman

Boris Pasternak 1890–1960
Russian writer

Pablo Picasso 1881–1973
Franco-Spanish painter

Dwight D. Eisenhower 1890–1969
U.S. general, President

James Joyce 1882–1941
Irish writer

Ho Chi Minh 1890–1969
Vietnamese communist leader

Virginia Woolf 1882–1941
British writer

Charles de Gaulle 1890–1970
French general, statesman

Franklin D. Roosevelt 1882–1945
U.S. President

Vyacheslav Mikhailovich Molotov 1890–
Russian statesman

Georges Braque 1882–1963
French painter

Erwin Rommel 1891–1944
German general

Igor Stravinsky 1882–1971
Russian composer

Averell Harriman 1891–
U.S. statesman

Eamon de Valera 1882–
Irish statesman

Haile Selassie 1891–
Emperor of Ethiopia

1876–1948

Franz Kafka 1883–1924
Czech writer

Francisco Franco 1892–
Spanish general, dictator

1967

Pierre Laval 1883–1945
French statesman

Tito (Josif Broz) 1892–
Yugoslav statesman

1879–1940

Benito Mussolini 1883–1945
Italian dictator

1879–1953

John Maynard Keynes 1883–1946
British economist

1894 ●
Franco-Russian alliance

1901 ●
Australia a Dominion

1905 ●
First Russian Revolution:
foundation of "soviets"

1910 ●
Union of South Africa
created

1898-1902
Boer War

1902 ●
Discovery of hormones

1905 ●
First moving picture
devised by Edison

1908 ●
Austria annexes Bosnia
and Herzegovina

1894–95 ●
Sino-Japanese War in
Korea

1900 ●
Planck's quantum theory

1904 ●
Entente Cordiale: Anglo-
French alliance

1906 ●
Algeciras Conference:
European hegemony over
Morocco

1910 ●
Japan annexes Korea

● **1895**
Sino-Japanese Treaty of
Shimonoseki followed by
the "Triple Intervention" of
Russia, France and
Germany

1901 ●
USA: assassination of
President McKinley;
Roosevelt President

1906 ●
Dreadnought launched

1910 ●
Mexican Revolution

1903 ●
Pogroms in Russia

● **1907**
Anglo-Russian Convention
on Persia, Afghanistan
and Tibet; Anglo-French
Entente expanded to
Triple Entente (Britain,
Russia, France)

● **1896**
Russo-Chinese defensive
alliance; railway con-
cession in Manchuria

1904 ●
Building of Panama Canal
under US protection

$E = Mc^2$

1905
An obscure civil servant in Switzerland revolutionizes the science of physics, with implications that are still not fully understood

1917
"Peace, Bread and Land!"
Lenin returns from exile to lead a Bolshevik coup that topples Russia's provisional government and establishes a new, Communist state

1922
The Blackshirts March on Rome
An ill-organized but highly effective march on Italy's capital brings Benito Mussolini and his Blackshirts to power

1933
The Burning of the Reichstag
Germany's ambitious Chancellor, Adolf Hitler, seizes upon a suspect incident to consolidate his control of the country

1914
Assassination Sparks the Great War
In the diplomatic confusion following the assassination of Austria-Hungary's heir-presumptive, Europe moves irrevocably toward war

1919
Treaty of Versailles
The vengeful settlement imposed upon Germany by the victorious Allies is exploited by nationalist extremists, culminating in the rise of Hitler

1935
Panic on Wall Street
Amid wild trading and wilder rumors, the speculative bubble of the late 1920s finally bursts, and America is plunged into a decade of depression

1929

1910
"Do or Die"
Tragedy overtakes the last great terrestrial voyage of discovery as Scott and his companions perish in the frozen wastes of Antarctica

1916
Slaughter at the Somme
The Allies mount an offensive to end the war – instead four months of slaughter follow

The New Socialist Offensive
Stalin creates a command economy and institutes political totalitarianism in Russia, thereby creating the modern U.S.S.R.

1928

Hermann Göring 1893–1946
German Nazi leader

J. Robert Oppenheimer 1904–67
U.S. physicist

Jonas Edward Salk 1914–
U.S. physician

Mao Tse-tung 1893–
Chinese statesman

Dag Hammarskjöld 1905–61
U.N. Secretary-General

Moshe Dayan 1915–
Israeli general, statesman

Jomo Kenyatta 1893–
Kenyan statesman

Jean Paul Sartre 1905–
French writer, philosopher

Francis Crick 1916–
British scientist

Nikita Khrushchev 1894–1971
Russian statesman

Samuel Beckett 1906–
Irish-French writer

Harold Wilson 1916–
British statesman

Harold Macmillan 1894–
British statesman

Leonid I. Brezhnev 1906–
Russian statesman

John F. Kennedy 1917–63
U.S. President

Georgi Zhukov 1895–1974
Russian general

Frank Whittle 1907–
British aeronautical expert

Gamal Abdel Nasser 1918–70
Egyptian statesman

Juan Perón 1895–
Argentinian statesman

Joseph McCarthy 1908–1957
U.S. Senator

Pierre Trudeau 1919–
Canadian statesman

F. Scott Fitzgerald 1896–1940
U.S. writer

Lin Piao 1908–71
Chinese statesman

Alexander Dubček 1921–
Czech statesman

Imre Nagy 1896–1958
Hungarian statesman

Salvador Allende 1908–73
Chilean statesman

Henry Kissinger 1923–
U.S. statesman

Trygve Lie 1896–1968
U.N. Secretary-General

Lyndon B. Johnson 1908–73
U.S. President

Robert F. Kennedy 1925–68
U.S. statesman

Bertold Brecht 1898–1956
German writer

John K. Galbraith 1908–
U.S. economist

Fidel Castro 1927–
Cuban revolutionary leader

René Magritte 1898–1967
French painter

Kwame Nkrumah 1909–72
Ghanaian statesman

Ernesto "Che" Guevara 1928–67
Argentinian revolutionary

Chou En-lai 1898–
Chinese statesman

Dean Rusk 1909–
U.S. statesman

Martin Luther King, Jr 1929–68
U.S. civil rights leader

Henry Moore 1898–
British sculptor

Andrei Gromyko 1909–
Russian diplomat

Hussein
King

Ernest Hemingway 1899–1961
U.S. writer

U. Thant 1909–
U.N. Secretary-General

Elvis
U.S.

Heinrich Himmler 1900–45
German Nazi leader

Georges Pompidou 1911–74
French statesman

Louis Mountbatten 1900–
British admiral

Jackson Pollock 1912–56
U.S. painter

Enrico Fermi 1901–54
Italian physicist

Willy Brandt 1913–
West German statesman

Hirohito 1901–
Emperor of Japan

Richard M. Nixon 1913–
U.S. President

Georgi Malenkov 1902–
Russian statesman

Benjamin Britten 1913–
British composer

1911
German gunboat at Agadir creates international tension

Votes for women in **1918**
Britain

1921
Russia: Kronstadt mutiny; ban on opposition in Party; New Economic Policy

1925
Sun Yat-sen dies; Chiang Kai-shek takes over Kuomintang leadership

1929
Lateran Treaty: papal recognition of Italy

1935-36
Italy conquers Ethiopia
League of Nations powerless

1915
First U-boat (submarine) attacks: sinking of the *Lusitania*

1928
A. Fleming discovers penicillin

1933
Hitler Chancellor of Germany; Germany leaves Geneva Disarmament Conference and League of Nations

1911
Revolution in China; imperial rule overthrown and republic proclaimed

1919
Gandhi's civil disobedience campaign in India: troops fire on Indians at Amritsar

1925
Locarno Pact guarantees Germany's western borders and allows her entry to League of Nations

1929
The Young Plan on German reparations

1935
The Saar is restored to Germany

1916
Battle of Jutland; Gallipoli and Salonika campaigns

Ireland: South gets a republican constitution; **1922**
Ulster remains British

1926
First television transmission

1930
The Allies withdraw troops from the Rhineland

1917
Battles of Passchendaele and Cambrai

1920
Votes for women in USA; prohibition of alcohol (until 1933)

Washington Naval **1927**
Disarmament Conference

1934
Nazi *putsch* in Austria

1915
Battles of Neuve Chapelle, Ypres, Aubers Ridge, Loos

1925
Trotsky asserts opposition to Stalin's "Communism in One Country": exiled 1929

1931
Sino-Japanese War: Japan withdraws from League of Nations

1935
First practical radar equipment

1914
Battles of Tannenberg and Masurian Lakes: Germany defeats Russia

1919
League of Nations, World Court, International Labor Organization established

1927
China: massacre of Communists by Nationalists in Shanghai begins civil war

1932
Geneva Disarmament Conference

1934-35
China: "Long March" north of Communist guerrillas under Mao Tse-tung

1923-25
French troops occupy the Ruhr

1931
Financial crisis reaches climax in Europe

USA enters World War **1917**

General strike in Britain **1926**

Insurance for the Elderly
For the first time in U.S. history, the American government underwrites social benefits for the elderly

1936
The Spanish Civil War
Assisted by the Axis Powers, General Francisco Franco lands an invasion army in his native Spain and overthrows the Second Republic

1935—
of Jordan

Presley 1935—
rock and roll singer

● **1936** Coup by military in Japan

● **1937** Italy withdraws from the League of Nations

● **1936** Rome-Berlin Axis: military pact

● **1937** Sino-Japanese War: fall of Peking, Shanghai and Nanking ● **1938** Hitler effects *Anschluss* (union) with Austria

● **1936** German troops enter the Rhineland

1938 Munich Agreement — ● Czech Sudetenland ceded to Germany: height of appeasement policy

● **1936-39** The great purges in Russia

● **1941** Lend-Lease allows Britain to buy war supplies from US on credit

● **1939** Molotov-Ribbentrop pact of non-aggression between Russia and Germany

● **1941** Beginning of the "Manhattan Project" for atomic research

1947 ● Independence for India and Pakistan; 1948 — for Burma and Ceylon

● **1944** Bretton Woods Conference (44 nations) sets up International Monetary Fund

1949 ● North Atlantic Treaty Organization established

1949 ● USSR demonstrates possession of nuclear weapons

1952 Hydrogen bomb developed

1957 ● Treaty of Rome establishes European Economic Community

1955 ● Warsaw Pact for mutual defense of East European countries

Cuban Revolution; Castro Premier (1959)

1958 ●

● US troops authorized to engage in offensive operations in Vietnam **1965** ●

1963 ● Assassination of John F. Kennedy; Johnson President

Krushchev falls from **1964** ● power: Leonid Brezhnev First Secretary, Alexei Kosygin Prime Minister

Assassination of Martin **1968** ● Luther King, Jr., and of Robert F. Kennedy

1961 Berlin wall erected

Officers rebellion in Libya **1969** ● topples King Idris; Col. Gaddafi Premier

Chancellor Brandt's **1970** *Ostpolitik,* leading to treaties with Soviet Union, Poland and East Germany

Jordan: Royal army **1970** defeats Palestine guerrillas

Hijacking becomes an **1969** ● international problem

Overthrow of Prince **1970** ● Sihanouk in Cambodia; combined US-South Vietnamese attacks on Communist bases there

1973 ● EEC: Britain, Denmark and Ireland admitted

1972 ● Rising violence in Ulster: direct British rule introduced

1971 ● China admitted to the United Nations

1973 ● Arab-Israeli "Yom Kippur" War

1972 ● President Nixon visits Peking and Moscow

1973 ● Peace treaty in Vietnam US troops withdrawn

Acknowledgments

The authors and publishers wish to thank the following museums and collections by whose kind permission the illustrations are reproduced. Page numbers appear in bold, photographic sources in italics.

12 Science Museum, London
13 Science Museum
14 (1, 2, 3) Science Museum
16 Science Museum
17 Science Museum
18 (1, 2) Science Museum
19 (2) Science Museum
20 (1) Illustrated London News (2) London Transport Executive: *Heinz Zinram* (3) Imperial War Museum, London
21 (1) *Paul Popper* (2) British Museum, London
22 Victoria and Albert Museum, London: *A.C. Cooper*
23 *Weidenfeld and Nicolson Archives*
24 *Novosti Press Agency*
25 *Culver Pictures*
26 Victoria and Albert Museum: *A.C. Cooper*
27 (1, 2) Victoria and Albert Museum: *A.C. Cooper*
28 *Novosti Press Agency*
29 Victoria and Albert Museum: *A.C. Cooper*
30 (1, 2, 3) *Novosti Press Agency*
31 (1) *Radio Times Hulton Picture Library* (2) National Portrait Gallery, London
32 *Erich Lessing/Magnum*
33 *Radio Times Hulton Picture Library*
34 *Eric Lessing/Magnum*
35 *Paul Brierly*
36 (1, 2) *Radio Times Hulton Picture Library*
37 *Radio Times Hulton Picture Library*
38 Culham Laboratory UKAEA: *Paul Brierly*
39 (1) *International Bilder Agentur, Zurich* (2) *Radio Times Hulton Picture Library*
40 (1) Cavendish Laboratory, University of Cambridge (2) National Portrait Gallery, London (3) *Mansell Collection*
41 (1) *Mansell Collection* (2) National Portrait Gallery, London
42 Museum of Modern Art, New York; Lillie P. Bliss Bequest
43 Museum of Modern Art, New York: Abby Aldrich Rockefeller Purchas Fund
44 National Gallery, London

45 Philadelphia Museum of Art: The A.E. Gallatin Collection (2) National Gallery of Art, Washington D.C.: Chester Dale Collection
47 Kunstmuseum, Basel: *Hans Hinz*
48 (1) Armory Show Papers, Smithsonian Institution, Washington D.C. (2) Philadelphia Museum of Art: The A.E. Gallatin Collection
49 Art Institute of Chicago: Gift of Leigh P. Block
50 (1) Roman Norbert Ketterer, Campione d'Italia: *John R. Freeman* (2) Mr. and Mrs. G. H. Foster: *Arts Council of Great Britain*
51 (1) *Weidenfeld and Nicolson Archives* (2) *Archivo Casasola, Mexico*
52 (1, 2) Ford Motor Company
53 Ford Motor Company
54 Ford Motor Company (2) *Sohio News Service*
55 *St. John Nixon*
56 (1, 2) The Montagu Motor Museum, Beaulieu
57 (1, 2) The Montagu Motor Museum
58 (1) *Paul Popper* (2) *Roger-Viollet* (3) National Portrait Gallery, London
59 (1, 3) *Radio Times Hulton Picture Library* (2) *Sport and General Press Agency*
60 Scott Polar Research Institute, Cambridge
61 Scott Polar Research Institute
62 *Paul Popper*
63 (1) Scott Polar Research Institute (2) Illustrated London News
64 (1, 2) Scott Polar Research Institute
65 Scott Polar Research Institute
67 By kind permission of Sir Peter Scott: *British Museum*
68 *Paul Popper*
69 (1) British Museum (2, 3) *Radio Times Hulton Picture Library* (4) *Weidenfeld and Nicolson Archives*
70 Bildarchiv der Osterreichischen Nationalbibliothek, Vienna
71 *Mansell Collection*
72 (1, 2) *Paul Popper*
73 (1) *Keystone Press Agency* (2) *Mansell Collection*
74 (1, 2, 3) Imperial War Museum
75 Imperial War Museum
76 (1, 2) *Radio Times Hulton Picture Library* (3) *Weidenfeld and Nicolson Archives*
77 (1, 2) Imperial War Museum
78 Imperial War Museum: *A.C.*

Cooper
79 *René Dazy*
80 (1, 2) Imperial War Museum
81 Imperial War Museum
82 (1) *Roger-Viollet* (2) Imperial War Museum
83 *Radio Times Hulton Picture Library*
84 Imperial War Museum: *A.C. Cooper*
85 Imperial War Museum: *A.C. Cooper*
86 (1) *Radio Times Hulton Picture Library* (2) *Camera Press*
87 (1) Imperial War Museum
88 *Keystone Press Agency*
89 *Novosti Press Agency*
90 *Novosti Press Agency*
91 (1) *Keystone Press Agency* (2) *Novosti Press Agency*
92 (1, 2) *Novosti Press Agency*
94 (1) *Flight International* (2) *Radio Times Hulton Picture Library*
95 (1) *Novosti Press Agency* (2, 3) *Radio Times Hulton Picture Library*
96 Imperial War Museum: *Eileen Tweedy*
97 *Radio Times Hulton Picture Library*
98 (1) *Roger-Viollet* (2) *Radio Times Hulton Picture Library*
99 Imperial War Museum: *Eileen Tweedy*
100 *Radio Times Hulton Picture Library*
101 (1) *Roger-Viollet* (2) *Radio Times Hulton Picture Library*
102 Musée de Versailles: *Photo Bulloz*
103 Imperial War Museum: *Eileen Tweedy*
104 (1) *Radio Times Hulton Picture Library* (2) The Turkish Embassy, London
105 (1) *Radio Times Hulton Picture Library* (2) *Mansell Collection*
106 Museo Aeronautico Caproni di Taliedo, Rome
107 *Phoebus Picture Library*
108 (1) *Editions Rencontre* (2) *Moro, Milan*
109 (1) *Foto Italia* (2) *Phoebus Picture Library*
110 (1) *Moro, Milan* (2) *Phoebus Picture Library*
111 *Moro, Rome*
112 (1, 2) *Radio Times Hulton Picture Library*
113 (1) *Radio Times Hulton Picture Library* (2) *Novosti Press Agency* (3) *Barnaby's Picture Library*
114 *Snark International*
115 *Radio Times Hulton Picture Library*

116 *Snark International*
117 *Novosti Press Agency*
118 *Snark International*
119 (1) *Radio Times Hulton Picture Library* (2) *Snark International*
120 *Novosti Press Agency*
121 (1) *Roger-Viollet* (2) *Radio Times Hulton Picture Library*
122 (1) *Novosti Press Agency* (2, 3) *Radio Times Hulton Picture Library*
123 (1) *Radio Times Hulton Picture Library* (2) *Edward Leigh*
124 United States Information Service
125 *Fox Photos*
126 (1) *Keystone Press Agency* (2) American Stock Exchange
128 (1) *Fox Photos* (2) *Phoebus Picture Library*
129 (1) *Mansell Collection* (2) *Culver Pictures* (3) *Phoebus Picture Library*
130 (1) *Ullstein Bilderdienst* (2) *Paul Popper* (3) *Archivo Casasola*
131 (1, 3) *Radio Times Hulton Picture Library* (2) *Keystone Press Agency*
132 *Keystone Press Agency*
133 *Phoebus Picture Library*
134 (1, 2) *Keystone Press Agency*
135 (1, 2, 3) *Keystone Press Agency*
136 *Wiener Library, London* (2) *Keystone Press Agency*
137 (1) *Wiener Library* (2) *Keystone Press Agency* (3) *Phoebus Picture Library*
138 (1) Imperial War Museum (2) *Keystone Press Agency*
139 (1) Imperial War Museum (2) *Paul Popper* (3) *Radio Times Hulton Picture Library*
140 *Snark International*
141 *Photo Research International*
142 *The Bettmann Archive*
143 Franklin D. Roosevelt Library Collection, New York
144 Franklin D. Roosevelt Library Collection
145 *Snark International*
146 (1) Imperial War Museum (2) *Archiv für Kunst und Geschichte*
147 (1) *Paul Popper* (2) *Radio Times Hulton Picture Library*
148 Karl Marx Memorial Library, London
149 Bibliothèque Nationale, Paris
150 (1, 2) *Keystone Press Agency*
151 (1) *Phoebus Picture Library* (2) *Keystone Press Agency*
152 (1) *Keystone Press Agency* (2) Musée d'Art Moderne, Paris
153 Museum of Modern Art, New York: © by S.P.A.D.E.M. Paris

Managing Editor   *Adrian Brink*
Assistant Editors   *Geoffrey Chesler, Francesca Ronan*
Picture Editor   *Julia Brown*
Consultant Designer   *Tim Higgins*
Art Director   *Anthony Cohen*

Index